Media images of desperate refugees drowning or washing up on the shores of the Italian island of Lampedusa have become all too common. But to European eyes these images mislead as well as they inform. They exoticize and distance immigrants from "normal life." So, how to humanize African migrants, whose trajectories seem alien to the experience of metropolitan Europe, without sentimentalizing them? This amazingly acute and timely reflection shows how the marginalized, in the form of African refugees, cast light on the actual norms of the dominant "center" – Europe, Italy, Rome – that they enter if they survive their arduous journeys. Crucially, migration across borders isn't the exception that normal European life today presupposes. All of humanity is descended from people who originally came out of Africa. We shouldn't forget this. The borders all came much later.

**John Agnew**, *Professor of Geography, UCLA, Los Angeles, USA*

Set in beautiful prose, Rinelli's illuminating study on the dynamics of African migration to Europe blends righteous indignation with penetrating analysis in ways that inform, engage, and inspire specialists on the subject and general readers alike. Focusing on instrumental security practices that seek to 'externalize' migration control and thereby render the plight of African immigrants invisible to the privileged eyes of the global North, Rinelli enriches his political analysis with an artist's attention to visual modes of representation. Given the enormity of the unfolding migration crisis in the Mediterranean, I can think of no other book that offers a more sophisticated approach to the topic.

**Manfred B. Steger**, *Professor of Political Science, University of Hawai'i-Manoa and Honorary Professor of Global Studies, RMIT University, Melbourne, Australia*

"What is Europe?" This is the compelling question this book asks, moving back and forth from the Sahara Desert to the Island of Lampedusa, from the choppy waters of the Mediterranean Sea to the city of Rome. Interlacing histories, experiences, and images of African immigration in Europe from the angle of a political understanding of the border, Lorenzo Rinelli has written a highly original and challenging book that questions Europe and Africa distinctions based on birth, citizenship and territory.

**Sandro Mezzadra**, *Professor of Political and Social Science, University of Bologna*

Lorenzo Rinelli's book is much more than a mere report on the humanitarian crisis associated with the contemporary migration flow from Africa to Europe. It's a compassionate, historically-informed reflection that brings nuanced ethico-political analysis to the issues; it's an extraordinarily articulate piece of writing that engages the historical trajectory of the flows with sophisticated conceptual thinking; and it's an expansion of the boundaries of the problem well beyond what one learns from international media. Everyone – governmental officials, scholars, students, and members of a global, policy-interested public – should read Rinelli's book.

**Michael Shapiro,** *Professor of Political Science, University of Hawai'i-Manoa*

# African Migrants and Europe

The process of migration control mirrors the trajectories of the people who traverse national boundaries, making today's borders flexible and fluid.

This book explores the transformation of migration control in the post-9/11 era. It looks at how border controls have become more diffuse in the face of increased human flows from Africa and presents a critical analysis of the *dispositif* of European migration control, including detention without trial, derogation of human rights law, torture, "extraordinary rendition," the curtailment of civil liberties, and the securitization of migration. By examining the role of Gaddafi's Libya in the last ten years as a gendarme of Europe, it argues for a revisioning of borders and frontiers in ways that can account for their dialectical nature and for the dialectical nature of political life.

This text will be of key interest to scholars and students of European studies, African studies, security studies, international relations, global studies, comparative politics, cultural geography, migration studies, and border theory.

**Lorenzo Rinelli** is a teacher and researcher at the University of California in Rome, Italy.

**Routledge Studies in African Politics and International Relations**
Edited by Daniel C. Bach, Emile Durkheim Centre for Comparative
Politics and Sociology, Sciences Po Bordeaux

# African Migrants and Europe

## Managing the ultimate frontier

**Lorenzo Rinelli**

Routledge
Taylor & Francis Group

LONDON AND NEW YORK

First published 2016
by Routledge
2 Park Square, Milton Park, Abingdon, Oxon OX14 4RN

and by Routledge
711 Third Avenue, New York, NY 10017

*Routledge is an imprint of the Taylor & Francis Group, an informa business*

*British Library Cataloguing in Publication Data*
A catalogue record for this book is available from the British Library

*Library of Congress Cataloging-in-Publication Data*
Rinelli, Lorenzo.
   African migrants and Europe : managing the ultimate frontier / Lorenzo Rinelli.
      pages cm — (Routledge studies in African politics and international relations)
   1. Europe—Emigration and immigration—Government policy.   2. Border security—Europe.   3. Boundaries—Political aspects—Europe.   4. Borderlands—Europe.   5. Libya—Emigration and immigration.   6. Africa—Emigration and immigration.   7. Europe—Emigration and immigration.   8. Africans—Europe—Social conditions.   9. Immigrants—Europe—Social conditions.   I. Title.
   JV7590.R56 2015
   325.4'096—dc23
   2015008640

ISBN: 978-1-138-80051-9 (hbk)
ISBN: 978-1-315-75541-0 (ebk)

Typeset in Times New Roman
by Apex CoVantage, LLC

For Mimmo and Preziosa,
Who moved first and strong until here

*Few men enjoy prolonged travel; it disrupts all habits and endlessly jolts all prejudice. But I was striving to have no prejudice and few habits.*

*Hadrian (Yourcenar 2005, p. 74)*

*Figure 0.1* Blue plaque
Source: Photograph by Lorenzo Rinelli

# Contents

# Foreword

"African migrants wash up on nude beach in southern Spain," news reports announced in late June 2004. "Two worlds collided," the reports retorted "as a raft carrying 42 destitute Africans …washed up on a nudist beach." (*Associated Press*, 2004) Suddenly, the frontier that "separated" the world of citizens and migrant world was no more. The frontier had been breached in the uninvited apparition of migrants, thus leading to the "collision" of two different worlds. Yet a more careful reading of the reports suggested that the sudden encounter of these worlds was more than merely a collision, a clash of humans coming from the midst of different experiences. It was also sudden and unexpected convergence of human lives, which, had it not been the very borders that give meaning to the idea of "different worlds," would have been unlikely, or unnecessary, to have come together in this fugitive fashion. Even then, as the reports unwittingly intimated, the sudden encounter of the "different" worlds turned out to be less a "collision" of two worlds and more an opening of these worlds into each other in the interactions that followed the initial shock.

> The migrants included four babies one just 11 days old. A group of bathers was shown [on a video taken by a bather and broadcast on Spanish television] gathered around one of the infants, gently counting the fingers on one of its hands and coming up with six.
>
> (*Associated Press*, 2004)

Ultimately, when the migrants washed up on the beach, thus washing over the nude citizen bodies, they also washed over the border, exposing the life of the border to be more than only collisions, terminations, and stoppages of human experiences. They showed that, not unlike the border a migrant poet's life, which can not prevent the bleeding of two worlds into one another, migrants and borders come together in transformative ways, pressuring, shifting, and changing the familiar routines and rhythms of lives. Perhaps most significantly, in washing over the border uninvited, these migrants highlighted an increasingly prevalent "insurrectional" dimension to the politics of frontiers, borders, and migration.

The book before you by Lorenzo Rinelli is an important intervention in conversations about frontiers migrants and borders. It is a timely intervention given the massive proliferation of transnational flows of bodies across European countries, including across Italy. More important than its interventions in the broad conversation on migrancy and control, the book demonstrates how a single site, such as the tiny Island of Lampedusa, can serve as a site of both migratory capture and transition — both stoppage of migrant flows as well as their accelerator. It shows how camps can be anywhere and nowhere.

Rinelli shows how efforts to regiment migrants, particularly African migrants, succeed and fail at once. They succeed in disrupting, if not in blocking, migrant flows in places like Lampedusa and elsewhere in Europe, but also, they, as practices of statecraft, are transgressed by migrants' extant and emerging agency and subjectivity. Even under duress, whether in captivity or during uncertain and dangerous journey, migrant stories, migratory images and sometimes, migrant subjectivity in death (in their posthumously enacted/granted citizenship) can act upon "host-societies" in transformative ways.

Rinelli situates his inquiries and insights in fundamental shifts in policies of migration regulation and control in the European Union: the externalization of control regime to the Mediterranean basin and beyond, focusing on the relationship between Italy and Libya. Prior to the recent outbreak of the Arab uprisings in the MENA region, the Italy-Libya nexus in North Africa had already become an active field of policy where the EU's migration controls were applied in an effort to stem the tide of the EU-bound immigrants before reaching the EU borders. While this arguably "extra-territorial" extension of the EU's political-legal powers through Italy is not entirely new, its methods and idioms are fairly unprecedented, not to speak of the intensity with which the extension practices are pursued in all of North Africa and the Sub-Saharan Africa. The EU-sponsored or inspired (either directly or indirectly) detention/asylum/immigrant camps that have sprung in North Africa and elsewhere are a testimony to the changing dynamics of the EU's migration control regime. Rinelli's project is located at this juncture of the old EU policies metamorphosing into new regime-forms through outsourcing and externalization (outside Europe and inside). Not surprisingly, given the emergent and still inchoate dynamics, this juncture of policy and conduct remains understudied. Rinelli's work in this book advances the analyses further in groundbreaking ways.

More specifically, Rinelli's project examines how this new policy environment regulates formal and informal placement of migrants within the EU countries, leading to a complex and flexible regime of "differently-included" labor force in respective countries. Hear Rinelli:

> The broad classifications of "immigrant," i.e. "permanent resident," "guest worker," or "illegal" (and the various subsets of these) affects (im)migrants' experiences of the labor market, access to rights, benefits and services as well as treatment by state officials. The process of category placement also shapes a migrant's subsequent mobility since one's status affects how, and whether, a person can leave the EU and/or return. Consequently, EU-wide apparatus of immigration laws and policies significantly shape the life conditions, choices, and expressions of migrants.

It is this regime of regulation and controls that Rinelli studies and maps. In this sense alone, Rinelli's book fills a significant void in our comprehension of political, economic and legal dynamics that derive the shifts in policy environment and regulatory regimes. Additionally, it sheds light on the new ways in which the "differently-included" migrants formulate responses to externalization policies from within the host countries of the EU as much they do from without. The focus on the Italy-Libya nexus, from the colonial era to the present turmoil in the relationship in the post-Qaddafi era, offers new insights into institutional behavior and formal policy-making in international law. This approach inverts the conventional logic and shows how internal differentiations of immigrant placement come to bear on external regulatory process. It demonstrates that the migration control regimes are dynamically shaped internally and externally through a regime that is at once orchestrated by the EU and driven by comparative factors beyond the EU. This is a very innovative approach and deserves special support.

In critically engaging the work of statecraft that spans immigration and citizenship in both productive and destructive ways across the Mediterranean basin, the book highlights how statecraft, which appears as a threat to cosmopolitan and pluralist projects, can also be redirected in ways that expand the horizons of citizenship and community beyond the narrow modern construct of the territorialized nation form. The book contends that "errantry" as a form of migrant agency exceeds the citizen-centric norm and points to the possibilities of community-making that are pluralist and democratic beyond the limitations of the citizen-nation-state form. The last half of the book is devoted to articulating how such pluralist politics can be imagined and supported. These are the promises of the book that I sympathize with and support.

The book treatment of Lampedusa's migrant legacy is exceptional, if not exemplary. The thesis and the conclusions are original within the field of migration broadly understood. Rinelli's scholarship both in depth and breadth is superb with a poetical flair that focuses the attention on the human stories without diluting the analysis. Rinelli shows how poetical is also always political. Clearly, the book situates an Italian island, an Italian community, and Italy as a country in the midst of a discussion that has both national and universal import. It is a contribution to migrant studies in showing how the European societies, localized and writ large are having to grapple with displaced humans (humanity) literally washing ashore on Spanish or Italian beaches, but also on their political consciousness.

*Nevzat Soguk*

# Preface

## Nabruka

One breezy morning in spring 2008, I found another story of the type that I had been hunting for a while. I read and collect them almost every day but still cannot get used to them. Perhaps that is not a bad thing. This particular story related to a place that I hold dear. Perhaps for this reason, I could not maintain the safe distance or impartiality that some would say is proper for a political scientist. Certainly, I felt a need to write about this event (Rinelli 2009a). So, back to setting the scene. Here I am one morning pouring my coffee and reading through *Il Messaggero*, a popular Italian newspaper. A tiny piece in the lower left corner of the local news section reads, "A 44-year-old woman was found hanged in her cell at the CIE (Center [or prison] for [migrants'] Identification and Expulsion) of Ponte Galeria in Rome." A couple of other local newspapers tossed in an acronym: M. M. But these papers reported her initials incorrectly. Her name was Nabruka Mimuni, and Nabruka was born in Tunisia. She had been living in Rome for thirty years and was on her way to renew her residence certification. Unfortunately, and tragically, she was arrested while in line to complete the certification. After her arrest, she was going to be deported/she would have been deported to Tunisia, where she had no family. Instead, she hanged herself in her cell, the night before I sat here drinking my coffee. Nabruka left a child and a husband behind – and us, to think about what had been done to her.

I can say, then, that this book was born out of indignation and inspiration, both caused by the relentless political strength I have encountered in those human beings who dwell in the borderscape (Anzaldúa 2007; Rajaram & Grundy-Warr 2008). In the spring of 2008, I had already started to organize and develop a narrative from my research on the African migrations to Europe. Europe's response to the externalization of migration control had already emerged from the wider debate on the notion of securitization in the area of migration. That was when migration entered the realm of high politics at the beginning of the 1990s. My understanding of externalization was initially in line with the views of most scholars who attend to the externalization of migration control policies primarily by using geographical terms. After all, the term *European externalization* suggests policies that are implemented in geopolitical spaces beyond that of continental Europe and that were first used on the subject of asylum policies with regard to the UK proposal to build transit processing centers outside the European Union (EU) in 2003.[1] Many scholars refer to externalization as a "remote control" (Fahrmeir *et al*. 2005) process or as "policing at a distance" (Guild & Bigo 2003), whereby a state's border control procedures are projected and implemented outside the territory of the state and thus limit the analyses of this phenomenon to simple geospatial characterizations. Most observers find this notion of externalization reasonable insofar as European policies have been implemented in, or outsourced to, North Africa.

However, the story of Nabruka made me think that perhaps the externalization of migration control in Africa was just the tip of the iceberg: the most visible feature of a complex European apparatus that is meant to exclude or, better, to differentiate among African migrants already in Europe or on their way to it. It is what Sayad (2004) defines as the *diacritical* function of the state – the function of "delineation" that turns African migrants into exceptions (from the Latin *ex-capere*, to capture outside) – to discriminate, select, and incorporate few differentially. If externalization only pushed Europe's gatekeepers beyond the geopolitical space of continental Europe, then how would one account for the role of the detention centers that now exist in many European cities?

Sipping on my morning coffee, I recalled the indifference of the media professionals who misspelled Nabruka's initials and the indifference of most Roman citizens about current immigration policies and legislation. Can we define geospatially local Roman practices of marginalization as externalization? Where does the internal end and external begin? In Nabruka's personal Möbius strip–like case, two allegedly geographically distinct and distant places – Tunisia and Rome – served as the alpha and omega of a life made invisible to Europeans who attend to the externalization of migration control policies using strictly conventional geospatial methodologies and conceptions of borders.

I then reflected more on how the phenomenon of externalization is not clearly defined in space and time. Where and when does it start and end? Eventually, I wanted to find out whether externalization (both in intent and in practice) is merely a structure for annihilating immigrants' identities or if it acts in response to African migrants' tactics to subvert control. Maybe the enormous amount of energy and capital that states expend and invest to manage migration from Africa is somehow productive. I questioned whether tensions generated at the border might cause certain types of politics, and lives, to proliferate and how they could cause this proliferation. In other words, I wanted to prove that it is possible to conceive of externalization as something other than a system of total control (the "Panopticon" of Foucault) or interdiction (the "Banopticon" of Didier Bigo) (Rajaram & Grundy-Warr 2008) through the collaborative arrangements of cross-border networks of security experts and state policies.

Along this line, the main ambition of this book is to reconceive the idea of the border as a process of negotiations and encounters in light of African migrations' interventions, moving it away from ossified conceptions that crystallize the border under the spell of the state. I argue that it is possible to theorize the border at the center of a new political project that reconciles the fracture between politics and policies. Citizenship characterizes the leading juridical width of individuals' belonging to a specific community, and the borders set the limits of the same juridical order.

It is consequential, then, that the contemporary multiplication, overdetermination, and ubiquity of the border have caused a short circuit between "territorial" and "relational" processes that calls for a reflection upon the same border. But, as I will explain further, how do we delineate something that by nature is a definer (Balibar & Hahn 2002)? In this book, inspired by African migrants' border struggles within what Soguk defines as the "economy of refugeeism and migration" (Shapiro & Alker 1995, pp. 285–326), I focus on the political power of migrations in shaping and modifying territories, borders and, indeed, states. If it is true, as Abdelmalek Sayad eminently wrote, that "thinking about immigration means thinking about the state, and that it is the state that is thinking about itself when it thinks about immigration" (2004, p. 279), it is also true that the state is thinking about itself because migrants stimulate that reflection. Reversing the lens, then, instead of analyzing migrations from the institutional point of view, this book looks at how migrations induce the dislodgment and re-definition of the nation state, as much as, global institutions. Approaching migration to interrogate the state, especially in relation to African states and the European Union member states, means to denaturalize it, and more importantly, to take into consideration the colonial history pertinent to those states and societies afflicted by historical amnesia. "Why? Because immigration constitutes the limit of what constitutes the national state. Immigration is the limit that reveals what it is intrinsically, or its basic truth" (Martiniello & Rath 2010, p. 166). Differently, stunting this methodological shift, we risk widening the gap between formal declarations of humanity and empirical human life.

On the contrary, one of the tasks of this book is to establish that the externalization of European migration control signifies the departure from an idea of community of people (politics) toward a community of institution (policies) that every day becomes more powerful and relies on a complicated apparatus or *dispositif*. Policies of migration control are not meant to resolve underpaid and unregulated employment or to eliminate "illegal" migration plainly because "it is precisely the control which states exercise over borders that defines international migration as a distinctive social process" (Zolberg 1989, p. 405). The goal of externalization is rather to reproduce an illegality that in turn justifies the necessity of a complicated apparatus of migration control "in a world characterized by widely varying conditions" where "international borders serve to maintain global inequality" (Zolberg 1989, p. 406). Intended in this way, I realized how much of an analytic understanding of the phenomenon of Europe's externalization of migration control is indebted to Foucault's concept of *dispositif* after that expanded by Giorgio Agamben (2009).[2] As Foucault explained about his vision:

> What I'm trying to pick out with this term is, firstly, a thoroughly heterogeneous ensemble consisting of discourses, institutions, architectural forms, regulatory decisions, laws, administrative measures, scientific statements, philosophical, moral and philanthropic propositions – in short, the said as much as the unsaid. Such are the elements of the apparatus. The apparatus itself is the system of relations that can be established between these elements.
>
> (Foucault 1980, p. 194)

Externalization as a *dispositif* consists of various elements, such as internment camps for migrants that are disguised as hospitality centers, architectural pretensions of urban alienation, mass deportations (also known as readmission agreements), high-tech border patrolling, ultramodern databases, and political economic labels of differential inclusion. Also, it operates in controlled departures and visa requirements. How to draw the list of those countries; how to decide which populations are dangerous and therefore should be banned? In fact, once we look at the phenomenon of externalization, we see that all of its elements are internally related even as they remain necessarily different. These are, for example:

- Biometrics, satellites, and databases, each of which is a technology that, by demanding answers to questions of truth and belonging, individuates, verifies, and controls migrants who the state imagines;
- Urban design, architecture, and urban planning within European cities commonly featuring immigrant detention centers;
- Frontex or the (in)security risk management rationale of European institutions and agencies that are in charge of coordinating European state strategies of migration control;
- Justices, tribunals, and domestic policies of intercepting migrants' boats on the high seas and returning them to imagined homelands;
- Diplomatic agreements, neighbor policies, and international treaties with non-European countries that are meant to disrupt migration flows;
- Camps inside as well as outside Europe to detain migrants and police training.

This assemblage of internal and external security elements offers a multiplicity of distinct vantage points from which to conceive and examine border effects. For instance, according to some angles and combinations, certain security agencies that in the past received great attention and visibility (e.g., gendarmerie, customs, border guards, immigration officers) become unintelligible. Though for some reason still maintaining a central role within the security field, the power of traditional border policing and control practices has now been distributed among different elements (some of them mentioned previously, and all variously beyond and/or within state geopolitical limits). These powers have had to become more fluid and less localized to effectively respond to contemporary, globalized challenges. In other words, the field of professional migration controls has had to function, much as Nabruka did, like a Möbius strip or a Klein bottle, with the locations and interventions of agents never fully fixed and never fully inside or out.

Of the many aspects of externalization that will be proposed and examined here, three are of particular significance: the configuration/design of the *dispositif* of the externalization of migration control, inside and outside Europe; the nature of the border; and, finally, the dialectical complexion of power struggles among (in)security professionals and migrants. Together, these show that, if different elements and agencies participate in the same *dispositif* – i.e. European externalization within a field of (in)security – then inherent differences between kinds of (in)security threats disappear. Consequently, the concept of externalization entails, logically, the design of a semantic continuum of threats, ranging from undocumented migration and diseases – "there is a link between imagining disease and imagining foreignness" (Sontag 1988, p. 135) – to terrorism. This continuum is Möbius twisted and has real consequences not only for host societies and their intended targets but also for security agencies and their activities and relationships in the prevailing political climate. Picture, for example, the phone- and Internet-tapping programs that Western countries have launched since 9/11 in their primarily "external" War on Terror. However, most importantly, the *dispositif* does not impose itself upon migrations, but it is influenced by those and shaped accordingly. In this sense, I diverge with Zolberg's prediction in the late 1980s when he affirmed that the shape of international migrations would depend in large part on how entry and exit doors would be manipulated by countries. It is important to note the ambivalence of the *dispositif* between molding migration routes and being influenced by the same. To assume a dialectical approach in analyzing the phenomenon of migration from Africa to Europe, it is not simply a matter of ethical choice. Other than that, it is a methodological stance to keep one's distance from a hydraulic and often econometric (Sayad 2004) analysis of migration that tends to privilege the point of view of host countries and migrants as victims of a crushing security apparatus.

## When the ordinary becomes beautiful: the role of images in discourses of migration

This research is based on a qualitative methodological approach that, even if it could not appear in its entirety in this particular publication, features prominently in many of my works. In particular, visual and oral memories of African migrants, and the practices of migration control, allow for a uniquely comprehensive analysis of the externalization of European migration and for the extension of this concept of "externalization" both beyond and within Europe's formal geospatial borders. Through samples of my photographic archive (although these will be limited to a few for editorial rationale) and an original video documentary made by an African migrant, this book aims to reveal aspects of recent migration control policy changes that have been concealed and, by tracing the interstices of migration discourses, reveals the importance and agency of the ordinary. Consequently, it pays as much attention to European and national policies as it does to visual representations of migrations and migrants visualizing their journey.

Why embark on a strenuous defense of photography or film as a legitimate tool to explain global migrations against the prevailing current of international relations scholarship? Do we have the luxury to entertain ourselves with questions of aesthetics when the world requires urgent action? I have come to the conclusion that aesthetics is too present in human life to be left outside our analytical toolbox. During a lecture delivered in 1975 at Wellesley College, Susan Sontag, invoking Oscar Wilde, said that the way we see the world (and therefore understand it) is "largely determined by art in the larger sense" (Wells 2002, p. 64). We should not be surprised, then, if realism, the most positivist approach to "seeing" international issues, presents an uncanny resemblance to the art of photography. Like photography, a neorealist approach presumes to merely describe the realities of world issues "independently of our values and assumptions" (Bleiker 2009, p. 5). This proceeds as if representation is neither a process nor a problem, as reality is self-evident and therefore only obscured by insufficient data rather than the subjectivity of the observer.

Can we then bring photography to the same level as other positivist approaches? It is worth mentioning that Hans Morgenthau, one of the founders of American political realism, wrote that "political science is an art and not a science" (Morgenthau 1965, p. 10). Can we go on, then, assuming that every methodological tool belongs to one or another form of art, a representation, intended or not, even if it is saturated with the discourse of scientific reason? Indeed, to decode world politics, we rely greatly on the art of numbers – otherwise named statistics – the art of mapping the Earth and its resources that is geopolitics[3], or the art of diplomacy that focuses on intricate sets of human correspondence among high-profile politicians and governors. Within the realm of international relations, each one of these arts and their own insights have been elevated to the status of common sense so that they are not recognized as being as inevitably partial as they are. Why, then, has one of the most scientific among arts – that is, photography and filming – not yet been taken seriously within the realm of world politics? Yet media images play a crucial role in representing and shaping world events, and more often than not, they alone set the level of security alert. Why, then, are we not taking advantage of a scientific art whose mechanisms have already been deconstructed to actively engage world politics? Perhaps only a few believe that a photograph can give a wide-ranging representation of world realities, but to be aware of its limits is already a respectable starting point. From that point, next we can explore its vast potentialities.

Foucault explained that knowledge and power are interrelated and that consequently the concept of truth is related to a certain knowledge, which never exists outside of power. The regime of truth is, then, the product of a system of procedures for the production and distribution of statements of truth. The scope, then, is to develop methodological tools of analysis able to detect the "political economy" (Foucault n.d., p. 13) within which the mode of production of truth operates while showing that a new politics of truth is possible. Photography and filming can serve the scope. The lens can get closer than anything else (think of a microscope lens and the politics of HIV diffusion in Africa) and perforate the veil of omniscient codes (thinking here of Barthes' *punctum* (Shapiro 2008, p. 23), opening up new possibilities for "seeing" the world. Beyond an academic interpretation of a photograph – that is, the cultural and linguistic structure if it – a photograph can determine a new relation between the viewer and the object of photography. This point becomes clearer when we pay attention to common approaches to migration analyzed through the lens of security in terms of integrity of the state's borders and the cultural integrity of the nation within it. Prominent statist modes of representation of migration insist on hierarchy of high – state and politicians – over low – migrants and their interlocutors. What can be heard and what can be viewed is, then, commonly filtered by these hierarchies. Framing migration through a security lens means to intend migration as a risk (contamination)/ opportunity (economic) for the state and distrust for those social relations that are structured on the basis of dangerous encounters. Similarly, framing migration as a humanitarian emergency in NGOs' fundraising images of starving African kids means to pose it as a security question that generates compassion without altering unidirectional hierarchical top-down relations. Dealing with migration and refugee subjects has become a way of thinking of the state and thinking in state categories (Sayad 2004).

The same is true for what cannot be heard and what must remain invisible. It is a (border) practice of consigning to the void not only the migrant but also social relations that prevent the identification of the migrant as one who does not belong. Photography and filming as a method, intended as the act of photographing/filming, opens up new perspectives and can expose the rationale of policies of security and migration control whose violence becomes mundane. Regarding my research project, the counterarchive I have assembled highlights "that which you cannot see" (Higgins 2001, p. 35) in present-day European practices of securitizing the Mediterranean. During the last decade, there have been many researchers[4] who have shown the indispensability of aesthetic sensibilities in rethinking world politics. Among those, Roland Bleiker reminds us that "aesthetics is neither good nor bad, progressive nor regressive. It works more like an amplifier" (2009, p. 11). Bleiker experiments with poetic modes of expression, transversal discourses, and aesthetic practices. In my case, I am trying to leverage aesthetics of the "ordinary" or the banal against the way statistics fetishizes data as an impersonal accounting of life. Then you will have a warrant for what makes your reading more "nuanced." An aesthetic sensibility can give us insights that cannot be detected by other practices like statistics; at the same time, it allows us a more nuanced way of reading international politics. There is a resonance between photographic depictions of Africa and contemporary discourses of African migrations into Europe. The stereotypical depiction of African migrants as the wretched of the Earth, desperate adventurers gambling with fate, systematically appears on European tabloids and TV news. Pictures of wrecked vessels adrift at sea or images of black bodies washed ashore inundate summer nights on European TV screens. This visual documentation is intimately connected to a persistent colonial depiction of Africa and justifies violence and death as the necessary price for migration control. The task here perhaps is to allow that which does not fit, that which has no part, to resound onto the boundaries of political space as permanence, allowing for the thinking of space as constituted by ongoing social relations that would refuse the arbitrary force of a particular form of political authority.

In particular, photography of the ordinary (Das 2007) as a method can locate and highlight symptoms of an epoch of any given society in the minute details of ordinary life. I am thinking here of seminal works like that of *A Seventh Man* conceptualized by John Berger with photos by Jean Mohr (Berger 1989) in the late 1960s that show how industrialized countries in northern Europe became dependent on the labor of southern migrants. That extraordinary work shows the biopolitical dimension of borders by intruding into recruitment centers where migrants were examined and underwent medical tests to prove that they had the physical and mental abilities to join the workforce. Through this disruptive archive, we can get a glimpse of migrants' gazes that turn away while the German medical examiner slips his hand under the underwear of an adult man from Turkey. In that moment, all the shame of a violent encounter explodes within the frame of an unbalanced cultural and economic relation. A collision like that sends us toward other zones of intelligibility with regard to the political economy of north-south relations. While *A Seventh Man* focuses on Turkish and Italian immigrant workers in Germany, it ignited a vast debate on the relation between labor and capital. It was translated into many languages and "began to be read by some of those whom it was about" (Berger 1989, p. 8).

In a similar way, perhaps more notoriously, former Brazilian economist Sebastião Salgado gathered in his monumental *Migrations: Humanity in Transition* hundreds of individual stories of migrations of our times. If we add the real time that the shutter was released for each photo to be composed, it equals to no more than one second of life on Earth. Commenting on Salgado's work on Sahel, David Campbell states that "photographs are a modality of power. They may conform to colonial economies of representation or can function as an ethical and responsibilizing practice in which the aesthetics repoliticizes" (Debrix 2003, p.89). Salgado succeeds in questioning modes of representing disasters, famines, and displacements. On one hand, he does it looking tirelessly for beauty in each of his shots. Most of the criticism departs from this point. While I do not deny the validity of this objection, I wrote elsewhere in conversation with Michael J. Shapiro that we often underestimate the political power of finding beauty in each ordinary gesture of life (Rinelli 2009b). On the other hand, Salgado questions the regime of truth of humanitarian intervention within institutionalized frameworks of action (IRC [International Rescue Committee], IOM [International Organization for Migration], UNDP [United Nations Development Program], etc.). He problematizes and confronts the conventional depiction of humanity in trouble – the malnourished bellies of African children – and the spectacle of atrocities. Where other photographers' work ends at pity and compassion, Salgado's begins there to explore dignity and determination. He catches a different angle, challenging viewers' perceptions of disaster, reveling in hope for new politics in every gesture without minimizing human suffering.

The work of Alfredo Jaar on the Rwandan genocide (Jaar, 1998) follows a similar path exploring the politics and representation of trauma. Although an exhaustive analysis is beyond the scope of this brief introduction, it is important to underline how his work exposes the power relations that constitute the political economy of representation of global traumatic events like Rwanda's genocide. Jaar reveals the power of editing in producing world news, and he opens up the intricate junctions between power and knowledge. Moving beyond his predecessors, Jaar couples images and, texts and sometimes recreates the environment during an exhibition. Only in this way, he argues, is it possible to overcome the "feeling" released by an image and amplify the limits of words for powerful counterinformation.

Jacques Rancière wrote that film and photography underline the ordinary moments of life and render those moments "beautiful as a trace of true. This phantasmagoric dimension of the true played an essential role in the formation of the critical paradigm of the human and social sciences" (Rancière 2006, p. 34). As I anticipated, I found that documentary films could render visible lives and experiences of those otherwise anonymous migrants who, once in Europe, managed to share stories of their efforts to navigate European borders. As Rancière, writing about Chantal Akerman's *De l'autre cote*, explains:

> The film's political impact consists precisely in the way it turns an economic and geopolitical issue into an aesthetic matter, the way in which it produces a confrontation between two sides, and a series of conflicting narratives around the raw materiality of the fence.
>
> (Rancière 2010, p. 150)

All of the elements of the *dispositif* of externalization will surface if we pay attention to the aesthetics of the documentary I chose, not only because it regards the geographical locus of my research, but also for two essential methodological reasons. First, while the arguably "extraterritorial" extension of the EU's political-legal powers is not entirely new, its methods and idioms are fairly unprecedented, not to mention the intensity with which the European migration control is pursued all over North Africa as well as sub-Saharan Africa. Although there have been several efforts to examine the dynamics of migration from Africa to Europe, scholarly analyses have either focused on policy and interstate relations and have disregarded the human dimension or have attempted to map the route of the flow, almost like a herd, along geographical lines, with each route confined within its proper academic locus. I, instead, attempt to frame my research inside the gaze of a camera lens that intrudes on the intimacy of a few young Ethiopians who, with hardly any prospects for their future, left Addis Ababa, their families, and society (Foucault, 1977).

This camera lens is the documentary film *Like a Man on Earth* (Segre & Yimer 2008). Without assuming that documentaries have any power of true representation, I believe that the memories, gestures, and body language of the persons in the film ably recall the challenges that these contemporary migrants had to face and reveal nuances between the lines of contemporary policies of migration control in Africa. This leads me to the second reason, which relates to the representational power of *Like a Man on Earth*. When I consider the aesthetic dimension of this film, I mean to pay attention to issues of time and space more than to its commercial or artistic rank among other video documentaries. What is important is to read the director's endeavor as an "attempt at reconfiguring the partitions of space and time" of discourses of migration that insist on a hierarchy of high (states, politicians, public figures) and low (migrants and their interlocutors), of subjects/agents, policies, and data over most persons' lives.

I met Dagmawi Yimer, also known as Dag, in December 2009, one year after the release of *Like a Man on Earth*. Dag was a student at the Faculty of Law of

Addis Ababa University when instances of political oppression and electoral corruption after the general elections (Anonymous 2006) of May 2005 made him leave his community. He embarked on a long and perilous journey to Rome, where eventually he was granted the status of a refugee. When in Rome, after surviving the violence of Europe's geospatial borders, Dag joined the school of Italian language in the Asinitas Cultural Association, a meeting space for African migrants in Rome. There, Dag not only learned to speak Italian but also became skilled in the language of video documentaries. Shortly after, in an attempt to shred the veil of silence shrouding how contemporary European policies of migration control are implemented in Africa, he decided to gather the memories of others who, like him, had journeyed from Ethiopia to Rome via Libya.

I then decided to regard Dag's film as a *leitmotiv* for my project. Like my work, his film examines a fundamental shift in policies of migration regulation and control in the European Union: the externalization of a regime of control to the Mediterranean Basin and beyond. North Africa, as his film shows, is an increasingly important field for the application of the EU's migration policies, and this shift of importance stems from invigorated efforts to stem a perceived tide of EU-bound immigrants before they even reach the EU's borders. Coincidentally, Dag's documentary resonates with all of the different loci of analysis of this book: the journey through the desert on trucks before reaching the coast of Libya, where migrants embark until they are intercepted at sea by the Italian Coast Guard and towed to the island of Lampedusa. After he obtained refugee status, Dag chose to visit Frontex's headquarters in Warsaw, where he managed to conduct an interview with the agency director. In the meantime, the backdrop to the stories of the African migrants who gather in the kitchen of the Asinitas Association is the city of Rome.

What can be heard: politicians arguing for the creation of new walls or media venting citizens' frustration about increasing unemployment and/or cultural loss/contamination, both allegedly caused by "illegals." And what can be seen: boats loaded with desperate people who police authorities rescue. Both kinds of sensory experience, and their limitations, depend on the discourses of migration mentioned previously. What cannot be heard and what must remain invisible: a migrant reclaiming her political subjectivity within the new host society. This documentary succeeds precisely in revealing what the recent transformations of policies of migration control in Europe and in Africa keep concealed. For instance, the interviews reveal to the audience the crude reality of the EU-sponsored or inspired (either directly or indirectly) detention/asylum/immigrant camps that have sprung up in Libya as a testimony to the changing dynamics of the EU's migration control regime.

In other words, I read Dag's documentary as an effort to reappropriate agency and voice his and his companions' experiences in a universal (visual) language that breaks the aforementioned hierarchy. The author's capacity of expression reclaims temporal and spatial mobility, not only within the host society (Italy in this case) but also in spaces and times that actively resist the host society's efforts to establish itself as a definite, clearly demarcated geopolitical territory.

Dag's agency as a person does not spring from his arrival in democratic but obviously radically hierarchic Europe. While breaking away from his society of origin along certain queer routes and at certain queer speeds, he reveals autonomy that, within the conventional geospatial logic of international relations, Third World migrants ought not to have outside of colonial and post-colonial ordering structures. This exemplifies what Rancière means by subjectification that is "the production through a series of actions, of a body and a capacity for enunciation not previously identifiable within a given field of experience, whose identification is thus part of the reconfiguration of the field of experience" (Rancière, p. 35).

To further underline the political significance of Dag's interviews, it is important to mention that *Like a Man on Earth* is part of a larger project, the Migrant Memories' Archive which, since 2006, has sought to recuperate both the memory and the dignity of the migratory path of many out of the Horn of Africa. The project is the outcome of conversations between social workers of the Asinitas Association, academic scholars specializing in the colonial and post-colonial history of the region of the Horn of Africa, and a group of refugees from the same area. According to Alessandro Triulzi, professor of history of sub-Saharan Africa at the University of Naples "L'Orientale," The project follows multiple paths. Certainly it explores the possibility of filling the lacuna between migrants and the host community.

Describing this alienation, Abdelmalek Sayad elaborates the idea of the double absence (2004), which is the social condition of the emigrant/immigrant who is condemned to be absent twice, both in respect to her origins and her new society. Through the migrants' active participation in narrating and setting the conditions for the narration, the archive facilitates the dispersion of the double absence, altering the usual process by which "we" (migration experts, academics, and journalists) speak on the "other's" behalf. While I have previously underlined the ways in which Dag and his companions reappropriate their capacities of self-representation, it is also important to note how their project seems to challenge the very limits of the concept of an archive conceived of as a "closed" system of memory storage.

This is extremely important with regard to Italy and its colonial past. The peculiar ending to Italy's half century of colonial rule, the fact that it ended not because of revolts but within a larger military defeat and political collapse, perpetuated images and memories of Italian colonizers as benign. It is well beyond the scope of this book to discuss Italian colonialism's burden, about which recent compelling studies (Ben-Ghiat & Fuller 2005; Aruffo 2003; Lombardi-Diop & Romeo 2012) have been published. Nevertheless, control of the colonial archives was crucial to maintain the general amnesia and construct what has been defined by Ernest Renan as "a willed remembering to forget" (Bhabha 1990, pp. 8–22). Perhaps there is too much to forget. There is the shame of military defeats among which stands out that by Ethiopian troops at Adwa in 1896. Also, there is the extreme poverty of the Italian population, a country of emigrants euphemistically promoted to the rank of explorers by the fascist rhetoric, and the financial precariousness of the diasporic state that was the trademark of Italian colonialism.

But, perhaps more than anything else, official memory presented Italian colonialism sugarcoated with respect to its capability for violence, while in reality it attained a notable primacy in military aggression: the world's first use of aerial bombardments during the Italo- Turkish War in 1911–1912; the first country to use gases in violation of the 1925 Gas Protocol in Lybia, Eritrea, and Ethiopia; genocidal tactics to crush the resistance of native populations with the exploitation of abusive relationships with colonial intermediaries such as *askari* (local soldiers serving in the European colonial army). Here, the documentary opens the archive with an image of *askari* fighting along Italian soldiers in Libya and Ethiopia. Dag's profile superimposes and resembles uncannily that of an Ethiopian soldier and while newsreels go on, his voice insinuates that we should begin back "when our grandfathers met" (Segre & Yimer 2008). A train leaves the Rome Central Station as the story continues on Dag's own archives, which incorporate that of his country built on the sediments of a colonial past. Along these lines, the active and continuous participation of migrants in the archive's construction renders the project a political act, *un fare politico*.

## Structure of the book

> *Il faut aimer les portes car elles sont le lieu où nul ne reste*
> *Le lieu par où l'on passé par où l'on part*
> *par où s'en viennent toutes rencontres.*
> *Il faut haïr les portes fermées fermées aux rencontres*
> *et fermées aux départs.*[5]

(Pierre 1955)

This book is divided into eight different chapters, each one dealing with particular levels of the phenomenon of African migration in Europe. The epigraph taken from the collection of poems "*Feuilles éparses*" of Abbé Pierre, founder of the Emmaus movement for helping refugees and the poor, traces out the direction to my conceptualization of the borders (see Chapter 2) and thus to the entire book. As a matter of fact, each chapter dealing with specific aspects of the apparatus, landscapes, technologies, and practices facing migrants' trajectories takes the name of a door. Each chapter is a door to open and point out the idea of the border as a possible passage but also as a barrier, a filter, and a violent break in migrants' journeys. It was with great contentment that I realized much later in the process of writing this book how a few African migrants actually shared the same vision of the border, not seen inevitably as a wall that impedes migrants' journeys but from time to time as a beacon of politics and life like the island of Lampedusa. Migrants are quite wary of those borders that shut down their hopes but know very well that others are meeting points where no one stops and continues the journey. Rose, for instance, explained to me that borders could save the life of migrants. She was three months pregnant when she was intercepted by the Italian Navy around Lampedusa and transferred to the nearest hospital. Today, she and her baby are safe and healthy. Many others told me that borders are necessary to provide security against bad people with evil intentions, and Morteza concluded: "Even clouds have a limit."

Therefore, the "brick door" deals with the city, the "sand door" with the Sahara Desert, the "blue door" with Lampedusa, and so on. As I previously stated in this introduction, I believe that it is naïve, if not risky, to keep considering the border a static standing wall. The border is not a neutral line but registers power relations between capital, institutions, and migrants. Unquestionably, borders' ubiquity and permeability generate a certain anxiety within the nation-state but, more importantly borders too often traverse with violence the lives of migrants who get caught in their thresholds in a contemporary world more open to flows of capital than to human bodies' circulation. In particular, Chapter 1 traces the genesis of the concept of the externalization of migration control at the European level. This chapter emphasizes how the process of Europe's disappearing internal border checks, the Schengen Area, has tremendously impacted constructions of the idea of Europe. The chapter concludes by problematizing the concept of borders and calling for a redefinition of them to be developed in the following section.

Chapter 2 introduces a personal reconceptualization of the border and provides a theoretical umbrella for the rest of my book. This theoretical approach, which stresses the essentially dialectical nature of borders and frontiers, will then be applied to each subsequent chapter. In general, these chapters seek to concretely apply the theoretical insights from the reconceptualizing of borders as they move away from ahistorical conceptions of borders and frontiers (which do not pay attention to the concrete conditions in which actors interact).

Chapter 3 shows how the externalization of European migration control has been implemented in North Africa and how African migrants deal with the crossing of the Sahara Desert. Consequently, as the growing trend of outsourcing of migration controls from Europe to Africa clearly shows, the border has moved outside, away from nominal European national borders. The chapter focuses attention on Libya and on the migrant route that connects the Horn of Africa to the coastline of Maghreb via Sudan and interrogates the impasse of conceiving the Sahara Desert as an enormous camp (à la Agamben) where migrants die without any hope or agency. I also trace the nationalist, developmentalist, and social anxieties and violence that accompany the uprising in Libya and the Western intervention in 2011 regarding a potential – which never occurred – migrant invasion in Europe. With a focus on the experience of migrants from the Horn of Africa in Tripoli, I explore the relationship between a securitization of migration and xenophobic attacks on migrants and the intensification of policing practices geared toward regulating the movement of migrant bodies and capital.

Chapter 4 moves north, where African migrants reach the coastline of Libya and attempt to cross the Mediterranean Sea. The chapter seeks to theorize the dynamics that emerge from the intimate relation between contemporary borders and biopolitics. Starting from the news of the seventy-three Eritreans who perished around the island of Lampedusa on August 2009 after being stranded at sea for three weeks, this chapter relies on narratives, personal observations, and photographs taken on the island of Lampedusa during the summer of 2009. The chapter also highlights changes to Italian migration control policies and how asylum seekers' receptions and concepts of borders and frontiers in the Mediterranean Sea have changed as a result.

Chapter 5 argues that the correspondence between law, institutions, and the actions of individuals modulates the visibility of the border and defines the southern limits of Europe in this particular historical moment. In the same waters on which Ulysses and Aeneas sailed for years, the Italian government has recently erected new borders that traverse two distinct legal realms, one national and one international. At the domestic level, with the introduction and subsequent enforcement of the crime of aiding and abetting clandestine immigration (Article 110 of the criminal code, Article 12 of Legislative Decree 286/98), the state criminalized de facto any action aimed at rescuing boatloads of African migrants who may become stranded in the Mediterranean Sea. At the international level, on 6 May 2009, following a bilateral agreement with Libya that skipped over parliamentarian debates, the Italian government unilaterally inaugurated a new strategy for stemming the flow of African migrants and asylum seekers. It consisted of intercepting migrants in Mediterranean international waters and sending them back to Libya.

Chapter 6 theorizes the role of technologies in changing the contemporary understanding of the border. It illustrates how border practices that are intended only to be re-enacted outside the geopolitical edges of states do not account for the reapplication of technologies that are overproduced in Europe's highly industrialized societies and re-employed by African migrants. Technologies of migration control (satellites/biometrics/radar) are therefore at the same time the means and ends of the same process. Through these technologies, migrants are detected and differently included within the host society in positions of vulnerability. However, at the same time, they become crucial economic components of research and industrial development for receiving countries within a comprehensive technécology of migration control. I call this approach *technécology* to stress the interconnectivity between technological practices of migration control and the utilization of the same technologies to migrate and transform one's environment.

Chapter 7 concludes the journey from Africa into Europe. Specifically, it follows a few African migrants into the city of Rome. In this chapter, I locate one of the new frontiers of Europe within a paradox of the city of Rome that is both fundamental and vital to its economic expansion. The chapter explores the inexorable growth of buildings together with the mounting rejection and marginalization of an emergent immigrant population and seeks to understand how contemporary Rome's urbanscapes are changing with the new immigrant communities that live within the nation-state and at the core of the city. The analysis of this paradox is crucial and reveals the way cityspace as a striated space is traversed by memories, sounds, images, and experiences – a sort of living and pulsing archive that is transformed and remembered in interesting ways by the new migrants. The chapter takes into consideration the ways in which migration control policies and migrants' lived experiences transform and have been transformed by the city.

Lastly, in Chapter 8, I highlight a series of processes, problems, and instances that allow us to theorize the political subjectivity of undocumented migrants. More specifically, the conclusions draw on fieldwork in Lampedusa that culminated in the *LampedusaInFestival* event without limiting itself to a single ethnographic study. This chapter looks at how the island of Lampedusa has acquired a symbolic status, serving as both the camp and the gateway of Europe, with the power to attract and catalyze different subjects, some of whom are active in political struggles, their undocumented status notwithstanding. By focusing on the material conditions that generate tensions at the border, I conclude the book by looking up to a political space within which new kind of political subjects do operate, beyond the logic of citizenship and established methods of political organization.

## References

Agamben, G., 2009. *"What Is an Apparatus?" and Other Essays*. Stanford, CA: Stanford University Press.

Anonymous, 2006. Ethiopian Protesters "Massacred." *BBC*. Available at: http://news.bbc.co.uk/2/hi/africa/6064638.stm [Accessed 3 October 2010]

Anzaldúa, G., 2007. *Borderlands/La Frontera: The New Mestiza*. 3rd ed. San Francisco, CA: Aunt Lute Books.

Aruffo, A., 2003. *Storia del colonialismo italiano: da Crispi a Mussolini*. Rome, Italy: Datanews.

Balibar, E. & Hahn, D., 2002. *Politics and the Other Scene*. London, UK: Verso.

Ben-Ghiat, R. & Fuller, M. eds., 2005. *Italian Colonialism (Italian and Italian American Studies)*. New York, NY: Palgrave Macmillan.

Berger, J., 1989. *A Seventh Man*. London, UK: Penguin Books/Granta.

Bhabha, H. K., 1990. *Nation and Narration*. London, UK: Psychology Press.

Bleiker, R., 2009. *Aesthetics and World Politics*. New York, NY: Palgrave Macmillan.

Das, V., 2007. *Life and Words: Violence and the Descent into the Ordinary*. Oakland, CA: University of California Press.

Debrix, F., 2003. *Rituals of Mediation: International Politics and Social Meaning*. Minneapolis, MN: University of Minnesota Press.

Fahrmeir, A., Faron, O. & Weil, P., 2005. *Migration Control in the North Atlantic World: The Evolution of State Practices in Europe and the United States from the French Revolution to the Inter-War Period*. New York, NY: Berghahn Books.

Foucault, M., 1977. The Political Function of the Intellectual. *Radical Philosophy*, RP017 (Summer). Available at: www.radicalphilosophy.com/article/the-political-function-of-the-intellectual [Accessed 20 September 2011]

Foucault, Michel, 1980. *Power/Knowledge: Selected Interviews and Other Writings, 1972–1977*. Vintage.

Guild, E. & Bigo, D., 2003. Le visa Schengen: expression d'une stratégie de « police » à distance. *Cultures & Conflicts*, n. 49 1/2003, pp. 22–37.

Higgins, N., 2001. Image and Identity: Mexican Indians and Photographic Art. *Social Alternatives*, 20(4), pp. 22–36.

Jaar, A., 1998. Let There Be Light: The Rwanda Project 1994–1998. Available at: www.imaginarymuseum.org/MHV/PZImhv/JaarRwandaProject.html [Accessed 21 September 2011]

Lombardi-Diop, C. & Romeo, C., 2012. *Postcolonial Italy: Challenging National Homogeneity*. New York, NY: Palgrave Macmillan.

Martiniello, M. & Rath, J., 2010. *Selected Studies in International Migration and Immigrant Incorporation*. Amsterdam, The Netherlands: Amsterdam University Press.

Morgenthau, H. J., 1965. *Scientific Man versus Power Politics*. Chicago, IL: University of Chicago Press.

Rajaram, P. K. & Grundy-Warr, C., 2008. *Borderscapes: Hidden Geographies and Politics at Territory's Edge*. Minneapolis, MN: University of Minnesota Press.

Rancière, J., 1998. *Disagreement: Politics and Philosophy*. Minneapolis, MN: University of Minnesota Press.

Rancière, J., 2006. *The Politics of Aesthetics*. London, UK: Continuum.

Rancière, J., 2010. *Dissensus: On Politics and Aesthetics*. London, UK: Continuum.

Rinelli, L., 2009a. Another Saddish Story Today. Available at: http://no-racism.net/arti cle/2934/ [Accessed 13 December 2010]

Rinelli, L., 2009b. To Get What We Have Lost. *JGCinema.com*. Available at: www.jgcin ema.com/single.php?sl=shapiro-cinema-politics [Accessed 21 September 2009]

Sayad, A., 2004. *The Suffering of the Immigrant*. Cambridge, UK: Polity.

Segre, A. & Yimer, D., 2008. *Like a Man on Earth*. Available at: http://likeamanonearth. blogspot.com/ [Accessed 21 September 2011]

Shapiro, M. J., 2008. *Cinematic Geopolitics*. New York, NY: Routledge.

Shapiro, M. J. & Alker, H. R., 1995. *Challenging Boundaries: Global Flows, Territorial Identities*. Minneapolis, MN: University of Minnesota Press.

Sontag, S., 1988. *Illness as Metaphor*. New York, NY: Farrar, Straus and Giroux.

Wells, L., 2002. *The Photography Reader*. New York, NY: Routledge.

Yourcenar, M., 2005. *Memoirs of Hadrian*. New York, NY: Farrar, Straus and Giroux.

Zolberg, A. R., 1989. The Next Waves: Migration Theory for a Changing World. *International Migration Review*, 23(3), p. 403.

## Notes

1   Blair, Tony. (2003). *New International Approaches to Asylum Processing and Protection*. Available at: www.statewatch.org/news/2003/apr/blair-simitis-asile.pdf [Accessed 7 March 2008].

2   Italian political philosopher Giorgio Agamben (2009, p. 14) defines *dispositif* when he writes:

> Further expanding the already large class of Foucauldian apparatuses, I shall call an apparatus literally anything that has in some way the capacity to capture, orient, determine, intercept, model, control, or secure the gestures, behaviors, opinions, or discourses of living beings. Not only, therefore, prisons, madhouses, the Panopticon, schools, confession, factories, disciplines, judicial measures, and so forth (whose connection with power is in a certain sense evident), but also the pen, writing, literature, philosophy, agriculture, cigarettes, navigation, computers, cellular telephones and – why not – language itself, which is perhaps the most ancient of apparatuses – one in which thousands and thousands of years ago a primate inadvertently let himself be captured, probably without realizing the consequences that he was about to face.

3   Geopolitics has been obsessed with a particular kind of photography, the most famous being the U2 photos of Cuba that started the missile crisis. Generally speaking, the world of intelligence gathering has been one of "realist" (in the art sense) photography. The possibility that the visible can "lie" has never been acknowledged despite the fact that images have often been misinterpreted or misrecognized. From Loch Ness Monster images to the obsessive scrutiny of satellite images searching in hopes of discovering clandestine nuclear silos, enemy troop movements, or "weapons of mass destruction" facilities in Iraq, the self-evident reality of the photograph is an important

part of geopolitics, just one that requires neither interpretation nor theory. It is fact, fact enough to invade.

4  I am thinking here of James Der Derian, Michael Shapiro, Cynthia Weber, Anthony Burk, David Campbell, and Nevzat Soguk, to name only a few.

5  We must love the doors because they are the place where no one stops. The place where we pass, where we leave from, where all the meetings take place. You have to hate the closed doors, closed to encounters and closed to those who leave (author's translation).

# Acknowledgments

Several of the chapters in this book appeared in academic journals and almost every conference, workshop, and public lecture I have taken part in. I am grateful to the editors and discussants who have engaged in stimulating conversations with me and helped me to carve out my intuitions along the way. I am forever indebted to my mentor and friend Nevzat Soguk who, first among others, professed the quality of my research. However, I could not even start thinking of crafting this study into the body of work that it is now without the careful reading, countless inspiring conversations, and enduring friendship of Sam Opondo, a brilliant scholar who has been so kind to accompany me, physically and figuratively, to his Africa. His intelligence has been so welcoming and refreshing that I often found myself at home, lost in it. I owe many thanks to the intellectual milieu I had the fortune to be part of during my life in Hawaii. In particular, sincere thanks to Rohan Kalyan, Amy Donahue, and Fabiano Mielniczuk for those spirited evenings of delicious food and writing. Thanks to Noah Viernes and Jason Adams, who have offered many critical insights on many occasions. Thanks also to Michael Shapiro, Sankaran Krishna, Nandita Sharma, and Manfred Henningsen for their guidance and help. Without a doubt, I feel in debt to Dagmawi Imer who, with his courage, tenacity, and film work, inspired me and introduced me to the school of migrants Asinitas in Rome where I met considerate social workers and extraordinary migrants. Ultimately, this book is for those who walk strenuously from one life to the next, always with courage and faith. Finally, I dedicate this book to my parents, Domenico and Preziosa who, as migrants themselves, taught me everything I know, but in particular to value migrants for their strength, which is the result of both hope and suffering.

# 1 Externalization

*The philosophy behind that is that border control cannot be carried out at the border only. We have to act before the border where the problem arises, we have to cooperate and act across the border, with our colleagues in third countries and then at the border and also behind the border.*

Colonel Ikka Laitinen, former Executive
Director of Frontex (Segre & Yimer 2008)

## 1.1 An introduction

For centuries in Europe, the territory between city-states was of no great concern to sovereign powers, which were more preoccupied with those who lived in the city and determining how many people could enter in relation to how many would leave. Admission decisions were made at the ports, riverbanks, and gates of the city. Even today, political analysts and historians of migration note strong similarities between contemporary gateways and those of the past. A renowned example is depicted, for instance, in Mimmo Gangemi's latest novel *La signora di Ellis Island* (*Ellis Island's Lady*, 2011), where Ellis Island is the quintessential mechanism of filtering in/out the US' foreign population. However, modern gateways such as Ellis Island also reveal differences between past and present-day practices of migration control. Perhaps the most striking is that whereas state immigrant selection used to be made at a country's gateway, today a process of extraterritorial selection is far more common. The globalization of extraterritorial immigration control that characterized our globalized world is perfectly embodied within the epigraph of this chapter that illustrates the role of Frontex acting as a linkage between European Union (EU) member states and other countries by coordinating immigration policies and legislations at the border, wherever it may be. This chapter deals indeed with the nature of extraterritorial European migration control.

In general, one can argue that the beginning of extraterritorial migration control practices began with the introduction of the visa (Torpey 2000). Nonetheless, while practices of extraterritorial migration control have been largely implemented by Western states in the past two decades since the introduction of visa requirements, after 9/11, this approach changed in kind as border controls have become more diffuse and less clearly localizable. Globalization's perception of increased human flows combined with the global war on terror has been infused with an idea of a permanent and disperse clash of civilizations (Huntington 1993). Thus, since 9/11, the category of the exceptional has been invoked to justify an array of violent practices that feature in the *dispositif* of the externalization of migration control: detention without trial, derogation of human rights law, torture, "extraordinary rendition," curtailment of civil liberties, and the securitization of migration. Concurrently, the concept of exceptionalism has prompted a switch from the mere control of immigration (e.g. determining how many people can enter relative to how many people will leave) to the detection of human movement within and away from the gateways of the state. In Europe, the space between and within city-states has become the field of migration control activity.

In this regard, while the practice of extraterritorial immigration control is at the core of the idea of European externalization of African migration control intended as the EU's endeavor to export its migration and asylum policies onto southern surrounding regions, this geospatial conception does not, as I envision it, account for all of externalization's features. McSweeney's (1999, p. 16) comments are apropos in this context. He argues that "the individual is ignored in conceptualizing the idea of security at the state level, only to be reinstated as its basic rationale – as it must be – in order to make sense of, and legitimize, the policy derived." The individual intended as the abstract legitimate member of any European society is the rationale of an apparatus securitization that actively ignores and is directed against actual, not abstract, individuals. This Other individual – vaguely dark-skinned, meager, most certainly undocumented, from the South – is the target of the policy of externalization. Thus, undocumented (read: untraceable) immigration has been singled out in security issues as an international threat to peace and stability.

A chain of syllogistic deductions is unleashed. There is migration. Therefore, there is a risk. Therefore, there is a possibility and perhaps a civil duty of intervention. Instead of focusing only on the extraterritorial aspect then, I contend that the discursive and deterritorializing nature of the European externalization of migration control makes it characteristically polycentric and polymorphic in response to the reterritorialization movements of African migrants. As much as it moves outside (Sahara Desert and Mediterranean Sea), it also extends and shapes the inside, including the domestic management of economic resources (Frontex), virtual dimensions (biometric databases), and urban spaces (Rome's urban plan) as specular reflections of African movements. Without denying the massive centripetal force that Europe exercises over Africa in terms of capitalism and neoliberal models, I argue that the system of externalization of migration control and African movements are affected by a reciprocal conditionality in an incessant cycle of deterritorialization and reterritorialization (Guattari & Deleuze 1987).

Significantly, to understand how migrations not only cross boundaries but also intervene in the true process of making boundaries, we start from the premise that the apparatus of externalization has been put into practice through a process of problematization. How might the Foucauldian concept of problematization function in this particular context? To problematize means to read practice in a certain way. As Soguk explains, Foucault intends problematization as the idea that "transforms the difficulties and obstacles of practice into a general problem for which one proposes diverse political solutions" (Foucault 1984) p. 389 in Soguk 1999, p. 50). This includes a necessary initial stage of analysis of a particular situation during which certain activities are understood as "difficulties": for example, the European member states conceive the influx of immigrants into the EU as trouble. Through the first stage of problematization, tension charges spaces where migrants' now-detrimental trajectories cross discourses of (in)security and neoliberal capitalism. However, "danger is an effect of interpretation" (p. 2). Indeed, African migrants help shape states and societies with their movements that intrude and spread a more intense globalization. One merges into the other. The border, as I discuss further later, is located at these points in time and space that are charged with a political force typical of globalization generating the border; it is not necessarily at the gateways of European countries.

It is also important to emphasize how the process of Europe's disappearing internal border checks has tremendously impacted constructions of the idea of Europe to the point that it has been underlined in Article 3, para 2, of the new Treaty on the European Union [TEU] as modified by the Treaty of Lisbon in force since 1 December 2009, as it states that:

> The Union shall offer its citizens an area of freedom, security and justice without internal frontiers, in which the free movement of persons is ensured in conjunction with appropriate measures with respect to external border controls, asylum, immigration and the prevention and combating of crime.
>
> (TEU post Lisbon, art. 3, para. 2 2010 O.J. C 83/17)

While the abolishment of passport control at old gates fortified the Union, it widened the separation with Africa, to the point that this internal process marked a crucial moment in the process of the externalization of migration control. These twenty years since Schengen have transformed the entire Mediterranean and Maghreb into the last major frontier of Europe and, not coincidentally, into a space to be vigorously, and violently, managed and controlled. However, to comprehend the intimate link between the project of the EU and contemporary European migration control policies, we must travel back in time to a period of twenty years ago when the Schengen Area became reality in Europe and opened the internal borders among the European states. Perhaps from the moment that the Schengen Treaty went into force (1995), it has been the most celebrated European pact since the signing of the Treaty of Rome that created the European Economic Community (1957). Call to mind the imaginative power of that moment. Like a good fairy tale ending, the Schengen Agreement defined the new dimensions of Europe:

> Hence the checks on persons are only carried out at the time of crossing of the external border of a member State, which then acts on behalf of all of the other States of the Schengen area.[1]

That instant, crystallized in cinematic form, remains in the images of Wim Wenders' *Lisbon Story* (Wenders 1994).[2] At the beginning of the movie, we drive with the protagonist Winter from Germany to Lisbon, Portugal, and we share his sense of freedom as he passes checkpoints abandoned at the border. Winter is intoxicated by this new experience; we watch him laughing frantically as he passes the border where no one is stationed and where nobody will search inside his trunk. Winter's exuberance was shared. At that time, European citizens were all inebriated by the image of a borderless Europe; Schengen marked perhaps the first time that citizens of European member states felt part of a great project or could at least enjoy the effects of a project, the EU, that had always been too far removed from everyday reality. Only later did people start to realize that the borders simply multiplied, thickened, and migrated where they were not before. Only later did people understand that ubiquitous border practices are intimately connected with the power of imagination. In this sense, the outside and inside are uncannily tied.

As a matter of fact, notwithstanding the force of international agreements, member states reserve the right to temporarily reintroduce controls at their internal borders when there is a serious threat to public policy or internal security triggered by special events such as the Olympic Games. According to the Migration Policy Institute, "between 2000 and 2003, Schengen member States reinstated border controls 33 times and, in almost half of the cases, they did so in anticipation of political events such as European Council meetings" (Migration Policy Institute, Paper No. 20/2007).[3] Recently in May 2011, the leaders of France and Italy asked to revise the Treaty of Schengen. The problem, as they explained it, was that over a thousand Tunisians were traveling with temporary visas issued in Italy: "the situation concerning migration in the Mediterranean could rapidly transform into a crisis that would undermine the trust that our compatriots have in the [principle] of freedom of travel within Schengen" (Anonymous 2011a). After this episode, home affairs ministers decided unanimously to allow member states to "reimpose border controls for six months, renewable for another six, when the control of an external border is no longer ensured due to exceptional circumstances" related to migratory pressures (Anonymous 2012). We are reminded with France's reintroduction of controls at its geographical limits with Italy specifically to stop Tunisians traveling through the Alps, of Schmitt's (1985, p. 5) assertion that the "sovereign is he who decides on the exception."

While protection and hospitality for 25,000–30,000 Tunisians was on the agenda, it seems obvious that relations between Europe and Maghreb were not part of the negotiations. Rather, "neither country wants to accommodate the North Africa migrants and both want to ensure the situation is not repeated in the future" (Anonymous 2011a). Thus, hundreds of Tunisians were rounded up in Paris and Marseille and put in prison for a night or two before being sent back into the streets, where they joined an invisible army of undocumented workers. Regime practices, therefore, work not so much to "solve" the "refugee problem" as to utilize bodies marked as refugees to stabilize various territorialized relations, institutions, and identities that afford the state its reason for being (Soguk 1999, p. 52).

What, then, is the externalization of migration control if not a regime practice, a *dispositif*, whose different elements work together for a common goal – namely, to manage the specific historical urgency of this new problem of unmanaged, excess African migrant bodies? When we pay close attention to the text of the Schengen website, it contains in itself the genes of the *dispositif* of externalization:

> To reconcile freedom and security, this freedom of movement was accompanied by so-called "compensatory" measures. With this in mind, the Schengen Information System (SIS) was set up. SIS is a sophisticated database used by the authorities of the Schengen member countries to exchange data on certain categories of people.[4]

Not only databases such as SIS and later SIS II but also other "compensatory" measures accompany the project of the Schengen Area of "free" movement, such as more effective coordination between administrations on border surveillance and police cooperation on forced repatriations (see Chapter 6 for a detailed analysis of these compensatory measures). It is gradually more clear that the inside and the outside are blurred (Walker 1992); there is not externalization without the idea of a homogenous space of Schengen. Externalization must be analyzed, then, along the discourse of Europeanization and be traced along this discourse's trajectory through time and space. I will therefore now proceed to examine those policy documents that constitute the process of externalization and how the nation-state attempts to retain its predominant position despite the apparent *communitarization* of migration control policies. Most likely, the key moment signaling the revival of the European integration after the institutional crisis of the 1970s was the making of the Single European Act (1986). According to its creator, Jaques Delors, this act was designed to allow the new economic Union to withstand challenges of economic globalization:

> The Single Act means the commitment of implementing simultaneously the great market without frontiers, more economic and social cohesion, a European research and technology policy, the strengthening of the European Monetary System, the beginning of a European social area and significant actions in environment.[5]

A further and important advancement was made in 1992 with the Treaty on European Union (TEU), signed in Maastricht, which established agreement on moves toward a single currency, among other institutional reforms. Namely, the TEU introduced a structure that consists of three "pillars" that remained in force until 1 December 2009 upon the entry into force of the Treaty of Lisbon when the EU obtained a consolidated legal personality. The three pillars were the European Community [EC] pillar that concerns common policies, monetary union, and citizenship; the Common Foreign and Security Policy (CFSP) pillar that relates to common defence; and the Justice and Home Affairs (JHA) pillar, which was shrunk and renamed Police and Judicial Co-operation in Criminal Matters (PJC) in 2003. The first two were distinctly intergovernmental; that is, the member states were powerful actors, and they controlled the nature and the pace of the process. The third pillar, PJC, is of particular interest to us since, under the TEU, member states cooperate in areas such as the formation of asylum policies, the control of people crossing the external frontiers of the Union, immigration policy, and judicial practice. A fundamental shift later occurred with the Treaty of Amsterdam (1997), which apparently made JHA communitarian.

This constitutes an important moment; plausibly since the beginning, the member states showed reluctance to bind themselves to any supranational law. However, JHA officials found other ways to establish autonomy at the European level, particularly by collaborating with counterparts of other member states. If we maintain a vision of the EU's architecture that is not just multilevel but also polycentric, then we can see how the member states could maintain their roles as keepers of national concerns through dialogue within EU institutions. Lavenex (2006, p. 331) clearly states that "by acting jointly at the intergovernmental level, national executives gain an information advantage over their domestic counterparts and act in the capacity of gatekeeper." The Treaty of Amsterdam's paradigmatic shift of immigration policy at the European level nonetheless allowed subsets of member states, such as particular parties, courts, and domestic civil societies, to operate relatively freely of supranational constraint. With the Treaty of Lisbon in force since 2009, the changes in the JHA area seem to be more of a technical nature rather than amounting to substantial changes. Nevertheless, the rules of the treaty constitute a further step in ongoing development in the field of JHA of the EU in terms of more harmonization among member state and European institutions.

An external dimension of the EU in terms of the control and filtering of asylum seekers was substantively embraced in 1999 at the Special European Council on Justice and Home Affairs in Tampere. There, the EU declared its intention to establish a Common European Asylum System to be based on the full and inclusive application of the Geneva Convention. The five-year agenda from 1999 to 2004 – the "Tampere Programme" – outlined the first set of legally binding EU-level asylum agreements. It also designated temporary protections for persons displaced by conflicts; established a common understanding of refugee status; and detailed subsidiary protections such as formal legal warranties, minimum procedural guarantees, minimum conditions for the reception of asylum seekers, and procedures for deciding which member state would be responsible for assessing which asylum claim.

Since then, the externalization of European migration control policies has played out at two levels: communitarian and intergovernmental. Nonetheless, the latter has developed much more quickly and powerfully. For instance, Lavenex (2006, p. 331) interprets the externalization of migration control as "a double-edged continuation of the transgovernmental logic of cooperation: in substantive terms through the prioritization of migration control over policy harmonization or a comprehensive approach; and in institutional terms preserving transgovernmental forms of cooperation despite intensifying communitarisation." Without dwelling on single documents, it will suffice to notice that, at the community level, attention to comprehensive economic and social issues has informed migration control approaches, while for single member states, these policies have always primarily been an issue of control. Through the years, member states have developed and implemented an extraterritorial system of immigration control that has centrifugally expanded out from the newly unifying EU. As a result, coordinated visa policies, national liaison officers at airports in countries of origin, and readmission agreements[6] became integral parts of the mechanism, officially celebrated by Article 3(3)[7] of Council Regulation No. 343/2003 of 18 February 2003 that replaced the 1990 Dublin Convention. The list continues.

It is even true that European member states sometimes enthusiastically exceed the letter of the aforementioned regulation, which clearly requires the state of destination to be "in compliance" with basic international refugee treaties. Instead, member states routinely organize group deportations to third, often unsafe, countries. Since unification, governments of Europe have increasingly found it advantageous to delegate the management of undocumented migrants and asylum seekers to third countries. As several authors (Castels 2004; Guirandou and Lahav 2000) demonstrate, different and multiple interests and loci of domestic dissent can clearly constrain governments' attempts to reject unwanted migrants. In other words, the EU and single member states are outsourcing their legal responsibilities to territories where those responsibilities are "subject to minimal scrutiny and accountability" (Oxfam 2005, p. iii), undermining established democratic checks and balances at the core of the EU.

Regarding migration control practices operated outside the purview of the rule of law, because of the methodology adopted, this book will focus mostly on Libya; it is worth recalling a well-publicized mass deportation that the Italian state organized first in the fall of 2004 and later in the spring of the following year. Both expulsion operations deported hundreds of migrants by plane to Libya, which is not a signatory to the Geneva Convention on the protection of refugees.[8] After detention in miserable conditions, these African migrants were deported to different countries of origin in clear breach of the basic principle of non-refoulment. According to the United Nations High Commissioner for Refugees (UNHCR) (2011), Italian authorities have not only breached the non-refoulment principle but also transferred de facto to Libya the responsibility of providing assistance to intercepted African migrants. Deportation flights still continue almost on a weekly basis to different African countries and are perceived by European state representatives as a viable "solution" for the management of an influx of people. For instance, regarding the Anglo-French effort to tackle illegal immigration:

> The joint action plan to tackle the migrant pressure at Calais will include exchange of data to enhance identification, cooperation on redocumentation and joint flights where necessary to deport illegal migrants. . . . In practice, most joint flights would be to Africa or the Indian subcontinent.
>
> (Borger & Wintour 2008)

From the Cimade's press communication of 5 November 2008:

> The French government, in cooperation with the British authorities, are pre-
> paring to send back collectively and by charter Afghan exiles placed in the
> detention centre at Coquelles[. . .] While the humanitarian condition and
> safety continue to worsen in Afghanistan and the non governmental organiza-
> tions like the secretary general of the United Nations declare themselves to be
> particularly worried about the situation Britain and France organize together
> charters destined for Kabul.[9]

It is clear enough that, even if Amsterdam readmission agreements fall within
the communitarian domain, member states actively work to secure bilateral cooperation across the Mediterranean. As a matter of fact, already in May 2002, a
Secretaries of Foreign Affairs conference held in Tripoli discussed the possibility
of integrated regional cooperation on immigration practices. The next year, Libya
officially moved forward at Alessandria (Egypt). Of particular relevance to my
research, in 2004 Italy and Libya concluded an agreement that includes, apart
from high-tech border control equipment, the establishment of reception centers to prevent asylum seekers and migrants from attempting dangerous journeys
across the Sahara and Mediterranean to European cities. At the time, Ferruccio
Pastore noted that:

> It is hard to consider it fortuitous that the EU Council agreed to lift all eco-
> nomic sanctions against Libya, . . . only a few days after Silvio Berlusconi,
> then Head of government, had gone to Libya to inaugurate with Muammar
> Qadhafi, 'Greenstream,' a gas pipeline linking Libya (Mellitah) and Italy.
>
> (Pastore 2007, p. 59)

Italy has been a forerunner when it comes to establishing centers for managing
asylum seekers' requests outside of the states, but the method had already been
utilized with Guantanamo for Haitian asylum seekers and, in the case of Australia's Pacific Solution (Rajaram & Grundy-Warr 2008), with offshore processing
centers in Nauru or PNG. This approach clearly contrasts not only with the tradition of safety havens for people displaced by war and conflicts but also with the
tradition of states processing asylum requests on their own territory (from which
the principle of non-refoulment is derived). Most importantly, for my purposes, it
indicates a recent modification of the concept of the territory of a state and, consequently, of the border. Today's borders accord with the exigencies of the *dispositif*
of externalization.

Bredeloup and Pliez (2011) maintain that intergovernmental initiatives such
as those between Italy and Libya make sense only in relation to certain tragic
events that occurred in 2002, when in June, forty-five Sudanese died in the Sahara
Desert; in September, fourteen Liberians died on their way to Sicily; and in
December, a hundred died in a shipwreck. As a matter of fact, the tragic event of
3 October 2013 when 300 migrants drowned next to the coastlines of Lampedusa

prompted the Italian government to initiate a massive rescue operation named *Mare Nostrum* (Our Sea) that until today has intercepted and rescued thousands of migrants in the Mediterranean Sea (see Chapter 8 for an in-depth discussion). If we hold this true, it underlines the political implications of forms of resistance operated by African migrants whose pressures and lives intervene in the shaping of governmental policies.

Once more, I am not celebrating the heroic resistance of African migrants that, in its basic survival mode, has often tragic and deadly implications. Rather, I intend with this approach to distance myself from a sort of scientific approach to migration that either privileges host societies or governments' point of view. It is true that numerous lives are lost every day along the frontier in the attempt to circumvent migration control that continues to operate in ever-stronger ways. According to Fortress Europe,[10] since 1988, at least 20,035 people have died attempting to cross the frontier because of the heat of the desert or the waves of the sea. On 8 May 2011, the *Guardian* reported the tragic story of a boat carrying seventy-two passengers. They were mostly Eritreans and were therefore most likely eligible to obtain the status of refugees. All but nine of the passengers died. According to the *Guardian*, they had run out of fuel and had been adrift since 27 March – that is, for more than a month. Although the boat encountered a number of military units, no effort was made to save the passengers. Eventually, they died of thirst and hunger. The president of the Council of Europe, Mr. Çavusoglu, called for an inquiry and seemed to voice the general indignation of Europe's elderly when he declared that

> if this grave accusation is true – that, despite the alarm being raised, and despite the fact that this boat, fleeing, had been located by armed forces operating in the Mediterranean, no attempt was made to rescue the 72 passengers aboard, then it is a dark day for Europe as a whole.
>
> (Shenker 2011b)

This is not the first time that African migrant and asylum seekers have been simply and actively ignored by the advanced technologies of European migration control. An almost identical story opens up Chapter 4. There, I explain how the desire of the *dispositif* of European migration control is to render migrants' bodies literally invisible instead of martyrs. Thus, I define externalization as a multifaceted *dispositif* that aims to problematize but also to ignore the movements of people inside, outside, and across the Schengen space. That is, externalization conceptualizes certain human bodies in motion as detrimental trajectories that must be managed by a fluid framework of practices that cannot help but continuously reproduce individualities in excess, such as the lives of those seventy-two migrants. The process of migration control mirrors those trajectories of people that pierce, perforate, and drill the most contested walls and cut across what maps attempt to colonize and make abstract (Certeau 2002, p. 129). Thus, today's borders have changed. They are more flexible and fluid and are characterized by an "erratic geometry"(Mezzadra 2005) which, more than distinguishing the inside from the outside, operates a sort of "differential inclusion"(Palidda 2008). As a result, to understand the *dispositif* of externalization requires a re-thinking of the idea of the border that I advance in the next chapter. Today's borders operate as a new control regime. They create states of permanent insecurity – or, better, a sort of "camp effect." As a complex mechanism, they function as a transnational and transversal regime practice that, like a strainer, makes up "the part of those who have no part" (Rancière 2006) and, simultaneously, merely sketches the silhouette of a hazy European identity.

## Notes

1   www.mediavisa.net/schengen-area.php
2   As a short methodological note, I do not interpret films as a mere cultural representation of what Europe was and is but cinema instead as a critical thinking apparatus that allows us the relation between space and imagination.
3   www.migrationpolicy.org/pubs/FS20_SchengenDisappearingBorders_121807.pdf
4   http://europa.eu/scadplus/leg/en/lvb/l33020.htm
5   www.historiasiglo20.org/europe/acta.htm
6   The first one being concluded in 1991 between the Schengen states and Poland.
7   "Any Member State shall retain the right, pursuant to its national laws, to send an asylum seeker to a third country, in compliance with the provisions of the Geneva Convention."
8   While Libya did not sign the Geneva Convention, it did sign the Convention on Refugee Problems in Africa by the OAU, which implicitly recognized the 1951 Geneva Convention.
9   www.cimade.org/communiques
10   http://fortresseurope.blogspot.com/2006/02/immigrants-dead-at-frontiers-of-europe_16.html

## References

Anonymous, 2012. EU Agrees Short-Term Border Closures to Block Migrants. *France 24*. Available at: www.france24.com/en/20120608-european-union-schengen-border-control-migrants-refugees/ [Accessed 18 August 2014]

Anonymous, 2007. The Lisbon Treaty. *Official Journal of the European Union*, 50(2007/C 306), p. 271.

Anonymous, 2011a. France-Italy Seek Schengen Reform. *BBC*. Available at: www.bbc.co.uk/news/world-europe-13189682 [Accessed 11 May 2011]

Borger, J. & Wintour, P., 2008. More Anglo-French Teamwork Makes Entente Formidable. *The Guardian*. Available at: www.guardian.co.uk/politics/2008/mar/28/foreignpolicy.gordonbrown [Accessed 16 November 2011]

Bredeloup, S. & Pliez, O., 2011. The Libyan Migration Corridor. Available at: http://cadmus.eui.eu/handle/1814/16213 [Accessed 18 January 2015]

Campbell, D., 1998. *Writing Security: United States Foreign Policy and the Politics of Identity*. Minneapolis, MN: University of Minnesota Press.

Castels, S., 2004. The Factors that Make and Unmake Migration Policies. *International Migration Review*, 38(3), pp. 852–884.

de Certeau, M., 2002. *The Practice of Everyday Life*. Oakland, CA: University of California Press.

Foucault, M., 1984 The Foucault Reader, Paul Rabinow ed. New York, NY: Pantheon Books.

Guattari, F. & Deleuze, G., 1987. *A Thousand Plateaus*. Minneapolis, MN: University of Minnesota Press.

Huntington, S., 1993. The Clash of Civilizations? *Foreign Affairs*, 72(3), pp. 22–49.

Lavenex, S., 2006. Shifting Up and Out: The Foreign Policy of European Immigration Control. *West European Politics*, 29(2), pp. 329–350.

McSweeney, B., 1999. *Security, Identity and Interests: A Sociology of International Relations*. Cambridge, UK: Cambridge University Press.

Mezzadra, S., 2005. *Derecho de fuga: migraciones, ciudadanía y globalización*. Madrid, Spain: Traficantes de Sueños.

Oxfam, 2005. *Foreign Territory. The Internationalisation of EU Asylum Policy*. Oxford, UK. Available at: www.compas.ox.ac.uk/fileadmin/files/Events/Events_2005/Foreign%20Territory%20Final%20(English).pdf [Accessed 20 August 2012]

Palidda, S., 2008. *Mobilità umane. Introduzione alla sociologia delle migrazioni*. Milano, Italy: Cortina Raffaello Editore.

Pastore, Ferruccio. 2007. Europe, Migration and Development: Critical Remarks on an Emerging Policy Field. *Development* 50(4): 56–62.

Rajaram, P. K. & Grundy-Warr, C., 2008. *Borderscapes: Hidden Geographies and Politics at Territory's Edge*. Minneapolis, MN: University of Minnesota Press.

Rancière, J., 2006. *The Politics of Aesthetics*. London, UK: Continuum.

Schmitt, C., 1985. *Political Theology: Four Chapters on the Concept of Sovereignty*. Chicago, IL: University of Chicago Press.

Segre, A. & Yimer, D., 2008. *Like a Man on Earth*. Available at: http://likeamanonearth. blogspot.com/ [Accessed 21 September 2011]

Shenker, J., 2011. Libyan Migrants' Boat Deaths to Be Investigated by Council of Europe. *The Guardian*. Available at: www.guardian.co.uk/world/2011/may/09/refugees-libya?intcmp=239 [Accessed 12 May 2011]

Soguk, N., 1999. *States and Strangers: Refugees and Displacements of Statecraft*. Minneapolis, MN: University of Minnesota Press.

Torpey, J., 2000. *The Invention of the Passport: Surveillance, Citizenship and the State*. Cambridge, UK: Cambridge University Press.

United Nations High Commissioner for Refugees (UNHCR), 2011. Submission by the Office of the United Nations High Commissioner for Refugees in the Case of Hirsi and Others v. Italy. Available at: www.unhcr.org/cgi-bin/texis/vtx/home/opendocPDF Viewer.html?docid=4de8e33c9&query=hirsi [Accessed 16 May 2013]

Walker, R.B.J., 1992. *Inside/Outside: International Relations as Political Theory*. Cambridge, UK: Cambridge University Press.

Wenders, W., dir., 1994. *Lisbon Story* (motion picture).

# 2 Frontiers and lives

*And yet I would invite you to pause and consider what Frontiers mean, and what part they play in the life of nations.*

(Lord Curzon 1907)

## 2.1 An invitation

Perhaps nobody more than Lord Curzon would want to pause and consider the consequences of the acts of drawing a line. During his second mandate as Viceroy of India, he presided over the partition of Bengal (16 October 1905) in two provinces: the eastern province, more rural and with a Muslim majority, and the western province, more industrialized with a Hindu majority. The colonial administration considered the eastern part underdeveloped and isolated by natural confines. In reality, the two provinces, although non-homogenously developed, were engaged in a rich set of interconnections. As a matter of fact, the division between eastern and western Bengal, operated by the British colonial government for administrative reasons, fueled one of the first national anti-British movements, to the point that the partition was revoked after only six years of violent opposition, mostly from the Hindu population. However – and this is what matters here – British policy of *divide et impera* was grounded on the idea of the inherent character of divisiveness of certain geographical features such as mountains and rivers. As a matter of fact, the colonial emphasis on difference arguably left an indelible mark on the population living on this geographical area that would be the stage of two other partitions: in 1947, when Bengal turned into East Pakistan, and in 1971, when East Pakistan became the independent state of Bangladesh.

Since Lord Curzon extended his invitation to the audience gathered in the Sheldonian Theater, Oxford, for the 1907 *Romanes Lecture* where he presented his considerations about frontiers, studies regarding frontiers and borders have proliferated. Certainly especially after WWII within the discipline of international relations, the border surged to the role of "mediator" among egotistic state-units, each one the "final judge of its own cause" ((Waltz 1959, p. 160) within an anarchical world system. Then again after the collapse of the Soviet system, the study of borders and frontiers moved beyond the contours of geopolitics and international law, more than ever, to invade the realms of sociology, anthropology, literature, and cultural studies (Anzaldúa 2007). Borders and frontiers were once mere corollaries of nation-states, crucial sites to hold the gate of territorial sovereignty. Today, this is still very much true within the political rhetoric that feeds the panic over the immigrants' invasion and fuels the violent reaction to it. Indeed, this book finds its incipit in a painful story of violent extraction within the urbanscape of the European Union, far from the conventional idea of the border as a fence that serves to exclude. In fact, to limit our understanding of the border to the mere function of banning, like much of the critical studies did (Lago 2009), is deceptive and unrepresentative of the complexity of the border. Not only are there different kinds of borders that perform different functions, but they have also indeed shifted to the level of signifiers, within differential exclusion and inclusion, for increasingly shifty globalized identities.

Notwithstanding the increase of interest on this subject, or perhaps because of this increase, the terms *border* and *frontier* are often interchangeable. As I will explain later in this chapter, the frontier has to be intended as a mobile and imprecise space within which the borders appear and operate, especially in reference to "colonial situations" (Mezzadra & Neilson 2013, p. 15) in Africa. On the contrary, the very search for a rigid classification of "border" may be misguided. As Étienne Balibar has noted, how can we possibly define a border if "to define or identify in general is nothing other than to trace a border?" (Balibar & Hahn 2002, p. 76). Thus, different theoretical approaches can at best underline different aspects of borders and frontiers: spatiality more than symbolism, their significance with regard to the labor market instead of their utility as military outposts, etc. In any case, in view of the theme of this book, to reflect upon borders and frontiers is essential to my analysis that considers citizenship and migration between Europe and Africa as its central theme. As Shapiro writes:

> Of all the forms of collective affiliation, modernity citizenship would appear to be the one whose constitution is almost exhausted by a model of space; the territorial boundaries of the nation-state system.
>
> (2000, p. 80)

Therefore, I propose that we take Lord Curzon's invitation seriously and pause to reflect upon the importance of borders and frontiers for the life of people who move between Africa and Europe. If a century ago Lord Curzon would state that "frontiers are indeed the razor's edge on which hang suspended the modern issues of war or peace, of life or death to nations," then frontiers and borders today are the dominant structures of intelligibility in terms of contemporary political identity. To open up alternative possibilities of belonging, we must intervene on them, as "they allow both the establishment of taxonomies and conceptual hierarchies that structure the movement of thought" (Mezzadra & Neilson 2013, p. 16).

Without any doubt, any investigation of the concept of border must depart from the fact that the border was never a comfortable place to dwell in. "Hatred, anger and exploitation are the prominent feature of this landscape" (Anzaldúa 2007, p. 19) because within border performativity dwells a violence that necessarily wants to silence alternative narratives. To realize that this violence is linked to spatio-temporal instances allows us to focus more on what is excluded and silenced instead of focusing on what is extracted, differently incorporated, and finally rendered visible within the nation-state's established frame. The border erupts when and where these contrasting forces, one migratory, the other attempting to control migration, meet. The scope of this chapter, then, is to liberate the study of borders from the perimeter of nation-states' governing narratives and underline their complex nature, focusing on specific intersections between African migrants' trajectories and national identities in order to "reactivate the constituent moment of the border"(Mezzadra & Neilson 2013, p. 17). Only by revealing what continually comes to be excised is it possible to mediate clashes over identity and belonging because, like before:

> Borders or frontiers are synonymous with questions of defense, war, citizenship or the right to punish criminals through collaboration with other states. It is essentially an interstate vision where frontiers delineate natural cultural containers and clear security barriers.
>
> (Bigo & Guild 2005, p. 54)

To revise the theoretical background of these concepts would involve relating contemporary world politics to the limits of previous methodological orientations based on the idea of the "natural," *in primis* the juridical one that considers the state the territorial paradigm of modernity with a well-defined interior separated by its exterior. Jurists define territory as "that section of the earth over which the State can legitimately exercise authority" (author's translation) (Martines 1992, p. 92). Understood in this way, territory is not only categorical but also becomes a source of juridical-political concepts such as extraterritoriality, extracommunitarianism, the enclave, and the camp, as Giorgio Agamben (1998) has superbly exposed in his influential work building on the Roman law institution of the *sacratio*. Unfortunately, too often, critical analyses that emerged from Agamben's work privileged and consequentially enhanced the role of the law and the state in excluding, processing, and detaining migrants, making the border a moving camp and obscuring migrants' political actions.

## 2.2   Lines and camps

In ancient Rome, the border was the line marked by the plow. Because marking land by a plow is indistinguishable from taking control of the territory, the border originally indicated sovereignty over a territory. Agamben (1998) reminds us how, in the Roman system, borders and sovereignty have been linked since the foundation of the Eternal City (753 BC). A life that is *sacer*, bare life, and a life that is sovereign are the two poles of the same system, the two elements of the space of exception that are found in the concept of the border as the perfect meeting point. As the myth of the foundation of Rome and the concept of *pomoerium* illustrate, one of the causes of *sacratio* – that is, the violation of a specific prohibition and the consequent ban from the community – was the cancelation of borders. The reason for this relies on the fact that the foundation of a city, Rome in this case, involved a complicated religious process. According to Lefebvre:

> The founding of Rome . . . was effected in a distinctly ritual manner. The founder . . . described a circle with his plough, thus subtracting a space from nature and investing it with a political meaning. Everything in this foundation story . . . is at once symbolic and practical: reality and meaning, the immediate and the abstract, are one.
>
> (1992, p. 244)

After an appropriate site was chosen, a first line or plow had to be drawn. Contained by the first line was the *mundus*, meaning "clean" or "pure," where all the positive religious symbols had to be put. Next, a second line had to be drawn outside the first one, and the space between the two was called the *pomoerium*. Inside this space between the first and the second line, priests would confine ghosts, demons, grubs, spirits of war, sicknesses, and any negative circumstance that could affect the city and its inhabitants. On the *pomoerium*, it was forbidden to eat, to build, to dwell, to cultivate, and even to walk. It was the area set apart where the walls would eventually have been built. Titus Livius' (Livy 2010), with his monumental *Ab Urbe Condita* (from the foundation of Rome), is the major source of information with regard to the myth of the foundation of Rome. As the story goes, Romulus and Remus, twin brothers, could not agree on where to build the city. As soon as Romulus drew the *pomoerium* on what today is Palatinus Hill, Remus, as a sign of defiance, crossed it. Romulus, furious, killed his brother to become the first king of Rome, declaring that he would have killed anyone daring to cross the *pomoerium* "sic deinde, quicumque alius transiliet moenia mea" (Livy 2010). Contrary to Hobbes' myth of the Leviathan, here the city is not founded on a social pact. Instead, it relies on an absolute "abandonment to an unconditional subjection to a power of death as if life were able to enter the city only in the double exception of being capable of being killed and yet not sacrificed" (Agamben 1998, p. 90). As in the story of Nabruka at the beginning of the book, migrants experience the border as a form of capture that includes them within the society excluding them, detaching their life from the political sphere. "And what this untying implies and produces – bare life, which dwells in the no man's land between the home and the city is, from the point of view of sovereignty, the original political element" (Ibid.).

Does the *pomoerium* ultimately relate to the frontier as the zone of mistiness? We intend the frontier with a sense of limit of a territory, even more a sense of extraterritoriality – where the wild things are. As I mention previously, ancient maps indicated the area of sub-Saharan Africa only with the line: *HIC SUNT LEONES* – only lions dwell there. As a result, the frontier has always indicated the zone of the unknown, a source of fear (but also of mutual enrichment). Certainly, the frontier marked the limit of the *sacrum*. To surpass the frontier often meant to violate the divine authority and to be contaminated and therefore banned from the community; interestingly, this was the case in passing the Pillars of Hercules (today, the Strait of Gibraltar), the limit of the Mediterranean Sea, between the world known and the unknown, as much as it was with the *pomoerium*. This space, intended in this way, then, is a space of exclusion rather than integration, the space where the fiction of a unitary concept of People is continually reified by excision.

Similarly, the concentration camp, according to Agamben (1998), is the primordial zone of exception: it is a zone outside/inside the law where the excision is performed, where the respectable citizen replaces the *homo sacer* via physical elimination. Therefore, it is possible to put side by side the concept of frontier in the ancient world and what Agamben refers to as the camp, because in the camp, as much as within the frontier, the intelligibility given by sovereign law is not evident. As a consequence, it is hard to distinguish what is outside or inside the law, what is wrong and what is right. As a matter of fact,

> one of the paradoxes of the state of exception lies in the fact that in the state of exception, it is impossible to distinguish transgression of the law from execution of the law, such that what violates a rule and what conforms to it coincide without any remainder.
>
> (Agamben 1998, p. 57)

In both spaces, it is possible to locate excised bodies, which are merely the surplus of the fabrication of accepted identities.

Agamben (1998) conceptualized this space of exception mostly within the hole of the camp isolating the border in its function of banning, and perhaps this appears to constitute one of the limits of his investigation. However, he astutely observed that the state of exception has already materialized in other spaces, such as waiting areas in international airports, the peripheries of megacities, or the soccer stadium in Bari in 1991 where hundreds of undocumented migrants from Albania were held. He suggested that we find the space of a camp anytime the state of exception materializes. Thus, undocumented migrants who dare to cross the Mediterranean risk being reduced to surplus human beings who may die without anyone being held responsible. But if we follow Agamben, we risk reifying a concept of borders as fences where the sovereignty is the only authority to exercise control, and we fail to perceive the filtering function of borders. It is also common to conceive the border as a physical wall attached to a specific space and geography because we tend to believe that specific geographical features are intrinsically borders.

## 2.3   Natural confines

> *Of all Natural Frontiers the sea is the most uncompromising, the least alterable, and the most effective.*
>
> (Lord Curzon 1907)

For a long time, and still somewhat today, a certain story dominated the space of imagination between Africa and Europe. As the story goes, proto-Europeans had been continuously surrounded by hordes of enemies living on the other side of the Mediterranean Sea. The basin thus had to be conquered as the least alterable frontier for Lord Curzon. From there, the idea of Mare Nostrum for Romans originated as the most effective protection to keep enemies at large. Yet "second in the list of Natural Frontiers may be placed deserts, until modern times a barrier even more impassable than the sea" (Curzon 1907). The great Sahara, this immense sprawl of sand that dominates the geography of the northern side of Africa, signified the inscrutability of the *finis Africae*. Nowadays, as I explain in detail in Chapter 3, along with the Mediterranean Sea, it represents the arena in which, in the last twenty years, the politics of European migration control have been enacted.

This spatial imaginary, which exploits the "natural" defensive attributes of the earth, continues to dominate the discourse of European migration control. It should be no surprise, then, that the natural defensive characteristics of geographical features, like rivers and oceans, are still maintained today and are considered indispensable conditions for migration control and political identity recognition. Therefore, when we look at contemporary states' policies of migration control in the southern frontier, Lord Curzon's reflections on the natural character of frontiers seem uncannily familiar. From a loaded conception of "territory" emerge both the idea that some borders are "natural" and the juridical abstraction of extraterritoriality (Ruggie 1993). "Natural borders," "territoriality," and "extraterritoriality" are all clearly artificial concepts. They seem otherwise only when geological features, such as seas, rivers, or great barren deserts, are incorporated within juridical constructions.

Despite general frustration with the nation-state narrative, contemporary discourse of international migration still seems to be dominated by a persistent idea to enclose population flows within naturalized geopolitical governing narratives.

> This idea is a very powerful one, so powerful, in fact that it is often taken for granted. In such a view, territorial borders must be about delimiting ownership, about delimiting authority, about establishing defensive lines and marking the difference between "us" and "them." Such functions may even be assumed to be natural, linked to the physical geographical features of rivers, deserts, seas and ridges of mountain ranges that often provide the topographical location of territorial borders.
>
> (Williams 2006, p. 5)

Territorial borders, then, along with their inherent geographical attributes, are never questioned; the border struggles, together with their violence, are never emphasized; and what these geopolitical narratives erase is never recovered. Those who are left behind on the boiling sand or at the bottom of the sea (Biemann & Holmes 2006) are bodies in excess: within the dominant narrative that on its critical aspect should include Agamben's idea of sovereignty, they are mere bumps on the road in a universal (Western), inevitable, irresistible drive to national modernity. The border-as-defense imaginary silences many stories of encounters between opposite shores and provides fertile ground for contemporary forms of antagonism, such as racism and anti-immigrant hostility, but cannot fully account for the complexities of the border. Alternatively, because the very concept of the border "implies the existence of people, languages, religions and knowledge on both sides" (Mignolo & Tlostanova 2006, p. 208), it is crucial to imagine that the sea, much like rivers, provides waterways that, like doors, connect different communities and allow for the diffusion of cultural traits and knowledge. "Hay tantísimas fronteras que dividen a la gente, pero por cada frontera existe también un puente" (Anzaldúa 2007, p. 107). Nowadays, with the advent of the "global," the border is the perfect viewpoint to analyze not only relations of class, race, and gender domination and migration control but also struggles, resistances, and desires to cross the bridge and enter the door that constitutes what we intend for political subjectivity. Now, standing out against the peril of a "borderless world" (Ohmae 1999; Pecoud 2007), borders have begun to assume ethical importance.

## 2.4    Ethics of confines

As I have mentioned previously, at the dawn of the new millennium, the study of borders and frontiers attempted to move beyond mere geographical and legal discourses. Recent studies have emphasized their mobility (Balibar & Hahn 2002) and their social origins (Wilson & Donnan 1998). Borders, even if often not clearly distinguished from frontiers, have been liberated from a certain territorial fixity and returned to the social world, to the world of humanity where they find their origins. In particular, according to the constructivist approach for instance, borders are not merely physical spaces but are also the fundamental elements for the organization of the state as a territorial entity. Thus, a classical constructivist like John Williams can declare that "returning borders to the social world, though, opens a host of possibilities for renewed investigation" (2006, p. 7). The series of possibilities that this turn presents are as unlimited as the choices of human beings. This shift, according to Williams, will liberate the analysis of international migration from the cage of economic forces (push and pull factors) and social constraints and will, at the same time, reconcile politics and ethics via borders. In the following pages, I will critically discuss the conceptual terrain on which Williams assembles his theoretical return of the border to the social world, and I will expose the limits and contradictions of this shift, presenting an alternative conceptualization that accounts for the border contestation of those in transit.

Williams starts from the premise that if borders are products of human choices and not something that has always existed in nature, then it is possible to reflect upon the ethical consequences of these socio-political artifacts:

> If the nature, meaning and role of, for example, territorial borders are not determined by some material structure, but are instead the result of a long series of human choices and decisions, then it is both reasonable and neces-
> sary to examine the thinking that saw some choices taken over others and to
> insist on the possibility of changing the way of thinking in the present and

future with a view to addressing injustices, inequities and other ethical problems with currently dominant ideas.

(Williams 2006, p. 8)

Williams does not believe that borders have an inherent ethical value but instead holds that borders can be used to obtain an ethical outcome: namely (and loosely) to tackle global injustices and inequities. In this sense, borders are ethical tools. Without borders then, "war and violence would become ubiquitous" (Williams 2006, p. 11). How, then, is one to make sense of a world where borders are multiplied and conflicts have become ubiquitous? In this regard, Williams has no doubts:

> The idea of territorial borders as the boundaries between sovereign states has enabled a rich skein of rules to develop about the ownership of property and the ways in which it can be transferred, about when it is permissible to resort to force and about who the actors are that are permitted to enter into international agreements and the kinds of subjects those agreements can cover. We tamper with this at our peril.

(2006, p. 11)

Borders, then, are synonymous with order, and in particular with the Westphalian order of self-reliant state-like units, of the sort that the realist approach has outlined. However, apparently Williams' approach does not lead to any fixed territorial demarcation between communities, races, or classes. Borders are, and have to be, mobile, as the title of his book *The Ethics of Territorial Borders: Drawing Lines in the Shifting Sand* suggests. However, despite a constructivist attention to the social processes that create borders and frontiers, this approach remains entrapped within the state framework. In this constructivist paradigm, migrant flows are pictured as a unitary mass that confronts the territorial subject par excellence: the sovereign state. What is more important, borders, intended as social practices, divide communities while being constructed by communities that need the borders to be defined as communities. In other words, borders are inherent to the very human condition. They are "natural" for the reason that they are vital to maintain an indispensable diversity and freedom between individuals, and this separation has to take a territorial form. Therefore, borders are, for Williams, still rooted in the territory, even though the ethical role they play is potentially detachable from their physical location. Otherwise, if borders were firmly, deeply drawn into the ground, many problems would arise, such as nationalist ideologies that tie certain communities to specific territories and generate eternal homelands. Williams finds cautionary examples, for example, in conflicts "over the location of territorial borders in places such as Palestine and Kosovo where the idea of 'holy land' comes into play" (Williams 2006, p. 14).

Williams' concern about the fate of the Palestinian community is odd if we consider that he completely neglects to consider the violence inherent to the expanding territory of Israeli settlers, shifting over the sands of Palestine. His argument concerning the ethical value of borders in preserving the life of the community is grounded on Hannah Arendt's political philosophy. According to Arendt, freedom of the individual is guaranteed through the political community, and totalitarianism is the political machinery that annihilates individuals by isolating them from their community. Her theory of the political community is somehow analogous to the Athenian agora; it is the public space where the individual is a rights holder and where plurality of decision is maintained. Policymakers must erect walls around the agora to defend the community against what she, referring to the genocide against the Jews, describes as "an attack upon human diversity as such, that is, upon a characteristic of the 'human status' without which the very words 'mankind' or humanity' would be devoid of meaning" (2010, pp. 268–269). How to effectively fight, then, she asks, against the "banality of evil" of a bureaucratic apparatus that aims to flatten pluralism (the diversity of communities) and plurality (the diversity of individuals)? Certainly not by claiming the respect of abstract legal principles of human rights, she proclaims. Appeals to abstract ethical categories like humanity offer little hope to those who seek to create philosophical foundations for tolerance. Does "the right to have rights" belong only to a member of a recognized community? After all, "the world found nothing sacred in the abstract nakedness of being human" (Arendt 1973, p. 299).

State-centered analyses of borders face a simple but devastating paradox: while the system of human rights is designed to protect those human beings who have nothing left but their naked body, it is also a result of a nation-state logic that is constructed around a concept of homogeneous and stable populations. Arendt traces the origin of the paradox within the text of the Declaration of the Rights of the Man and Citizen that was adopted between 20 and 26 August 1789. She notes that the ideas of the French Revolution were aimed at subverting the old system, one of aristocratic power, with a new one. Men are born equal and free because they are members of the nation, as clearly stated in Article 3 of the Declaration. Once incorporated into the nation, once within the protective wall and sitting on the steps of the agora, men (neither women nor slaves) would be considered active members of the polity regardless of their origins or diversities. In that instant, the community and the territory become consecrated together as protectorates of a newly democratic state. Its institutions will continuously shape an otherwise merely nominal national identity. But to mold is to draw a line; it is to identify who belongs and to expel others beyond the margins. Therefore, theories that maintain the fiction of the rigidity and permanency of the border while failing to take into consideration those who live "smack in the fissure" (Gomez-Peña 1993, p. 37) keep this system, and its paradoxes, intact.

## 2.5   A new world (b)order

Although Williams' study helps to recognize the multiple roles and functions that borders and frontiers play in the realm of contemporary global politics, few contradictions that are inherent to state-level analyses persist within Williams' ethical exploration of territorial borders. In fact, even if we welcome the theoretical turn toward abandoning the obsolete "border-as-fence" analogy, it remains the case that the power to question the legitimacy of borders continues to be monopolized within the community in a blatant reification of an exclusive territoriality of the nation and linearity of borders. The author even observes that:

> There is a need for division and distinction between communities and this can take, and frequently has taken, a territorial form. This territorial form does not to have to be via exclusively sovereignty but this has proven to be a durable and attractive mechanism, and, despite the undoubted costs that cosmopolitan critics are quick to highlight, such durability and attractiveness ought not to be dismissed out of hand.
>
> (Williams 2006, p. 105)

In other words, the international order is based upon the concept of borders because borders, and a need for division and distinction between communities, are part of human nature. However, how is it possible to reconcile a constructivist position with this contention that borders are natural? The first incongruence leads to a second: if borders are inherent to human nature, they are necessarily timeless. This position clashes against the author's post-positivist pronouncement that it is necessary to pay attention to history and to the fact that criteria of legitimacy are always historically located and therefore relative. Borders, as practically normative concepts, have histories, but Williams appears to efface the historical differences of borders in favor of a homogeneous, ahistorical concept, which he locates in a universal human need to divide and distinguish between communities. This represents the danger and contradiction of a foundational approach, which reproduces a series of practices of exclusion to reaffirm the political right to exclude alternative approaches.

It is certainly urgent, then, to dig out the bricks of the wall "because borders have history; the very notion of border has a history. And it is not the same everywhere at every level" (Balibar & Hahn 2002, p. 77). And what is more, it is important to note that the history of borders cannot be limited to territory but also to knowledge. In this direction, the world map drawn by Gerardus Mercator and Johannes Ortelius "worked together with theology to create a zero point of observation and of knowledge: a perspective that denied all other perspectives"(Castro-Gomez, 2002, as cited in Mignolo & Tlostanova 2006, p. 206). In the case of Africa, as Mbembe explains, little effort has been made to comprehend the imaginaries and indigenous practices of space, oversimplifying the genesis of current delineation of states' limits that "long antedates the Congress of Berlin held in 1884" (Mbembe 2000, p. 265). As a matter of fact, although it is crucial to comprehend how the tracing of the internal borders of Europe reflected colonial attempts to reorganize the worlds of Africa (Schmitt 2003), a truly critical investigation that would finally provincialize Europe would move beyond colonial demarcations.

If, on one hand, the Pan-African Congress, in a resolution adopted in 1958 in Accra, Ghana, denounced "the artificial frontiers drawn by imperialist powers to divide the peoples of Africa, particularly those which cut across ethnic groups and divide people of the same stock" and called for "the abolition or the adjustment of such frontiers at an early date" (Legum 1962, p. 228),[1] on the other hand, to avoid an increasing fragmentation of the post-colonial status quo, the Organization of African Unity in 1963 declared the intangibility of colonial boundaries, giving them legitimacy. Still, the history of borders in Africa cannot be reduced to limits drawn by colonial powers and through the lens of international law; otherwise, the concept of territory makes sense only in relation to state sovereignty, excluding other forms more fluid of appropriation, like migration. Instead, as Mbembe explains:

> Far from being simple products of colonialism, current boundaries thus reflect commercial, religious, and military realities, the rivalries, power relationships, and alliances that prevailed among the various imperial powers and between them and the Africans through the centuries preceding colonization proper.
>
> (2000, p. 265)

Rethinking borders or *border thinking* (Mignolo 2000) then configures as an ethical endeavor that emerges as a response to the violence of colonial epistemology. As I have noted previously, however, this is not the violence that interests Williams, because maintaining a generic reference to indefinite injustices without digging in depth into the genealogy of violence allows a reification of the sanctity of borders. In the case of Africa's Rwanda, it is imperative to investigate the role of Belgium and its act of colonial partitioning with regard to the violence that erupted between Hutu and Tutsi. Borders signify the violence of the space between the interior and the exterior, the concrete gap crystallized between imagined communities.

Paradoxically, Williams emphasizes Arendt's recognition that "the world lies between people, and this in-between . . . is today the object of the greatest concern and the most obvious upheaval in all the countries of the globe" (2006, p. 103). Only being open to the world and recognizing the familiar as well as the unfamiliar allows one to reconceptualize the space that a constructivist approach opens and to move ideas of borders beyond the realist approach of anarchical world order, as well as nationalistic imaginings of them as geographical marks of glorious pasts. The stories that take place in the space between Europe and Africa can help us to reconceptualize borders in ways that attend to the roles of practice, rather than to mere geographical tropes. Nowadays, the Sahara Desert and the deep blue Mediterranean Sea constitute the two most evident features of the last frontier of Europe whose limits operate beyond the geopolitical limits of the Union with perpendicular incursions, revealing the essential violence on which ultimately it relies to secure states' legitimacy. As I attempt to show, we should not conceive these geopolitical confines as a definite line that coincides with the sovereignty influence of states' territories, "for the border is not a thing but a materialization of authority" (Chambers 2008, p. 6).

## 2.6   For a reconceptualization

As I have stated previously, Williams' analysis that reifies the essentiality of borders as justification of a certain community is fated to reach only a partial visualization because non-citizens/"illegals" are not considered adequate political subjects of social processes. Starting with these premises, his approach fails to completely explain how and why borders move and multiply. To reclaim a dialectical character of borders fundamentally means to question the myth of the social contract from Hobbes to Rawls, secured within the shell of the classic Westphalian sovereign state, which hardly has ever been stable. Such a conception of the state, its rigidity, cannot stand the changes caused by the emergence of a global economy nor the vacuity of legal proclamations of human rights when these are confronted with the unbearable nakedness of human life in the move across sovereign countries. But how to make sense, then, of the vast mass of human beings that cross the distinct borders of the sovereign state if not only by problematizing the dichotomy of inclusion-exclusion, citizen-alien? Isn't it the effort to make sense of their magnitude that produces the dichotomy in the first place? At the moment that we are experiencing the presence of camps in multiple forms, disseminated everywhere within the frontier of the first world, we perceive that these spaces of containment are leaking already what is contaminating the artificial transparency of the nation-state. Today, millions of people "in excess" are moving across nation-states' territory, their numbers having multiplied since WWII along with the number of borders and conflicts.

> Once they are in circulation in larger contexts, movements of individual bodies have significant implications; they play an important part in the historically contingent practices and processes by which peculiar identities (of citizen and domestic community) are constructed, assigned, negotiated, resisted, and most importantly, "fixed in the image of the modern state."
>
> (Soguk 1999, p. 27)

It is important to highlight, then, the role of the excluded subject in participating in the unstable dialectic of inclusion and exclusion, the spatio-temporal dimension of borders and frontiers. "It is precisely when one enacts the rights that one does not have that one becomes a political subject" (Isin & Rygiel 2007, p. 189). Therefore, I suggest that the border emerges whenever practices of statecraft enter in relation or, rather, collide with migrants' obstinate trajectories. In this way, the new frontier between Africa and Europe is to be located around points of interaction between the implementation of policies of migration control and acts of flows – that is, at the juncture of multiple discourses of migration. When borders materialize, then, they localize in time and space the acts of power and resistance, which conversely mold new emerging and shifting frontiers. In this sense, the last frontier of Europe, the Mediterranean and the Sahara Desert, resembles Foucault's heterotopias– that is, spaces *animées encore par une sourde sacralisation* (still nurtured by the hidden presence of the sacred), (1986, p.23) a sacred space reserved to those that are in a state of crisis in relation to the society in which they live, and for that reason always temporary, and fleeting, in their self-constitutive excess. Borders are spaces, in the Foucaldian language, where it is difficult to locate power on one distinct point and resistance on another.

So, therefore, the concepts of frontier and border are twofold: on one hand, they amount to two key elements of the statecraft aimed at preventing people from acting politically – that is, from being heard – but, paradoxically, on the other hand, they are fluctuating space entities that emerge and are shaped by people's ability to reclaim their political subjectivity. In this sense, migrants seem to challenge the classical logic of international relations, considering that migrants' physical mobility interferes with the principle of territoriality that results in being shaken. The intent here is not to draw a sequence of points to be unified in order to identify a line that will split the outside from the inside. In that case, a spatial representation would take up the stage, obfuscating the necessary attention we must pay to the reterritorialization moment. As an alternative, it is helpful to mark out points of action/non-action without laying any claim of totality, knowing that "some borders are no longer situated at the border at all" (Balibar & Hahn 2002, p. 84). Instead, "they are dispersed a little everywhere, wherever the movement of information, people, and things is happening and is controlled" (Balibar 2003, p. 1). Synchronic (timeless) conceptualizations of borders do not apply to contemporary political communities that nowadays have to adapt to an increased mobility and multidimensionality of migrations. As a matter of fact, "fixed boundaries are displaced by flows and diversions that undermine as well as reinforce existing spatial divides" (Agnew 1995, p. 214) in a dialectical way.

Still, the border is contingent on power practices whose perennial fluctuations, like in Williams', make the border seem natural and inevitable. It is important to shake this assertion and demonstrate the border's reliance on a complex interconnection of historical contingencies and thus to reveal its violence and, at the same time, its precariousness. In the case of Europe, the idea of fixity of the border reinforces the discourse of a fortress (Gebrewold-Tochalo 2007) as a socio-political body under a permanent state of siege that sets off (often violent) panicked reactions. Privileging an ahistorical perspective, as I mentioned previously, synchronic approaches interpret conflicts in Africa, for instance, as disconnected to politics and colonial histories and instead interpret them as security issues that threaten an imagined stable political space of Europe. A discourse of securitization and risk analysis conceals the real functions of the frontier and borders to filter out certain individuals while crystallizing the imagery of the nation-state as the only place in which "authentic politics" (Walker 1992) is possible. This is the logic behind the state's strategy of leveling human trafficking charges against fishers who help castaway refugees or the Italian government's recent bordering practice of intercepting migrants/asylum seekers in international waters to disrupt their trajectories, as we will discuss in the following chapters.

## Note

1   See the Resolutions adopted by the All African People Conference Accra, in December 5–13, 1958, in Legum Colin, 1962, *Pan Africanism: A Short Political Guide*.

# References

Agamben, G., 1998. *Homo Sacer: Sovereign Power and Bare Life.* Stanford, CA: Stanford University Press.

Agnew, J., and Corbridge, S., 1995. *Mastering Space: Hegemony, Territory and International Political Economy.* New York, NY: Routledge.

Anzaldúa, G., 2007. *Borderlands/La Frontera: The New Mestiza.* 3rd ed. San Francisco, CA: Aunt Lute Books.

Arendt, H., 1973. *The Origins of Totalitarianism.* New York: Harcourt Brace Jovanovich.

Arendt, Hannah. 2010. *Eichmann in Jerusalem: A Report on the Banality of Evil.* New York, NY: Penguin Classics.

Balibar, E., 2003. *We, the People of Europe? Reflections on Transnational Citizenship.* Princeton, NJ: Princeton University Press

Balibar, E. & Hahn, D., 2002. *Politics and the Other Scene.* Londo, UK: Verso.

Biemann, U. & Holmes, B., 2006. *The Maghreb Connection: Movements of Life across North Africa.* Barcelona, Spain: Actar.

Bigo, D. & Guild, E., 2005. *Controlling Frontiers: Free Movement into and within Europe.* Burlington, VT: Ashgate Publishing.

Chambers, I., 2008. *Mediterranean Crossings: The Politics of an Interrupted Modernity.* Durham, NC: Duke University Press.

Curzon, G.,1907. Frontiers – Introduction. *International Boundaries Research Unit.* Available at: www-ibru.dur.ac.uk/resources/docs/curzon1.html [Accessed 14 August 2010]

Foucault, M., 1986. Of Other Spaces. *Diacritics*, 16(1), Spring, pp. 22–27.

Gebrewold-Tochalo, B., 2007. *Africa and Fortress Europe: Threats and Opportunities.* Farnham, UK: Ashgate Publishing.

Gomez-Pena, G., 1993. *Warrior for Gringostroika: Essays, Performance Texts, and Poetry.* St. Paul, MN: Graywolf Press.

Isin, E. & Rygiel, K., 2007. Abject Spaces: Frontiers, Zones, Camps. In D. Elizabeth & C. Masters, eds. *The Logics of Biopower and the War on Terror: Living, Dying, Surviving.* London, UK: Palgrave Macmillan, pp. 181–203.

Lago, A. D., 2009. *Non-Persons.* Vimodrone, Italy: IPOC di Pietro Condemi.

Lefebvre, H., 1992. *The Production of Space.* New York, NY: Wiley-Blackwell.

Legum, C., 1962. *Pan Africanism: A Short Political Guide.* London, UK: Pall Mall Press.

Livy, T. 2010. *Titi Livii Patavini. Historiarum Ab Urbe Condita Libri Quinque Priores: Ad Optimas Editiones Castigati.* Charleston, SC: Nabu Press.

Martines, T., 1992. *Diritto costituzionale.* Milan, Italy: Giuffrè. Available at: www.ciao.it/ Diritto_costituzionale_Martines_T__173364 [Accessed 25 July 2010]

Mbembe, A., 2000. At the Edge of the World: Boundaries, Territoriality, and Sovereignty in Africa. *Public Culture*, 12(1), pp. 259–284.

Mezzadra, S. & Neilson, B., 2013. *Border as Method, or, the Multiplication of Labor.* Durham, NC: Duke University Press.

Mignolo, W., 2000. *Local Histories/Global Designs: Coloniality, Subaltern Knowledges, and Border Thinking.* Princeton, NJ: Princeton University Press.

Mignolo, W. D. & Tlostanova, M. V., 2006. Theorizing from the Borders: Shifting to Geo- and Body-Politics of Knowledge. *European Journal of Social Theory*, 9(2), pp. 205–221.

Ohmae, K., 1999. *The Borderless World: Power and Strategy in the Interlinked Economy.* New York, NY: Harper Paperbacks.

Pecoud, A., 2007. *Migration without Borders: Essays on the Free Movement of People.* New York, NY: Berghahn Books.

Ruggie, J. G., 1993. Territoriality and Beyond: Problematizing Modernity in International Relations. *International Organization*, 47(1), pp. 139–174.

Schmitt, C., 2003. *The Nomos of the Earth in the International Law of the Jus Publicum Europaeum*. New York, NY: Telos Press Publishing.

Shapiro, M. J., 2000. National times and other times: Rethinking citizenship. *Cultural Studies* 14(1), 1 January, pp. 79–98.

Soguk, N., 1999. *States and Strangers: Refugees and Displacements of Statecraft*. Minneapolis, MN: University of Minnesota Press.

Walker, R.B.J., 1992. *Inside/Outside: International Relations as Political Theory*. Cambridge, UK: Cambridge University Press.

Waltz, K., 1959. *Man, the State, and War: A Theoretical Analysis*. New York, NY: Columbia University Press.

Williams, J., 2006. *The Ethics of Territorial Borders: Drawing Lines in the Shifting Sand*. Houndmills, UK: Palgrave Macmillan.

Wilson, T. M. & Donnan, H., 1998. *Border Identities: Nation and State at International Frontiers*. Cambridge, UK: Cambridge University Press.

# 3    The sand door

*The sand, the stones, the sky, the sun, the silence, the suffering, not the metal and cement towns with the sounds of fountains and human voices. It was here – in the barren order of the desert – where everything was possible, where one walked shadow-less on the edge of his own death.*

*(Clezio 2010, p. 12)*

## 3.1    The great desert

The edge is a stroke on the sand. Thousands of tire marks left by the trucks that from Sudan head up north through the vastness of the Sahara Desert, loaded with hundreds of migrants squeezed one on top of the other, holding on to something, hoping not to fall off and fade away like a creek in the sand. In the kitchen of the Asinitas school in Rome, as Senait, Mimi, and Dag (Segre & Yimer 2008) call back fragments of "the journey," one may wonder if one must be provided with supernatural strength to walk balanced over the edge of one's own death, along the route that goes from East and Central Africa toward Libya. Indeed, the great Sahara and, within it, the state of Libya, functions as a limbo where, especially today when rival militias are shelling Libyan cities, migrants often find a precarious destination. Nonetheless, at the same time, because of the impervious character of the land, the Sahara provides a perilous but promising path – "where everything was possible" – to the Maghreb and eventually to the southern coast of the Mediterranean Basin. The desert is therefore opaque, muddled, shielding and, at the same time, longed for, although for too many, we must remember that it signifies a tragic end. In this chapter, I attempt to clarify the ambiguous role that this desolate terrain has acquired for African migrations as both a crucial tool for Africans and a major instrument within the European management of migration control.

What emerges at first sight is that with over 4,000 km of desert borders, each of the six countries bordering Libya on its southern, eastern, and western frontiers acts as a point of entry for refugees and migrants to the point that even Libyan officials recognize the impracticality of sealing the country's borders (Herzog 2009). It is interesting here to reflect upon conclusions that Frontex's officials drew about the Sahara Desert at the end of their mission in Libya.

In the same way, seeking to improve controls of a vast desert space may require imaginative thinking, perhaps by viewing the desert as a sea – a brown sea – rather than a land space.

(Frontex 2007, p.11)

Frontex's gaze resembles that of earlier colonial European scientists, geologists, and engineers who dreamt of conjoining the Mediterranean and the Sahel, the southern shore of the Sahara Desert. This colonial fantasy was one of mastering natural forces, a delirium of positivist omnipotence over the most arid desert of the world. Ferdinand de Lesseps, a prominent scientist of that time, member of the Academy of Sciences, and designer of the Suez Canal, carried the idea of pouring seawater into the desert. But as Ali Bensaâd notes:

Long before the colonial fantasies, this conception lay at the basis of the spatial perceptions of the Arab geographers of the Middle Ages. They used almost exclusively maritime terminology to identify and describe the Sahara: the very name of the Maghreb finds its origin there, since it was called *Djerizet El Maghreb*, the Sunset Isle and it was identified as an island surrounded by the Mediterranean, the Ocean and the Sahara.

(Biemann & Holmes 2006, p. 14)

Today, trans-Saharan trajectories traverse the vast sea of sand, alive more than ever, revitalized by sub-Saharan migrants who, led or carried by skillful Bedouins, venture into the north. If "three main migration routes can be identified in the African continent, namely the western, northern and eastern routes" (Sørensen & Dansk institut for internationale studier 2006, p. 48), the eastern route is the route chosen by those who from the Horn of Africa intend to reach Libya, today the most traversed and certainly the most dangerous. The incredible adventure of crossing the desert requires extraordinary resources that only the fittest possess. The echoes of this intense circulation reach the bureaucratic heart of the old Europe, which reacts anxiously, sending a contingent of risk management experts to investigate the desert and, possibly, to bring the ancient *Limes Tripolitanus*, the Roman-fortified frontier in Libya, up to date. Frontex, then, as the European Agency for the Management of Operational Cooperation at the External Borders of the Member States of the European Union, operates through a meticulous risk assessment, deploying the most advanced technologies to bolster local police and de facto delocalizing the dirty job of migration management (see Chapter 6 for further discussions on Frontex).

Given the lack of clear demarcations and the size of the terrain, fixed border crossing points will play a limited role in controlling illegal immigration. This should not preclude however the need for a change in border management strategy and investment in premises and overall infrastructure.

(Frontex 2007, p. 17)

Yet, migrants go on, continuously opening up new routes as soon as European forces intervene to secure a door and masterfully altering European technologies

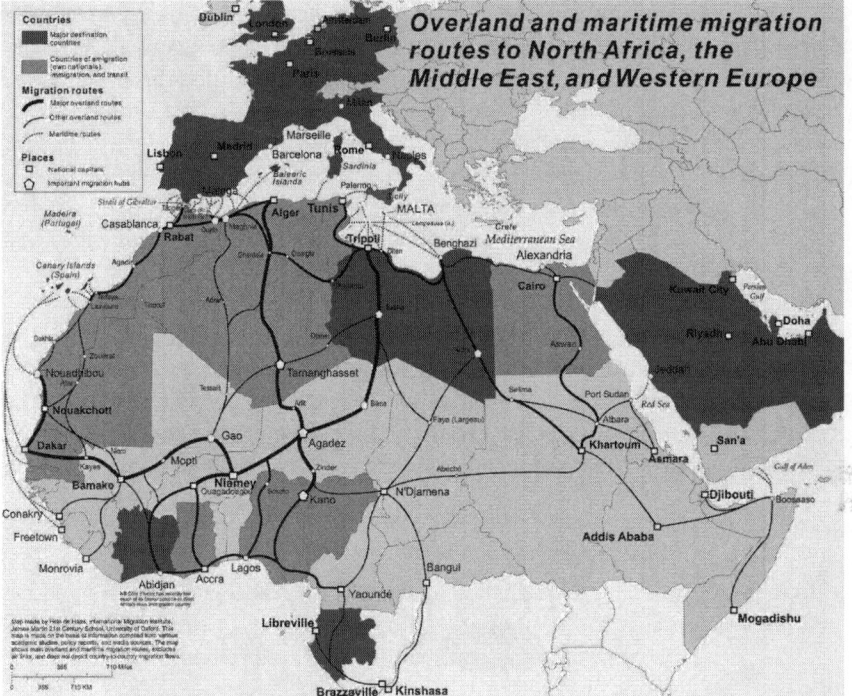

*Figure 3.1* Trans-Saharan migration routes.
Source: www.oxfordmartin.ox.ac.uk/opinion/view/230

of detection (see Figure 3.1). As I will explain later (see Chapter 6) in reference to the dynamic nature of technological borders, migrants are indeed true entrepreneurs of today's technological era. Where possible, refugees and migrants have adopted existing trans-Saharan caravan routes, which have operated for centuries in the transport of goods and slaves between Libya and neighboring African countries, notably Sudan and Chad. Depending on the political and security circumstances, routes regularly change. Like the desert facade, they shift.

## 3.2   Give me a reason to leave

> The decision to migrate is more and more made by individuals. One day, they have just disappeared, they didn't inform their family and even their mothers don't know where they are. They only call their family when they have reached Europe.
> Representative of the local NGO ANAFA in Saint Louis
> (Senegal) (Schapendonk & van Moppes 2007, p. 7)

The epigraph of this section functions as a reminder that migration is sometimes an individual decision that is taken because of and notwithstanding many social and economic factors. At the beginning of the documentary *Like a Man on Earth*, Dag confesses that when he decided to leave, he did not tell anyone. Above all, he did not tell his father because "he would have probably interpreted my decision as an escape from my responsibilities as a student, and a betrayal of all his sacrifices to make me study in the most prestigious school of Addis Ababa" (Segre & Yimer 2008). Thus, first and foremost, it is a personal and individual motivation to improve one's life and/or that of one's family that leads young Africans to embark on their journey. This point is often underestimated by mainstream analyses of migration, which mostly focus on economic and structural push/pull factors to make sense of a human process (that of migration) that has to be contained and managed.

> In this domain economic practice and econometric calculation assume that their definition of costs and benefits has an absolute value . . . and that the arbitrary dividing line between the two is necessary and immutable. As the distinction has been established once and for all, nothing remains to be done except to refine the investigation so as to establish a balance sheet for each column.
>
> (Sayad 2004, p. 77)

To focus on an econometric method of analysis leads scholars to exceptionalize the migration process and to portray migration as a consequence of determinate factors that can be controlled and adjusted; the presence of the individual is lost inside myriad data and charts. Dag's documentary recuperates a form of presence that overcomes "the traditional scheme of rationality in terms of ends and means, causes and effects" (Rancière 2005, p. 16). Through what is said and unsaid, and especially within moments of silence, the camera is able to capture what cannot be said to any interviewer: the burden of real human sorrow that these people carry. Young migrants often leave with close friends without saying anything to others, but at other times, the entire community is involved. Migrants who are "sponsored," whether by families or by the whole community, feel enormous pressure to complete the journey and to find some way to send money back to repay the investment made to support their endeavor. Because of the responsibilities they bear, migrants often prefer to continue their journeys even in the face of unbearable conditions and risks to their lives. What is worth noting here is that only the most audacious and skilled individuals decide to leave or are chosen among the community. This element conflicts with conventional discourses of migration that contend that war and endemic African misery are the root causes of migration and depict African migrants as desperate people. As a result of this form of intelligibility, I have noted previously how enormous capital is invested in "development" plans to improve education. Allegedly, these investments will eventually curb the desire to emigrate; in effect, they help nation-states consolidate their territorial borders.

The actual relation between development and migration is rather more complicated. Hein de Haas (2008, p.1314) contends that "economic and human development increases people's capabilities and aspirations and therefore tends to coincide with an increase rather than a decrease in emigration, at least in the short to medium run." The link between improved economic conditions, better education, and increased mobility is evident when we consider the impact of new information and media technology on the lives of migrants (see Chapter 6). The perception of the West that filters out from images on TV and the Web certainly builds a strong desire in the minds of many young Africans to join the First World; therefore, even if the exact extent to which Internet access affects migration decisions is unclear, it is undoubtedly high. Ros *et al.* state, for example, that "technology providers, (migration) webmasters and Internet café holders should therefore be viewed as new actors in the migration scene" (Schapendonk & van Moppes 2007, p. 9). The same analysis can also be extended to the advertisements of companies that profit from the business of migrant remittances, the control and management of which seems to be at the top of the agenda of NGOs, international organizations, and financial institutions. If media play an important role by building desire and aspirations, migrants rely on accounts made by other migrants who have already settled in Europe. For different reasons, these migrants provide incomplete if not simply biased information about life conditions at their destinations:

> My name is Negga, I am 19 years old. . . . We did not know how difficult reaching those places would be. We only knew that life in Europe was better than ours. That is how we got the desire to leave.
>
> (Segre & Yimer 2008, p. 46)

As they emerge from the many interviews in the documentary, many stories and rumors circulate among aspiring migrants within their society of origin, but nobody knows the exact difficulties and coordinates of the journey. The most significant reason behind this important aspect of migration – apart from personal motivations to provide families with accounts that are "cleansed" of all horror stories – relies on the fact that migration routes constantly change. They open and close depending on different circumstances. There might, for instance, be increased security at the borders and/or changed economic/political/social conditions along the preferred route. Sometimes new opportunities emerge from these changes, always in a dialectic way.

### 3.3   Along the eastern route

But these are not just rumors. Sub-Saharan Africans living in North Africa do find jobs in specific niches of the informal service sector: construction, agriculture, petty trade, and fishery. Trans-Saharan migration also causes trade to flourish and helps revitalize desert towns. The foundations of contemporary trans-Saharan migration were laid in the 1970s and 1980s when nomads and traders started migrating to work at construction sites and oil fields in southern Algeria and Libya. Such immigration was often openly welcomed because migrants filled local labor shortages and meshed with policies to revitalize underpopulated desert regions. It is also important to note that patterns of labor migration in and through these countries have roots in the long history of Saharan caravan routes.

It has only been since the mid-1990s that Libya became a primary destination for increasing immigration flows, not just from neighboring Sahel countries but also from the wider sub-Saharan region. As oil revenues and their production and use became the basis of relating to Libya, we have been determined to situate the locus of this increasingly complex society as something that is always mediated by oil. Such an analysis trims down the multiple ways in which the Libyan society is differentiated, the multiple ways in which power is articulated and contested, the way bodies encounter each other, and the role played by various diplomatic entanglements. Indeed, a negotiation that privileges Libya's production and purchasing power has made it possible for the Gaddafi regime to redeem itself on the international scene while allowing its atrocities against various groups to either go unnoticed or be accommodated, albeit uncomfortably. Libya's purchasing power manifests itself in its ability to salvage its reputation and even buy its way back into the core of "international community" (after the Lockerbie settlements, participation in the war against terror, and the Megrahi release are some examples) or into Africanness under entities like the African Union and the Libya Arab African Investment Company (LAICO), which has interests in hotels, telecommunications, banking, agriculture, and fuel distribution in a number of African countries.

In a flawless example of a push/pull factor analysis, Ferruccio Pastore explains that "besides preexisting and still strong Libyan demand for foreign labor, the specific determinants of the quick rise in inflows from Sub-Saharan Africa were political" (Pastore 2007, p.3). The proliferation of conflicts in Western Africa and the Horn of Africa throughout the final decade of the twentieth century and beyond offers a final set of broadly political conditions that can be factored into the rapid increase of sub-Saharan immigration to Libya. Several wars within the area impacted the eastern Saharan route: Liberia (1989–1996 and 1999–2003), Ethiopia-Eritrea (1998–2000), the Second Sudanese Civil War (1983–2005), and the conflict in Darfur (2003–present). In addition, Somalia has been without a central government since President Siad Barre was overthrown in 1991. What is more, the end of the conflict between Libya and Chad (1987), the bilateral freedom of circulation agreement (1994) that followed, and the repression of Tuareg rebellions in Niger (1995) and Mali (1996) all facilitated cross-Saharan transit. Above all, the spectacular pan-Africanist turn in Qadhafi's foreign policy, which was mainly motivated by the leader's disappointment with the other Arab regimes' lack of support following the gradual hardening of United Nations (UN) sanctions against Libya after 1992, helped to establish Libya as a primary destination for trans-Saharan migration. Repeated and widely advertised promises by the colonel that sub-Saharan migrant workers would be welcomed as brothers obviously represented a good reason to leave.

For different reasons then, during the past twenty years, the route to Europe that goes toward the coast of Libya has been the most trafficked. In addition, in 1998, Italy concluded a series of agreements with Tunisia to curb migration flows through the region, which effectively closed that route. Migrants then started using alternative paths, including the one that goes through Libya. Consequently, the number of clandestine landings on the Sicilian coast increased, which put significant social and political pressure on Italian authorities. It is worth noting that, at the end of the 1990s, the international community still considered Libya a pariah state, and Italy still had unresolved symbolic and economic issues dating back to its occupation of Libya.

As a result with the shift toward global securitization strategies to halt terrorism, Libya re-entered the international political community. The political climate around international migration therefore started to change. Colonel Gaddafi was cunning enough to exploit paranoid European and Italian visions of invading immigrants and the discursively associated risk of international terrorist attacks. The gradual cooperation of the Libyan regime with the West and the Colonel's clear disapproval of the 9/11 attacks certainly signified Libya's redemption. With a lobbying campaign at the European level – the process of which Italy sped up – Libya went from being at the top of rogue state lists to achieving status as a seemingly responsible member of the international community. It is uncanny how the histories of these two colonially intertwined states became linked once again through bilateral cooperation in the fields of security and undocumented migration.

### 3.4   Migrant = terrorist = cheap labor

It is worth noting that the majority of African residents in Europe originated from north African countries (Migration Policy Institute 2013), which conversely plays a central role in the implementation of European policies to curb African sub-Saharan migration. It is also worth noting that a perception still prevails in Europe that a multitude of hundreds of thousands of Africans are all set to leave the coast of Libya to invade Europe. It is also it is possible that the attack by the NATO allies on Gaddafi's[1] forces in the summer of 2011 was justified, in part, by the urgency to re-establish a geopolitical order and then to prevent an immigrant invasion. On 7 July 2011, British Foreign Secretary William Hague, when pressured on the cost and time length of the military operation in Libya, clearly linked it with the necessity to avoid risking a migration invasion in Europe. On that occasion, he stated that:

> If we had just allowed Gaddafi to re-conquer the rest of the country by force . . . causing thousands of casualties, creating a humanitarian crisis, with uncontrolled migration to Southern Europe as a result, the cost for [the] UK and our European partners could be vastly greater than the cost of this military operation.
>
> (Hague 2011)

Two points are worth noting here: first, that migration is often problematized in terms of costs and economic efficiency to the point that "using the language of economics to rationalize a problem that is not (or not only) economic is tantamount to converting ethical and political arguments into pure technical arguments"

(Sayad 2004, p. 77). The idea of migration management goes on with the *dispositif* of European externalization of migration control in North Africa to the point that migration from Africa becomes exceptional and invasive, as if it were a virus that could infect the entire European continent. What I am trying to assert here is that the significance of a management approach to African migration is a symptom of the widening gap between a Europe of institutions and a Europe of people. Second, that the idea that there are 1.5–2 million sub-Saharan African migrants ready to migrate into Europe is based on a poor understanding of African migration and the role of Libya in the economic and socio-economic milieu of that continent in the last twenty years. In particular, Gaddafi consistently fostered a threat of a migration invasion as a tool to blackmail his European negotiation partners. Together with oil, the migration control issue was one of the main negotiation tools he utilized to regain international credibility with the European Union (EU) and with Italy in particular. When a slight increase in migrants' boats crossing occurred toward Italy and Malta in the early 2000s, he immediately fomented that fear. It is therefore essential to shed light on the foundations of these assertions, these allegations, of masses of Africans ready to sail to Europe.[2]

While large numbers of migrants, regular and irregular alike, fled Libya during the uprising of 2011, a high number of irregular migrants remained, with continued inflows into the country – 12.2% according to the International Organization for Migration [IOM] in 2011, and only a small percentage of those who reside there, a few thousand, decide to cross the Mediterranean Sea. Therefore, when an increase of crossings has occurred and still occurs, this increase is due to several factors. Primarily and frequently, new migration routes open due to increasing controls on other parts of the Mediterranean coast, such as over the western route via the Strait of Gibraltar but also due to a change in Libyan domestic economic policies that open and close job opportunities for seasonal workers. Lastly, this is also a partial reaction to an increase in racist violence in Libya against sub-Saharan migrant workers and nowadays to the shelling of Libyan cities by militias.

These conclusions therefore clash with the dominant European discourse on African migration, which instead perpetuates the myth that millions of sub-Saharan Africans are waiting on the shores of Maghreb, driven by desperation, to invade Europe.[3] The reality of African migration into Europe is more complicated than this discourse allows, and the reasons behind these alarming proclamations are deeper than what emerges on the surface. The direct consequence of this approach is undermining the difficulties of the journey through the desert. Ignoring the reality of the trans-Saharan routes and avoiding public debates over bilateral agreements between Europe, Italy, and north African states counts as a manifestation of the externalization of European migration control, as defined previously. First and foremost, picturing migrants as victims who must be saved from brutal human traffickers and associating migrants with terrorism (Edwards & Ferstman 2010) is an effect of convenience, not truth. The majority of smugglers, *dallala*, are former migrants or nomads who have some small networks connected to other networks. In pre-colonial Maghreb, nomadic tribes such as the Maqil, the Arib, the Requibat, and many others always supported the north-south link, acting as a sort of shifting hyphen between Maghreb and the Sahel (Biemann & Holmes 2006). In fact, because of its severe climate, the great Sahara cannot be occupied. It is a space of permanent transition over an extension of hot sand that takes four hours to fly over. To acknowledge this is not to disregard the involvement of criminal organizations in exploiting migrants, but rather to avert from discussing the increased militarization of traditional migration paths and the consequent need for migrants to look for alternative, more dangerous routes. As long as fewer legal channels for immigration are opened and as long as asylum seekers are denied access to legal procedures, it is likely that a significant number of African migrants will refer to smugglers to cross the desert. Ironically, to practically travel these routes today often requires tools and means that only criminal and state organizations possess. Attention to the complexities of migration in the region also calls into question, although only incidentally, the efforts of intergovernmental/nongovernmental organizations [IGOs/NGOs] to prevent migration by spurring development and launching awareness campaigns, since at this point it is evident that increased schooling and wealth boost human mobility (de Haas 2008). The militarization of frontiers and the business of international aid and development are only two different sides of one approach that aims to control, manage, and orchestrate human mobility for the sake of convenience and profit. Containers are often the tools to extract that gain.

## 3.5   Containers

> With us, there was a kid, four years old, with his mother. During the whole journey, I was looking at the kid, asking myself how it was possible to let him travel together with 100 other people, crammed in like animals inside a container, like those that deliver vegetables, where there is no air to breathe or space enough to move. For a twenty-one-hour journey, where one urinates in front of everybody because the door of the restroom is blocked by the people sitting in front of it. We traveled from 4 p.m. until 1 a.m. the next day. Every time the driver would stop to eat, we stayed locked inside the container under the sun. There was no air and everyone stood up panicking because it was impossible to breathe and we wanted to get off. For those at the end of the trailer it was even harder. Watching the kid gave us courage, and every time the truck would stop, we took him and lifted him close to the window.
>
> (Segre 2009, p. 67, author's translation)

The image of the container recurs in many interviews with migrants who have experienced the unforgiving Sahara Desert and the brutality of the Libyan police. Like caravans and camels before, these containers carry neo-slaves from detention centers to oases where migrants will be sold. According to Sir Harold Evans, it was Malcom McLean (2012), a truck driver, who came up with the idea of the container to move goods more rapidly and efficiently, and we have learned how, for many, the containerization of the world has become synonymous with globalization. This may be true for the plain reason that containers move not only goods but also human cargo.

Those containers sailing the great sand sea may, at first, recall the concept of boats as heterotopias described by Michel Foucault. At the end of his excursus, Foucault writes that the boat is a floating piece of space, a place without a place that exists by itself. "It is closed in on itself and at the same time is given over to the infinity of the sea" (Foucault 1986, p. 27). However, as the analogy of overcrowded sand containers fails to resonate with the celebration of boats sailing toward limitless seas, we may instead tie the container to Foucault's crisis heterotopias, or places of loss and death where migrants often die and become one with the sand. Thus, these containers are perhaps places without places that house those who live in a condition of crisis within their surrounding societies and who, once confined to non-spaces, are then abandoned to the infinity of the desert.

For those who attempt to reach Libya from the sub-Saharan region, trucks head up north, while containers carrying migrants captured by the Libyan police head south toward the Sahel, "the shore" of the great sea of sand. There, the Libyan police will eventually abandon the migrants to their fate, unless the migrants have the financial resources required to pay the price of their existence and resume their journey, hoping not to be arrested again. Officially, according to agreements that Maghreb countries signed with the European Union, Libyan police take undocumented migrants back beyond the Libyan border. Sadly, the expulsions do not occur very often. It is more profitable to spread the migrant resources sporadically over the territory and thereby stimulate the economy around camps and oases in the middle of the arid desert, like that of Kufra for instance. Kufra is an oasis located at the southeastern limits of Libya, one of the most arid parts of the Sahara, and therefore a vital post for any who attempt to cross the desert. Ironically, history tells us that it was often used by the Italian Army as a stop on the way to Italian East Africa (AOI) when the Suez Canal was closed to them (Aruffo 2003). Today, the oasis is a place where people are detained upon entering the country, as well as when they are about to be deported across the land borders with Sudan and Egypt. But deportation does appear to be what externalized European migration control efforts in Kufra are primarily about. "Before it was the place where the expulsions were carried out, but now it is a city of commerce," Fikirte remarks (Segre 2009, p. 68). According to migrant testimonies, Kufra's prison functions more as an employment office than a place for detention. For example, although there is a government-run migrant detention center at Kufra, smugglers also operate their own detention facilities there.

> There is no doctor or nurse on site or available. Everyone sleeps on the floor. . . . At most, people are allowed outside once per day when the guards conduct their count of detainees. Although this is the one chance to breathe fresh air, it is also the time when the most beatings occur.
>
> (Human Rights Watch 2009, p. 81)

Because smugglers run their own facilities and wear military uniforms, migrants do not have a clear distinction between "illegal" smugglers and "legal" authorities. Therefore, they have the impression that the two forces work together.

In this sense, the renowned opacity of the desert, exemplified by sand that covers all traces, does not relate only to its geological aspects. As soon as the prison starts to fill, the local *dallala* come to visit the "legal" facility and, if they think that they can extort some money from migrants, buy them for 30 Libyan dinars. Many Christian migrants point out that this was the price that Judas requested to betray Jesus. The migrant-slaves are then moved into a field (*misrah*) where they work until they can reimburse the *dallala* the price they paid to buy them and save enough money to head again to the north. The migrants are then sold to Libyan smugglers and cross the desert again via truck. Very often, when they reach the coast, they are again arrested, tortured, expelled, and sold in what amounts to a vicious circle.

## 3.6  Camps in the desert

'How can you forget the concentration camps built from Italian colonists in Libya into which they deported your great family – the Obeidats? Why don't you have the self-confidence, why don't you refuse?' the Libyan intellectual Abi Elkafi recently asked the Libyan ambassador in Rome . . . in an open letter. 'The reasons I write to you are the odious new concentration camps set up on Libya's soil on behalf of the Berlusconi government.'

(Dietrich 2004)

It is not difficult to relate to the grief of Abi Elkafi when he recalls the history of his country under the brutal occupation of fascist armies. Records of concentration camps in Libya's desert date from 1929 to 1934 and signal the end of the heroic resistance of Chief Omar al Mukhtar who, although more than seventy years old, managed to keep the fascist army in check until his capture and hanging on 12 September 1931. To subdue him and the civil population, fascist airplanes delivered gas and chemical bombs (Boca 1996). His legacy, thanks to his deep religious devotion, military cunning, and bravery, helped to keep alive the Libyan rejection of Mussolini's colonial fervor. The colonial regime's reaction was no less dreadful than it had been twenty years earlier when the Italian government, seeking to crush Libyan resistance, set a world record for the first aerial bombing on the oasis of *Ain Zara* on 1 November 1911 (Aruffo 2003). Because of General Graziani's loyalty to the fascist ideology and his notoriously cruel and rigorous methods, Benito Mussolini directly ordered General Graziani to Libya in 1930. His strategy was to totally annihilate any form of dissent among the civil population by creating an empty buffer zone between the rebels and the population, including the construction of a 270-km-long fence along the perimeter with Egypt to cut any aid to the resistance (Ahmida 2007). The area of Gebel experienced mass deportations (amounting to 110,832 total units and 100,000 units alone in 1931 according to Libyan historian al-Barghathi), with the consequent relocation and internment of 80,000 people among sixteen concentration camps of different sizes: from *el Abiàr* with 3,100 prisoners to *al-Agaila* with 20,000 prisoners (Evans-Pritchard 1949). By and large, living conditions in these camps were precarious at best. They were built in the middle of the desert and provided detainees no ability to make use of their nomadic mètis. What is more, the whole endeavor was tainted by a layer of hypocrisy, since the fascist ideology pretended to use the camps to "educate and civilize" the imprisoned Libyan population. Scholars of Italian colonialism, such as del Boca, Rochat, and Ahmida, have accused the Italian government of systematically censoring and obstructing the disclosure of sources and notes of camps in Libya. Ahmida (2007) ended up turning to Libyan oral history to reveal the atrocities of Italian camps, especially with reference to Ma Bi Marad ("ضرم يب ام" – "No Illness but This Place"] written by the famous Libyan poet Rajab Hamad Buhwaish al-Minifi at the concentration camp of al-Agaila.

The concentration camp system was formally dismantled in 1932; although Italy and Libya formally agreed on a common document (BBC 1998) in which Italy recognized some of its responsibility for the atrocities committed during the colonial enterprise, in fact, the Libyan desert is punctuated nowadays by several detention camps for migrants. These are real structures with concrete walls where, every year, more than 60,000 migrants are imprisoned (Herzog 2009). Each camp is connected to other, smaller camps where migrants are arrested. Together, these camps function like a macabre web or strainer; they capture, select, and filter excess human bodies. The capture and moving of migrants via container from satellite camps to principal ones bears an uncanny resemblance bearing an uncanny resemblance to the lager network mechanism set during the Nazi Germany. The trucks that pull the containers are brand-new six-tire Iveco Trakker 420s – an Italian brand that the Italian government sold to Libya after the 2003 bilateral agreements to stem the flow of undocumented migrations. I will dwell upon the role of these technologies in Chapter 6.

Although no video is yet available, the configuration of the Libyan system of migration control and the poor conditions within detention centers where migrants are incarcerated are well documented via audio (Herzog 2009). Some of the camps are old prisons or military bases; others are warehouses where Qadhafi used to store chemical weapons (in fact, according to some testimonies, because chemical residuals still pervade the building, everyone held in Kufra's prison catches a skin disease called *asasia* (Segre & Yimer 2008). At least since 2004, when the European Commission published its report (European Commission 2004), Europe has known about the desperate conditions of inmates in these centers. The report also confirms that Italy provided funds for the construction of three of these camps for migrants along with technical resources to support Libyan police patrol operations. According to the report, in 2003 Italy financed the construction of a camp for undocumented immigrants, in line with European standards, to be built in the north of the country; the construction started by the end of November 2004. A final report provided at the end of a 2004 European Commission technical mission foresees a special allocation in the financial exercise for 2004–2005 to effectuate two more camps in the south of the country in Kufra and Sebha. Among the items provided by the Italian government, the European Commission's report mentions the provision of "1,000 sacks for corpse transport" (2004) to the Libyan authorities. Dead migrant bodies are more than a natural eventuality in these detention centers. Therefore, hundreds of sacks are needed to remove those bodies from their cells.

The milestone for cooperation on immigration control was laid on 13 December 2000 when "Italy and Libya concluded a bilateral agreement for the promotion and protection of investments, which entered into force on October 20, 2004" ("Italy-Libya BIT" or "BIT").[4] Most importantly, the two countries agreed to cooperate against terrorism, drug trafficking, and undocumented immigration. On 29 December 2007, Mr. Giuliano Amato, then–Italian Minister of the Interior, and Mr. Abdurrahman Shalgam, his Libyan counterpart, signed an important treaty to conduct joint patrol operations to stem the flow of undocumented migration. This treaty perfectly crowned one year of intense economic and diplomatic relations between Italy and Libya. In October 2007,[5] the Italian State Hydrocarbons Authority [ENI] and National Oil Corporation [NOC] of Libya signed a wide-ranging agreement to amplify drilling operations off the Libyan coast. The new agreement set oil and gas production expiry dates for 2042 and 2047, respectively. I will not dwell upon the specific content of these bilateral agreements. It is enough to say that all these agreements were concluded at the executive level between the two governments without parliamentary debate. As Lavenex clearly states:

> Government representatives gain autonomy because their action at the intergovernmental level is shielded from the pluralistic domestic arena, where they compete with other actors on the "right" interpretation of social problems and possible policy solutions.
>
> (2006, p. 331)

Without any doubt, this kind of cooperation management faces some legitimacy problems. For instance, between 16 August 2003 and December 2004, the Italian government organized forty-seven deportation flights via Air Libya Tibesti and Buraq Air of more than 5,000 captive passengers, including Sudanese and Ethiopians. They were deported before their requests for asylum were examined, which was in violation of the principle of non-refoulment that several international conventions protect. In May 2005, the European Court of Human Rights "declared admissible complaints against Italy submitted by eighty-three refugees expelled to Libya from Italy" (Pastore 2007, p. 9). In fact, in concluding the report, after having visited the camps to verify the overall conditions in which migrants were held, notwithstanding room for improvement, the European mission contends that "in general, conditions in the camps were found to be difficult but relatively acceptable in the light of the overall general context" (European Commission, 2004, p. 34). In contrast, the testimonies of migrants held there seem to point in the opposite direction:

> Kufra it is a place of death. When you hear the noise of the keys turning in the lock, your blood freezes. You must turn your eyes towards the wall. If you dare to look into their eyes, they beat you up. . . . We were at least 700 . . . we used to sleep one over the other; there were no space enough to

lie down on the ground. Single meal: a fistful of white rice for the whole day, 20 grams each . . . during the night they brought me in the courtyard. Every night. They asked me to do push-ups. Once exhausted they kicked me and cursed my Christian faith and me. Every night. . . . Personally, the first time I saw Kufra I wanted to hang myself. . . . I cannot describe the filthiness, the hunger, and the incessant humiliations. There were also kids and women. They kept them separated. Women they will never tell you because of shame, but it is important that everyone knows what they (Libyan guards) do to women in Kufra. They rape them in front of their husbands, in front of their brothers. They used iron sticks, wood sticks . . . it is shocking. They treat us like animals . . .

(Del Grande 2007, p. 126)

The impression that emerges from reading the direct experiences of migrants held in these camps is not one of tolerable conditions given exceptional circumstances. Rather, these voices describe the methodical, permanent, and unexceptional maintenance of inhuman conditions for these captured migrants. Nowadays, in the aftermath of Libya's revolution on the verge of a total civil war, the situation of migrants in detention centers is also deteriorating. There are eighteen camps for migrants, normally containing between 4,000 and 6,000 people, most of which are at this moment experiencing shortage of food and sanitation, turning into death traps for African migrants without proper documents. Detention is a mode of transience that is imposed on people who are categorized as temporary or in transition. Their detention is therefore perpetually indefinite. According to migrants' stories, it may last anywhere from two weeks to many years. The temporary condition of permanence, of being trapped in a state of exception, a state of siege, as if perpetually adrift in a sailboat or a life raft, is a state of absolute suspension; migrants find themselves lost in a void created by the immanent collision of two contradictory temporal states: permanence and transience.

As with twentieth-century camps, these zones are zones that annihilate human conditions through incessant torture, indifference and invisibility. Families, relatives, and friends often do not receive any news of arrested migrants for years and believe that they simply died during the dangerous desert crossing. While the number of people who perish during the crossing is high, many migrants who are arrested and lack any financial resources end up being enslaved; they use their bare bodies as their last resort to buy their freedom. Many die alone in cells, which are lonely and miserable regardless of whether they are deemed "illegal" or "legal," after experiencing recurring tortures, humiliations, and deprivations.

The end or aim of this web of detention facilities is not to physically eliminate migrants, as I mention elsewhere, but to treat them as if they were invisible, or visible yet non-existent, like ghosts. Their spirits will often be crushed, their determinations nullified, their voices unheard. By design, their presence will be rendered invisible and inaudible. Roman Herzog managed to record an audio documentary from within migrant detention camps in Libya for the first time. In Zlitlen's camp, he meets a detained Nigerian woman who is unafraid to speak openly against the forces in charge of the prison. She states:

> I have been here for 3 months. I cannot talk with my husband. People suffer in here. The water we drink is salty . . . many women got sick because of food. Sores cover us. . . . Nobody care about us, some are at the point of dying, and some women are pregnant. Please, someone help us. We need to get out of here.
>
> (Herzog 2009)

## 3.7 Filter them out/in

Camps are only one element of the complex system of migration control that uses geographical isolation to render migrants invisible and inaudible. As a camp effect, the desert also filters out. For example, in an interview a few months ago, Dag said clearly that only those who are the most fortunate and strong succeed. Those who perish on their way across the desert vanish inside the golden dunes; their bodies are instantly mummified by "quartz-sand about to turn into liquid gas" (Biemann & Holmes 2006, p. 45). Therefore, the testimonies of detainees in the camp of Kufra are merely one part of a continuum of hardship and abuse that is characteristic of a sort of permanent limbo faced by those trapped in a slave economy, viciously circular, that seeks to render migrant political voices silent. Much like twentieth-century Italian colonial projects, by halting migrants' trajectories, the externalization of European migration control seeks to halt their ability to raise their voices, to be political subjects; ultimately, therefore, it aims to render migrants discursively, if not always physically, non-existent. Only in this way can Europe uphold a contradiction of waving legal principles of individual rights as its own distinctive ensign while simultaneously orchestrating an apparatus of migration control with visibly obvious deadly effects.

Nonetheless, echoes of these practices in the Sahara Desert sometimes reach Fortress Europe, along with clamoring within European society. Saharan itineraries are being projected into Europe now that migrant detention camps are in every city in Europe (see Chapter 8). This proliferation of the external within the internal partially calls to mind the concept of overdetermination that Balibar assigns to colonial and, later, post-colonial borders. The French philosopher referred to overdetermination (Balibar & Hahn 2002, p. 79) as the tendency of European empires to project their existence beyond Europe by replicating their borders within the colonies (e.g. Francophone Africa versus Anglophone Africa). Today, however, the process is reversed: the camps and the containers that mark out the routes of migrants in Africa arrive within the territory of Europe. These echoes highlight the interaction and interdependence of borders and camps and can serve as stopwatches to count down the collapse of the system of inclusion that the end of the era of colonialism proclaimed. European politics of migration control in Africa reveal not only the limits of who is left out and who is included in European society, but also how the system of limiting, of bordering, works. Borders are a pre-condition of the political economy of international migration insofar as they construct social relationships and determine the legal positions of people on the move in ways that are required for state- and territory-based political analysis.

The colonial camps that were once used to clarify otherwise unclear distinctions between the colonizer and the colonized have today mutated into international airport waiting zones and miserable housing projects on the margins of European cities (Agamben 2000). These places within a place filter people and leave certain bodies, but not others, in a condition of crisis within the surrounding society. While "inside," they nonetheless function as borders. Migrants, refugees, and asylum seekers frequently find residence within these contemporary camps or zones of exclusion within the state. These persons represent a surplus that is every day more convenient to reallocate and reorganize within the cracks of the global economic system. At the core of the concept of borders, at its essence, lays a process of differentiation, which in turn constitutes the most important gear of political economy. Selections that are made at border sites are translated into different wages and divisions of labor. Transnational chains of value mechanisms (Piore 1979) that are manifest in wage differentials link price differentials and segmented labor markets between as well as within countries. This is the background in which the desert and the sea are transformed into camp effect areas. In the abyss of the sea and within the opacity of the desert, we see reflected the emptiness of the universal human being, into which the shadow of the European citizen collapses.

## Notes

1   The Arabic name القَذَّافِي مُعَمَّر of the Libyan leader will be here romanized as Muammar Gaddafi according to BBC and mayor British publications. However, there are several spellings from many transliterations of regional Arabic, as journalists already noted more than twenty years ago: www.straightdope.com/columns/read/513/how-are-you-supposed-to-spell-muammar-gaddafi-khadafy-qadhafi

2   Numbers in this case come from different sources, mostly think tanks and national authorities, and often are not mutually corroborating. Still, it is possible to draw some conclusions or, better, to raise questions from the data that inform current European policies of migration control. For instance, Libyan authorities currently estimate that the foreign population residing legally in Libya is 600,000, and that a further 700,000 to 1.2 million are residing illegally – 2 million according to IOM (Human Rights Watch 2009).

3   Incidentally, I would like to recall statements expressed in a resounding declaration made on 21 July 2004 by Mr. Giuseppe Pisanu, then–Minister of the Interior in the second Berlusconi government (2001–2006). He specifically rang the alarm bell problematizing the "2 million" desperate people waiting on the coast of Libya ready to reach Europe. Later on, the next Minister of the Interior, Mr. Roberto Maroni, together with the current Minister of the Interior, Mr. Angelino Alfano, both reiterated that hundreds of thousands of migrants "are massing in Libya now with the intent of reaching Italy" at the same time as Libya's interim Interior Minister, Salah Mazek, recently warned the European Union that Libya had had enough of being a way station for migrants heading to Europe and that it was "Europe's turn to pay" (The Editorial Board 2014).

4   www.cgsh.com/treaty_rights_and_remedies_of_italian_investors_in_libya/

5   www.africanoiljournal.com/10–18–2007_eni_signs_contracts.htm

# References

Agamben, G., 2000. *Means without End: Notes on Politics*. Minneapolis, MN: University of Minnesota Press.

Ahmida, A. A., 2007. Marad: le ferite aperte dei campi di concentramento fascisti della Libia 1929–1933. *Afriche e Orienti*, (1), pp. 80–95.

European Commission, 2004. Technical Mission to Libya on Illegal Immigration. Available at: eu-report-libya-ill-imm.pdf [Accessed 27 January 2007]

Aruffo, A., 2003. *Storia del colonialismo italiano: da Crispi a Mussolini*. Rome, Italy: Datanews.

Balibar, E. & Hahn, D., 2002. *Politics and the Other Scene*. London, UK: Verso.

BBC News, 1998. Italy-Libya statement. *BBC*. Available at: http://news.bbc.co.uk/2/hi/130378.stm [Accessed 19 July 2011]

Biemann, U. & Holmes, B., 2006. *The Maghreb Connection: Movements of Life across North Africa*. Barcelona, Spain: Actar.

Boca, A. D., 1996. *I gas di Mussolini: Il fascismo e la guerra d'Etiopa (Primo piano)*. Rome, Italy: Editori riuniti.

Clezio, J.M.G.L., 2010. *Desert*. Boston, MA: Verba Mundi Books.

De Haas, H., 2008. The Myth of Invasion: The Inconvenient Realities of African Migration to Europe. *Third World Quarterly*, 29(7), p. 1305.

Del Grande, G., 2007. *Mamadou va a morire: la strage dei clandestini nel Mediterraneo*. Rome, Italy: Infinito.

Dietrich, H., 2004. The Desert Front. Available at: www.noborder.org/nolager/more/display.php?id=4 [Accessed 28 April 2010]

The Editorial Board, 2014. Europe's Migration Emergency. *The New York Times*. Available at: www.nytimes.com/2014/05/19/opinion/europes-migration-emergency.html [Accessed 21 August 2014]

Edwards, A. & Ferstman, C., 2010. *Human Security and Non-Citizens: Law, Policy and International Affairs*. Cambridge, UK: Cambridge University Press.

European Commission, 2004. *Technical Mission to Libya on Illegal Immigration*. Brussels, Belgium: European Commission.

Evans-Pritchard, E. E., 1949. *The Sanusi of Cyrenaica*. Oxford, UK: Clarendon Press.

Foucault, M., 1986. Of Other Spaces. *Diacritics*, 16(1), Spring, pp. 22–27.

Frontex, 2007. Frontex-Led EU Illegal Immigration Technical Mission to Libya. Available at: www.statewatch.org/news/2007/oct/eu-libya-frontex-report.pdf [Accessed 5 November, 2009]

Hague, W., 2011. Time Is Against Gaddafi. Available at: http://news.bbc.co.uk/2/hi/programmes/hardtalk/9532641.stm [Accessed 14 July 2011]

Herzog, R., 2009. *Noi difendiamo l'Europa*. Roma: Audiodoc productions

Human Rights Watch, 2009. *Pushed Back, Pushed Around*. Available at: www.hrw.org/reports/2009/09/21/pushed-back-pushed-around-0 [Accessed 7 April, 2010]

Lavenex, S., 2006. Shifting Up and Out: The Foreign Policy of European Immigration Control. *West European Politics*, 29(2), pp. 329–350.

Migration Policy Institute, 2013. International Migrant Population by Country of Origin and Destination. Available at: www.migrationpolicy.org/programs/data-hub/charts/international-migrant-population-country-origin-and-destination [Accessed 21 August 2014]

Opondo, S. O., 2011. Libya's "Black" Market Diplomacies: Opacity and Entanglement in the Face of Hope and Horror. *Globalizations*, 8(5), pp. 661–668.

Pastore, F., 2007. Libya's entry Into the great migration game: Recent Developments and Critical Issues. Rome, Italy: *Cespi*. Available at: www.cespi.it/PDF/Pastore-Libia-great%20game.pdf [Accessed 20 May 2008]

Piore, M., 1979. *Birds of Passage: Migrant Labor and Industrial Societies*. Cambridge, UK: Cambridge University Press.

Porsia, N., 2014. Libia, milizie contro i trafficanti: da Zuwara niente più barconi per l'Europa. *Redattore Sociale*. Available at: www.redattoresociale.it/Notiziario/Arti colo/467255/Libia-milizie-contro-i-trafficanti-da-Zuwara-niente-piu-barconi-per-l-Europa [Accessed 10 September 2014]

Rancière, J., 2005. From Politics to Aesthetics? *Paragraph*, 28(1), pp. 13–25.

Rinelli, L., 2012. European Alternatives – Global Health, Global Security. Available at: www.euroalter.com/2012/global-health-global-security [Accessed 10 September 2013]

Sayad, A., 2004. *The Suffering of the Immigrant*. Cambridge, UK: Polity.

Schapendonk, J. & van Moppes, D., 2007. *Migration and Information: Images of Europe, Migration Encouraging Factors and En Route Information Sharing*. Nijmegen, the Netherlands: Radboud University.

Segre, A., 2009. *Come un uomo sulla terra*. Rome, Italy: Castel Gandolfo.

Segre, A. & Yimer, D., 2008. Like a Man on Earth. Available at: http://likeamanonearth.blogspot.com/ [Accessed 21 September 2011]

Sørensen, N. & Dansk institut for internationale studier, 2006. *Mediterranean Transit Migration*. København, Denmark: DIIS Danish Institute for International Studies.

# 4　The blue door

## 4.1　Lampedusa: the blue door

Imagine this space. Visualize the Mediterranean Basin like a vast blue plaque.[1] Now, imagine the *dispositif* of migration control, freezing migrants' motions in an endless temporary limbo: a zone that is inside as well as outside the water. This is a space "in which the intention is to treat people neither as subjects (of discipline) nor as objects (of elimination)" (Isin & Rygiel 2007, p. 184). The plan is to render undocumented people's existence "invisible and inaudible" (Ibid.) – therefore, to transform the sea into a clear plaque, wiping out migrants' presences by absorbing their *motus* and not allowing them to be recognized as subjects. This has to be done without generating new martyrs who could upset the imaginary of European public opinion.

Unfortunately, sometimes life is too stubborn, and cracks appear inside the clear space of the plaque. "We sweat and cry salt water, so we know that the ocean is really in our blood," cries poet Teresia Teaiwa (Hau'Ofa 2008, p. 41). The chaotic environment of the Mediterranean becomes a space to be appropriated and properly managed. It represents the limits that define Europe. But the same agency can be attributed to resistance's tactics. In fact, tactics rely on opportunities because "what it wins it cannot keep," making use of the cracks within strategies' space. The inherent fluctuation of this *motus* constitutes the intrinsic characteristic of borders and frontiers. One of the sites where this interaction occurs is the Italian island of Lampedusa.

Lampedusa is just one, yet a critical, point around which Europe is defined. To write about this island is to take into consideration the dimension of the Mediterranean that ends and begins on its shores. Even if for centuries, fishers and sailors took advantage of its port to find refuge and protection, surprisingly, Lampedusa does not appear to be a crossroad of different identities. Instead, its buildings and the urban structure of the village convey a sense of carelessness and anonymity timidly covered with a flimsy layer of make-up barely enough to compete with other shining tourist destinations around the Mediterranean. To write about this rock that emerges from the abyss of the sea is also to reflect upon the fact that, geologically speaking, this is Africa and not Europe. Closer to Tunisia than to Sicily, Lampedusa has been, in the past twenty years, the fulcrum of the European and Italian management of migration flows from Africa. As a result of this orientation, the island suffers because of a policy that diverts money toward security and the control of immigration instead of paying attention to an enduring lack of basic education and health services. It has been referred to as both the advanced extreme of two continents and the most southern European outpost. Is Lampedusa just the appendix of Europe, or is it the Trojan horse of new hordes at the gates of the fortress?

This chronic condition has exasperated its inhabitants, who have reacted in different ways. On one hand, the resident population has incorporated a governmental discourse of blaming migrants for any problem to the point that in the regional election of 2007, the *Lega Nord* (Northern League), the most prominent anti-immigration Italian political party, performed among the winning coalition, securing the position of vice mayor for one of its elected representatives, Mrs. Angela Maraventano. On the other hand, others have opposed the governmental resolution to relegate Lampedusa to the role of military outpost in the war against African migrants' flows, while others have recognized that the presence of migrants provides stable revenue during the desolate winter season when the island is populated by detained migrants, officials, and humanitarian operators. In many ways, then, the multifaceted character of this island makes it a central site in which to investigate the implementation of European migration control and the effects that it has on the process of African migrations.

## 4.2   At the airport

Landing at the airport of Lampedusa, one can clearly see what remains of the detention center for migrants that operated from July 1998 as the *Centro di Permanenza Temporanea* (Center for Temporary Permanence [CPT]) until 1 August 2007 when former barracks in the *Contrada Imbriacola* were transformed into a new structure for migrants and asylum seekers, nowadays defined as the Center for Identification and Expulsion (CIE). The old construction next to the airport was designed as a CPT following Law No. 40/1998, the so-called *Turco-Napolitano* law. Designed by a center-left government, it is the earliest Italian organic immigration law that established detention centers for immigrants and asylum seekers. The center in Lampedusa was designed to contain only 186 people, but soon it was clear that that would be inadequate to deal with the number of migrants who were rescued and transported to the island by Italian and European authorities. Already going through the very first years of implementation of European migration control, it is plain, then, that Lampedusa has never been a voluntary destination for African migrants who sail from Africa. Migrants are often located on radars around the Mediterranean Sea and then transferred to the island. Better still, it is a mutual counterpunctual relationship between security and migration. Migrants follow fisher routes between Sicily and Tunisia to increase their chances of being intercepted in case of (frequent) engine breakdowns.

Lampedusa has been defined as the quintessential heterotopic space, a true touristic gem of the Mediterranean seascape and a space of exile, one within the other, apparently separated and coexisting. Pugliese argues that this is possible because

> in the schema of heterotopic space, the absolutely other space, the penal colony, becomes invisible and unintelligible within the enframing discourse of western tourism: spectacular sunsets, sparkling waters and serviced luxury – all effectively work to disappear the squalor and suffering of the immigration prison just over the horizon.
>
> (Pugliese 2010, p. 118)

The center at the airport is extremely close to the runway in order to have easy access to carriers and therefore more easily manage the relocations of undocumented migrants to other structures in Italy or even deportation to the countries of North Africa. In fact, the airport of Lampedusa was the stage of well-publicized mass deportations, the first of which took place between 2 and 9 October 2004. *La Rete Antirazzista Siciliana* (the Sicilian Antiracist Network) broadcasted images of the deportation[2] in both 2004 and 2005 in which the camera gives a wide shot of African migrants being escorted by police officers.

Migrants walk in line formation from the detention structure next to the runway to the Adriatic Air Charter, a small Croatian company. The whole scene has something surreal about it: it is bright midday, and the migrants are handcuffed to each other. It looks like if they are holding hands, as if seeking comfort before embarking toward the unknown. They do not know where they are going, but they imagine that they will be reallocated to some other facility in mainland Italy. Suddenly, an activist on the other side of the fence shouts out in Arabic that they will be deported back to Libya. Here, the scene acquires its tragicomic character. Like in those silent movies that inevitably culminate in an eruption of physicality, every man runs for his own life in different directions; most of them are arrested in a few seconds. With a mix of sympathy and compassion, we follow the last one, chased by a few officers running along the runway, looking for a way out that does not exist. On the other side of the fence, there are overhanging rocks and then the deep blue sea, where now the Door of Europe (Dodman, 2011) has been built to signify the narrow entrance to the European world. The motion does not have the grace of a great escape à la Steve McQueen, but it still retains the grandiosity of a rebellion.

Following the deportations of October 2005, a group of ten NGOs from France, Spain, and Italy filed a complaint addressing Mr. Barroso (at the time, the President of the European Commission) to take action against Italy for the violation of various principles of human rights law that constitute the flagship of the European Union (EU). The complaint cites, first of all, the violation of the right of defense and of all parties to be heard according to Articles 6 and 7 of the European Convention for the Protection of Human Rights and Fundamental Freedoms. At the same time, the deportations could be considered an infringement of the prohibition of torture and inhuman or degrading treatment, provided for in Article 4 of the European Charter of Fundamental Rights and Article 3 of the European Convention for the Protection of Human Rights and Fundamental Freedoms. What is certain is that the Italian government operated in violation of the prohibition of collective expulsions provided for in Article 4 of the fourth protocol of the European Convention for the Protection of Human Rights and Fundamental Freedoms and Article 19 of the European Charter of Fundamental Rights and was also in violation of the non-refoulment principle, as specified in Article 33 of the 1951 Refugees Convention. Specifically, we read in the complaint that

> by deporting over 1,000 migrants and potential asylum seekers between the 2nd and the 9th of October 2004, as part of collective expulsions to Libya, the Italian authorities contravened the right to asylum as recognized by the Amsterdam Treaty . . . whose principles are referred to by the European Court of Justice in its rulings.[3]

Here, the relation between the law and the person and that between the law and the territory intersect. The unremitting deterritorialization of the internal and external borders of Europe not only renders its legal space discontinuous but also allows private and public subjects at the national and local levels to shuffle the hierarchy of European law. As I explained in Chapter 2, the function of the contemporary border is to differentially include/exclude single migrants within one political system instead of two separate worlds and cultures. Lampedusa condenses the characteristic of the contemporary border and its contradiction since it has been transformed into a contemporary gate where tourists' and migrants' bodies meet. What my research demonstrates is that the externalization of migration control must be viewed as a system of relations between migrations and control that has elected Lampedusa as one of the preferred stages.

## 4.3    Tourists and bodies

Because the island of Lampedusa is a gem of the Mediterranean, its economy relies heavily on tourism. Consequently as far as the migrant detention center was next to the airport runaway, the proximity created a disturbing juxtaposition characterized by both tourists' mobility and migrant capture. As Pugliese notes,

> nothing more geographically exemplifies the manner in which incompatible heterotopias and heterochronies coexist within the one locus, yet remain seemingly invisible to each other, than the images of washed up corpses of refugees on the beaches of Europe in the line of sight of tourists continuing to enjoy their vacation.
>
> (Pugliese 2010, p. 673)

In the summer of 2009, the detention center next to the airport did not function – no more "illegals" leaning against the fence like spectators of the exhibition they embodied for holiday makers on their way to a much desired vacation, their encamped bodies juxtaposed with the ease with which tourists can enjoy the island. The bodies of the migrants behind the fence reveal the politics of disparity between those that have legitimacy and those that do not. They carry the border within themselves. But when I visited the island, there was a glaring absence of undocumented migrants. I kept asking around about the unusual emptiness, covering my curiosity with the indignation of a northern tourist who does not want to look at such a display of misery while on vacation. The locals reassured me that Lampedusa was empty and was back to being one of the treasures of the Mediterranean, echoing Mr. Andrea Ronchi, Minister for European Policies, who had visited the island a few days before. With a sort of profuseness, he could affirm that:

> Lampedusa today has zero immigrants in the CPA [Center of First Reception]. Lampedusa returns to Italy as a tourist gem. Today the Mediterranean Sea does not convey anymore those terrible images of illegals and desperation. This is the most tangible evidence of the great work of the Italian government.[4]

Thus, Lampedusa functions as a mechanism of the political apparatus of control. As I mentioned previously, no immigrant or asylum seeker arrives on the island if the authorities do not want them there. They have been always intercepted, captured, dragged here, to be filtered and distributed through the network of detention centers around the peninsula. Further peregrinations will confirm this hypothesis. Where are the hordes of immigrants, the Third World's invasion, which for years has been the spotlight of news every summer?

## 4.4 Underwater signposts

I had just left the island of Lampedusa when, on 21 August 2009 after three summer months of uncanny stillness, news from Lampedusa made national headlines. It was reported that five Africans had docked at the island's small harbor. The news described them as if they were ghosts; they could barely walk and had to be dragged off the military boat by Italian authorities. Still, the arrival of yet another few Africans is hardly material for nationwide news. At least since 2002, every summer, African migrants have been intercepted and dragged onto the island of Lampedusa; almost 22,000 (according to fortresseurope.blogspot.com) migrants have died since 1988 while attempting to cross the frontiers of the EU. In this story, however, there was something new, something so shocking that it was worthy of a front-page headline for an audience that otherwise has become inured to violent stories. The five ghosts were the only survivors of a dreadful journey to escape the brutal war-torn reality of Eritrea; to get to Lampedusa, these voyagers went through the harsh climates of the Sahara Desert and survived the brutality of Libyan police control. They managed to sail, at the end of July, toward the shores of southern Europe.

There were seventy-eight passengers in total who sailed from the Libyan coast. After only a few days, their vessel began to drift, and they ran out of food and water. It is a near impossibility to navigate the Mediterranean Basin without being sighted on radar monitors or intercepted by an army of helicopters, airplanes, vessels of any single state, or European agencies. The externalization of migration control also exists at the virtual level of satellite mapping of the area of the Mediterranean. Still, while several boats crossed their path, the survivors said that no one gave them any assistance. They had been navigating for more than three weeks when the Italian authorities decided to intercept them. When they were finally rescued, only five of the initial seventy-eight remained.

For a few days, the Italian government refused to accept their version of the story. To the Italian authorities, the most logical explanation was that they were human traffickers themselves. It would have been useful to inspect their boat, but the authorities left it to be swallowed by the sea, as much as the other seventy-three companions, who became, to paraphrase Glissant, "underwater signposts" (Glissant 1997, p. 6). However, as the days passed, those signposts started surfacing in the channel of Sicily, persistently one after the other, and the public realized the shockingly crude accuracy of their story.

> They died in the sea, but politics, outlined in dispatches sent from the West, murdered them. They built walls in the water, they demanded that visas should appear out of thin air; politics assured that people will be moving on from one place to another.
>
> (Rajaram & Grundy-Warr 2008, p. 205)

Today their corpses join the thousands of bodies that mark the route between Libya and Lampedusa. Within that moment of indignation, one may become conscious that a new border practice around the European continent has materialized.

## 4.5    Borders and frontiers

As I explained in Chapter 2, I consider it critical not to use terms such as *border* and *frontier* interchangeably. I concur with Didier Bigo in contesting the unproblematic overlapping of the two terms in canonical International Relations discourse where the frontiers are the state frontiers and the state is a political entity sealed by borders. Following the analogy, Bigo remarks that "borders or frontiers are synonymous with questions of defense, war, citizenship or the right to punish criminals through collaboration with other states. It is essentially an interstate vision where frontiers delineate natural cultural containers and clear security barriers" (Bigo & Guild 2005, p. 54). I instead believe the nature of the frontier to be more complicated, being a space, in the Foucaldian sense, where it is difficult to locate power on one distinct point and resistance on another. It is the moving localizations of borders in time and space of the emergence of power and resistance that mold the frontier. I suggest that at these points of encounter the border emerges – that is, whenever practices of statecraft enter into relation/collide with migrants' obstinate trajectories. In this sense, as I have anticipated in Chapter Two, the last frontier of Europe, the Mediterranean as well as the Sahara Desert, is a space "still nurtured by the hidden presence of the sacred" ("[toutes sont] animées encore par une sourde sacralisation") (Foucault 1986, p.23). The frontier, then, is a sacred space reserved to those that are in a state of crisis in relation to the society where they exist. They are part of the society, but they are excluded at the same time from it, always temporarily and in excess, but at the same time indispensable for the society to be complete. To revise the theoretical background of the concepts of borders and frontiers essentially means to question the myth of the social contract from Hobbes to Rawls secured within the shell of the classic Westphalian sovereign state as their foundation and basis. It is evident that such a conception of the state cannot withstand the changes caused by the materialization of a global era. At the same time, it is important to recalibrate the power of legal proclamations of universal human rights at the moment we face the unbearable bareness of human life. I maintain that the new frontier of Europe is to be located around points of interaction between the implementation of policies of migration control and acts of flows – that is, at the juncture of multiple discourses of migration. My understanding of the concepts of frontiers and borders is twofold: on one hand, they amount to two key elements of the statecraft aimed at preventing people from acting politically – that is, to prevent their voices from being heard. Paradoxically, on the other hand, as space entities, they surface and are shaped by the ability of people to reclaim their subjectivity.

Once the need to locate the border emerges, the intention is not to draw a sequence of points to be unified in order to identify a line that will split the outside from the inside. In that case, a spatial representation would take up the stage obfuscating the necessary attention I pay to the operational moment. Rather, I mark out points of action/non-action without laying any claim of totality, conscious that "some borders are no longer situated at the border at all" (Balibar 2002, p. 84). Thus, the border manifests itself within the periphery of a metropolitan area as well as within the scorched Sahara Desert every time the authority of the state encounters someone or something that challenges it. In fact, concepts such as rigidity and immobility do not apply to the contemporary idea of border that nowadays has to respond to the increased mobility and multidimensionality of migrations: "fixed boundaries are displaced by flows and diversions that undermine as well as reinforce existing spatial divides" (Agnew 1995, p. 214) in a dialectical way.

Still, the border is contingent on power practices whose perennial fluctuations make the border seem natural and inevitable. It is my intention to shake this assertion and demonstrate the border's reliance on a complex interconnection of historical contingencies and thus to reveal its precariousness (see MigMap, by Labor k3000). The idea of the fixity of the border reinforces the discourse of Fortress Europe as a socio-political body under a permanent state of siege that conceals the real functions of frontiers and borders to trap the subjectification of migrants and asylum seekers while crystallizing the imagery of the nation-state. This is the logic behind the state's strategy of charging fishers who help people adrift at sea with the accusation of human trafficking or the latest practice of the Italian government to intercept migrants/asylum seekers in international waters to deviate their trajectories. The most resourceful methodology will be, then, to draw attention to where and when different "practices" happen and the conditions before their existence at the moment that they become visible. As Foucault put it in *Questions of Method*:

It is a question of analyzing a "regime of practices" – practices understood here as places where what is said and what is done, rules imposed and reason given, the planned and the taken for granted meet and interconnect.

(Burchell, Gordon, & Miller 1991, p. 75)

These practices, once implemented or just acted out, attain their own life and indicate a direction to follow or simply serve as an example of what has to be done. But fundamentally, I believe, they signal the new contour of the frontier and delimit the space of the political.

## 4.6   Strategies and tactics

Relying on the difference between strategy and tactic outlined by Certeau (2002, p. 36), I maintain that how Europe is configured or bordered is largely conditioned by the weaving interaction between strategies of migration control and tactics of resistance. The difference between the two, as explained by Certeau, relies on their different approaches toward space and time. While a strategy postulates a place that belongs to the agent and it requires time that the agent keeps, because of its favorable position, a tactic instead 'is a calculated action determined by the absence of a proper locus' (2002, p. 37). According to Certeau, as in management every 'strategic' rationalization seeks first of all to distinguish its 'own' place, that is, the place of its own power and will, from an 'environment.' (ibid.).

But the same agency can be attributed to tactics. In fact, tactics relies on opportunities because "what it wins it cannot keep," making use of the cracks within strategies' space. The extreme necessary mobility of this *motus* constitutes the intrinsic characteristic of borders and frontiers. Because the very trajectories of these migrants aim at the hyphen of the nation-state, the chaotic environment of the Mediterranean becomes a space to be appropriated and properly managed. As Joseph Pugliese writes, this idea "is perhaps best encapsulated by the Roman imperial tag: *mare nostrum* / our sea. The Mediterranean as *mare nostrum* is already conceptualized as a homogenous space of confinement, possession, and colonization" (Pugliese 2010). The definition of *Mare Nostrum* appears at the beginning of Caesar's *De bello gallico* (Caesar 2006) indicate the confidence to have acquired full control over the Mediterranean and thus a change in Rome's foreign policy, now reoriented to the north toward the Atlantic. The idea of *Mare Nostrum* entailed a totality of control over that sea that, ironically, was considered by Roman emperors to be a mere lake. Instead, the Mediterranean Sea was never a homogenous space both during the Roman occupation and today when European policies of migration control attempt to purge it of foreign bodies. It is then crucial to accept the fact that "to talk of the Mediterranean – of its past, present and future – is to move in this disquieting place" (Chambers 2008, p. 5). It is perhaps ironic, then, if it were not tragic, that the Italian government decided to name a military operation "Mare Nostrum" with the scope to rescue the migrants and arrest the traffickers of immigrants following the worst shipwreck of the twenty-first century that occurred just a few miles off Lampedusa when 366 African migrants died on 3 October 2013. Ambiguous and ubiquitous like the European approach to African migration, this operation retains essentially an emergency nature that continues to define any policies of migration management and control. As a consequence of this emergency approach, detention centers remain necessary corollaries into which to cram African migrants intercepted in the waters around Lampedusa.

## 4.7 Boats and bodies

I had wanted to locate the new center for undocumented migrants (today, the Center for Identification and Expulsion [CIE]), but I cannot find it. It seems incredible that a prison could be invisible on this tiny rock. While I am looking for the new detention center, something else catches my attention. Next to various sorts of rubbish, old rusty cars, and refrigerators, there is a separate space where hundreds of wooden boats lay on one side, a few still intact. These are the boats of the immigrants captured and dragged here. Most of the boats have names written in Arabic – they are well built, they seem able to navigate high seas. This is so different from the representation that the news shows us of old wrecks with a crew of desperate people on their last chance, gambling with the border: to win or to die, but at least willing to die trying.

Why are these boats here and not at the port? Why are residents not recycling the good ones and using the material to build/repair their boats? Why does the local administration spend money and energy to move these boats to the most remote corner of the island, the farthest point from the coast? I start to feel the ubiquity of the border. Alone, I am inside the only geographical depression of the island where the cemetery of migrants' boats is located. And I feel the sacredness of these remnants, their disruptive power. The boats have to be hidden away, destroyed, and what is left eliminated. As I mentioned, how the border functions has to do with what is said and what is seen or concealed. If the migrants arrive on solid boats, contradicting the image of desperate people sailing on wrecked vessels, it does mean that migrants' patterns are stable, organized, and regular. It means that migration is not just an "accident," the ultimate decision taken out of desperation, but a human practice that relies on established patterns. According to Castells, the morphology of the structure has more importance than the individual's willpower, which ends up being channeled by different elements of control such as the state, socio-cultural obligations, and different organizations (Castells 2000). The individual mobility, then, tends to be captured within lines that ultimately privilege some trajectories instead of others. Thus, a migrant relies on well-defined routes marked by previous experiences and personal contacts (*Métis*), as well as juridical and economic restraints.

On the other end, migration is not a mere trajectory from a defined point A to a clear point B; instead, it includes the autonomy of the individual as much as the importance of the unknown and, undeniably, the adaptability of the migrant to the latter. Ultimately, the mobility of the individual is restrained by the extension of the structure that, vice versa, is modified by the flow in itself. This observation seems to pertain to the case of Lampedusa. The policies of migration controls put in force and the capacity of the institutional structures built to accommodate a

*Figure 4.1.* Tunisian boats in Lampedusa
Photograph by Lorenzo Rinelli

certain number of migrants highlight the strategy to capture and direct any vessel in this zone of the Mediterranean toward the island.

Finally, let me map out the new detention center at the Contrada Imbriacola. As appears in one of the pictures taken on site, it is located at the center of the island surrounded by the only geological depression. Even if the CIE has been built only recently to accommodate 381 people [1 August 2007], it has been already renovated because of the riots of February 2009 when migrants held inside the center [860 were held at that moment] tried to break out . . . sparking a clash with security forces that caused several injuries. . . . A fire broke out in one of the buildings housing the illegal immigrants, largely destroying it (Anonymous, 2009). It is after lunch when I arrive there. Under the midday heat there are no sounds coming from inside the structure: no guards, no movements but the drone of cicadas. The center is completely empty. What is invisible nonetheless exists and often constitutes the most essential aspect. Slowly, between the blinding rays of the merciless African summer the silhouette of a new border and its location becomes visible. What are the motives behind the construction of a big center of permanence for migrants on the island?

At the time this book goes under revision, the center is being renovated and inaugurated by the first anniversary of the above mentioned October 3rd trag- edy, ready to receive new African migrants intercepted around the Mediterranean. What then if the island functions as a tap that can be turned off and on according to political climates? 'They are all dragged in here' on the island, insists Giusy Nicolini, Mayor of Lampedusa. 'They have been always intercepted, captured, and dragged here to be filtered and distributed through the network of centers

*Figure 4.2.* Detention center at Contrada Imbriacola
Photograph by Lorenzo Rinelli

around the Italian peninsula.' (Interview recorded by the author on 7 July 2009, Lampedusa)

## 4.8 Locating the border

What is the real function of Lampedusa? Bruno Siragusa (a member of the neoliberal political party Forza Italia) was mayor of Lampedusa from 2002 until 2005 and since then, every summer, locals have witnessed another "emergency" of immigrants' landings. Interestingly enough, in an interview with Roman Herzog, Siragusa admits that there are no landings in Lampedusa since migrants' boats are intercepted sixty miles out in the sea. Instead, it would be more appropriate to declare that the government is performing a humanitarian rescue operation. In his own words, the former mayor recalls that:

> When 10 years ago the center did not exist yet and the phenomenon started, these people indeed were landing on these shores and they (migrants) were wandering around the territory and the people of Lampedusa would provide blankets, warm soup, to eat, expression of a great human solidarity. Now that the phenomenon is under control there is no reason to complain about.
>
> (Herzog 2009)

This interview is remarkable for two reasons: on one hand, it shows how the visibility of the migrants created a sense of immediate solidarity with the local inhabitants, but it also demonstrates implicitly that the wall that creates invisibility often provokes insensibility and hostility. I will return to this important point in the last chapter, as I will discuss joint projects between African migrants and locals. More importantly, it is acknowledged that Lampedusa functions as a gathering place but not necessarily as a voluntary destination for migrants. Surprisingly, the Italian Prime Minister, Mr. Silvio Berlusconi, clarified the location of the border when last summer he declared that:

> It is much easier . . . to examine individual situations in the country of origin, otherwise they come here and go to a camp which, I should not be saying this, is very similar to a concentration camp.
>
> (Squires, 2009)

This would seem to just be a faux pas, although it reveals further complexity when one examines the statement more in depth. On one hand, Mr. Berlusconi acknowledges the unbearable conditions of the permanence of migrants in the camps. On the other hand, he announces a change of strategy, revealing once again the inherent mobility and ubiquity of the border. On 6 May 2009, Italy unilaterally inaugurated a new policy for stemming the flow, consisting of intercepting migrants on high seas and sending them back to Libya. Only a week later at the port of Gaeta, Italy, represented by Maroni Interior Minister of Italy and Libya, with its ambassador to Italy Hafid Gaddur, celebrated the pact with a solemn ceremony. In that occasion, the head of Italy's Guardia di Finanza, Cosimo D'Arrigo, added that members of the Libyan coast guard would be stationed in Lampedusa.[5] Mr. Maroni observed:

> For the first time in history we succeeded in sending directly back to Libya *clandestines* whom we have located yesterday on the sea on three boats. Until today we had to take them into custody, identify and send them back to the nations of origins. . .
>
> (Respinti in Libia migranti presi in mare, Onu preoccupata, Reuters Italia, 7 May 2009)

The strategy seemed to be effective, as 500 boats were intercepted and sent back to Libya in the first week. The number of arrivals suddenly dropped, and the *Times of Malta* published an article titled "Where have all the immigrants gone?"[6] As I have explained, tactics differ from strategies in their different approach to time. A tactic relies on improvisations and an immediate response. It is presumable that migrants did not attempt to sail during the first phase of the joint patrol operation and tried different routes. The European elections of the members of Parliament held between 4 and 7 June 2009 supported this shift. The European People Party (EPP), to which Forza Italia and the Northern League belong, then became the largest group in the European Parliament with 256 members.

Since the WWII, this is the first time that a European state had openly violated the principle of non-refoulment as indicated in the 1951 Refugee Convention. Notwithstanding what Berlusconi and his ministers have declared, intercepting boats carrying potential refugees on high seas and therefore outside territorial waters still constitutes a violation of the Refugee Convention. "As we will see the conflict over the state of exception presents itself essentially as a dispute over its proper locus" (Agamben 2005, p. 24). Apart from the fact that Italian military boats are part of the territory of the state, jurisprudence and scholars have repeatedly stated that non-refoulment obligations are not limited by the territorial boundaries of any state. As a matter of fact:

> [The] principle of non-refoulment does not imply any geographical limitation. . . . Given the practice of States to intercept persons at a great distance from their own territory, the international refugee protection regime would be rendered ineffective if States' agents abroad were free to act at variance with obligations under international refugee law.[7]

What is left of the legal principle of non-refoulment when more than 1,000 people have been intercepted and sent back to non-secure (that is only a euphemism) countries like Libya that do not recognize the existence of refugees? "The world found nothing sacred in the abstract nakedness of being human," Arendt (1973, p. 299) cries. The paradox is simple but devastating: the system of human rights designed to protect those human beings who have nothing left but their naked bodies has been reduced to a derivative of the nation-state logic that is constructed around a homogenous and firm concept of population. The very fact that the idea of nation has squatted in the place of the state has necessarily provoked a *caesura* between people and People (Agamben 2000) – hence the issue of refugees, stateless, exiles in the first place. On one end lies a compact corpus of citizens and on the other end the banished and wretched of the Earth.

Like Arendt, Julia Kristeva (1994) traces the origin of the paradox within the text of the Declaration of the Rights of the Man and Citizen that was adopted between 20 and 26 August 1789. As she notes, the ideas of the French Revolution were aimed at subverting the old system, one of aristocratic power, with a new one based on nationality. Men are born equal and free because they are members of the nation, as clearly stated in Article 3 of the Declaration; once incorporated into the nation, men are considered active members of the polity. At that moment, the life of the citizen becomes sanctified under the protection of the newly democratic state's institutions that will continuously shape the national identity. But to shape means also to draw a line; it means to identify who belongs from who has been expelled to the margins. Theoretical conceptions that maintain the fiction of the rigidity and permanency of the border state have helped this system to remain intact while not taking into consideration those who live "smack in the fissure."[8]

## 4.9 And then came the Arab spring

The uprising started on 17 February 2011 as a peaceful demonstration of the Libyan population in the eastern province of Benghazi, but the brutal military response led the country into a civil war. As far as this research is concerned, it is worth remembering how, since the occurrence of the popular uprisings, European media and politicians have been obsessed with the imaginary fear of massive waves of north Africans invading Europe:

> The fear of thousands of people like him [a Nigerian migrant worker], combined with the chaos still reigning in Libya, raises the prospect of a massive new influx of migrants to Europe in coming months, with no guarantee that the fledgling rebel government will have the resources or inclination to stop it.
>
> (Meo 2011)

Indeed, as the conflict intensified, all foreigners hastened to leave the country; however, an attentive analysis that privileges "biopolitics over geopolitics" (Opondo 2011, p.21) will reveal that the civil uprising had many more significant implications for migration and mobility in the region itself. Using road transportation, most people rushed to neighboring countries such as Tunisia and Egypt, and many were not able to return home because it was too hazardous, as they had fled insecurity, persecution and deprivation in their own country and/or because they lacked the money and contacts to flee after having lived in Libya for many years. Many people were stuck in temporary camps for refugees erected close to the borders and remained trapped in the most deplorable conditions until they found a safe means to return to their country or until a host country would accept them as refugees. For some, the temporary state of being a refugee lasted a year or more in a sort of limbo of immanent permanence.

The overall climate of insecurity and suspicion against foreigners that more often than not pervaded Libyan society[9] increased during the civil uprising because sub-Saharan Africans were associated with the "black mercenaries" that Gaddafi reportedly employed to battle rebels and carry out rapes and other violence. Indeed, some sub-Saharan migrants decided to stay and fight with Gaddafi's forces, hoping to be well paid and possibly becoming permanent nationals by obtaining Libyan nationality. Still others were brought to Libya during the revolt specifically to join Gaddafi's forces. "Some among those were the offspring of families who had been living in the southern part of Libya for decades – Chadians or Nigerians or even Libyans with no legal status, eager to get naturalized" (Attir 2012). Almost completely ignored by the geopolitical analysis of the Libyan crisis, the tragedy of the sub-Saharan migrants was subsumed under the supervision of NATO forces and added to the frequent xenophobic attacks against workers and families from sub-Saharan Africa. As Amnesty International crisis researcher Donatella Rovera reported:

> We examined this issue in depth and found no evidence. The rebels spread these rumors everywhere, which had terrible consequences for African guest workers: there was a systematic hunt for migrants, some were lynched and many arrested.
>
> (Human Rights Investigations 2011)

As an alternative reading of the tragedy of African migrants, this research ponders the diplomatic transactions that make it possible for such violence to take place for such a long time and the implications for the society of Libya, which has become increasingly unbearable as a result of the current uprisings. As Opondo points out:

> It involves locating both processes within the history of political relations that have made Libya and Gaddafi possible. As "we" look at . . . Gaddafi's departure, we should pay attention to the reproduction of values, exchanges, violence and erasures of bodies and voices that characterize the passage to the "new."
>
> (2011, p. 21)

The story of relations between Italy and Libya is illustrative in locating the process that made Gaddafi and Libya the way they are today. It a story that does not end with the completion of the colonel's rule only because Italian politicians have stopped getting together under his Bedouin tent set on a given garden in Rome. It is a story that continues today – for instance, with a bilateral cooperation agreement signed on 18 May 2012[10] to support Libyan troupes in detecting and intercepting African migrants. It a story in which the black body is the white canvas on whose skin the annals of the diplomatic entanglements are recorded and that made the regime and the revolution against it possible. Whether understood as intruders, foes, or victims, black Africans' bodies are incarcerated, conceptually and physically, within single paradigms of international aid, development, and security. The contingency, multiplicity, and complexity of African migration are not recognized to take the voice coming out of the black body seriously. It is the blackness of sub-Saharan migrants that is at once the locus of estrangement/displacement and its relevance. Yet, the migrant remains voiceless, oversimplified, appearing only as a lack, empty as naked black life, out of balance then, only a body in excess, whereas too resilient as worker, too dangerous as military sexual maces, and/or as infected body that carries super bugs into the nation.

The issue of African migrants carrying deadly disease came out recently regarding the recent outbreak of the Ebola virus in West Africa. Without going into a much-needed discussion of the issue of virus containment and origins, it is crucial here to note how Libyan society, nowadays worn to shreds by a spiral of endemic hostility among different factions, has been able to coalesce against the threat of virus infection that the Sahara Desert allegedly has not been able to keep out. In the city of Zuwara, close to the Tunisian border and nowadays the main migration hub for those who venture to Europe, dead bodies of African migrants surface on the shore, generating terror among inhabitants, as these bodies are suspected of carrying the germs of a devastating plague. Photos of mutilated bodies and old wrecked boats are posted in several cafés in the city. People have taken to the streets to protest against the traffickers and smugglers of migrants. "A boy wearing a sanitary mask was holding a sign saying 'We won't allow traffickers to turn Zuwara into a vampire town'" (Porsia 2014). Without underestimating the deadly effects of the Ebola virus, the discourse connecting Ebola and African migrants has taken a geopolitical and military turn instead of one related to a community health approach. What the United Nations and international organizations could not do – that is, impose a cease fire and legitimize a newly elected Parliament – the coming plague scenario did. This has happened by unifying civil society and rebels in the common effort to search, capture, and remove black African migrants from the city and take them to the desert, again leaving the migrants to disappear into the sandy haze of the great Sahara.

Hence, we return to the incipit of the previous chapter, to the vital role of the desert and the sea within the "colonial grammar of signification" (Fernandes 2007, p. 83), as the dividing sea over the Sahel, on the dark side, freezing the sub-Sahara and its inhabitants within the usual rigid discourse of colonial encounters. The recent spread of Ebola has reactivated, if this was ever needed, the imaginary of sub-Saharan Africa as primitive, mysterious, and deadly, as the nest of pathogens that proliferates before taking over the rest of the world, carried through the desert over and inside migrant shoulders. I have illustrated elsewhere (Rinelli 2012) how the discourse of containment and encampment is the matrix, then, that interlaces discourses of sanitation and geopolitical security to fortify the surveillance apparatus of migration control.

What is worth noting here is that by privileging the security discourse, European authorities overshadow a widening gap between places and gender, race and class. It is against the leveling power of pathogens that threat to eliminate the gap, that the European apparatus of externalization is mobilized, to quarantine, isolate, and freeze the movement of African migrants. The discourse must shift then from a scientific approach – keeping in mind that science is far from being apolitical – to economic and social differentials toward a socially global community approach to address the roots of the outbreak instead of leaving this to the desert and the sea.

Thus, it would be erroneous to configure the idea of consensus as a hegemonic and homogenous space, a Mediterranean plaque, where political life occurs separately from naked life. In this space of purity, we will all be living dominated by an overwhelming power – as Rancière put it, "entrapped in the complementarity of bare life and exception" (Rancière 2010, p. 11). Only if we intend the space of exception to be a space of politics, as Primo Levi remarkably revealed in *Survival in Auschwitz* (1996), can the imperturbability of the space of exclusion be disrupted. In this sense, the bipolar impasse of Agamben's argument of the state of exception, sovereign/bare life, can be overcome. A political space

> is not established solely by actions (with material violence generating a place, a legal order, a legislation): the genesis of a space of this kind also presupposes a practice, images, symbols, and the construction of buildings, of towns, and of localized social relationships.
>
> (Lefebvre 1992, p. 245)

Consider, for instance, the three boat stories in the following chapters.

## Notes

1 I use the term *plaque* in a way that partially resembles its microbiological sense. According to britannica.com, plaque, in microbiology,

> indicates a clear area on an otherwise opaque field of bacteria that indicates the inhibition or dissolution of the bacterial cells by some agent, either a virus

or an antibiotic. It is a sensitive laboratory indicator of the presence of some anti-bacterial factor.

Therefore, we can imagine the Mediterranean as a European plaque where the migrants' trajectories are wiped out by a plethora of technological devices of migration control.

2  www.ngvision.org/download/487/ngv.bradipz.net/new_global_vision/disc75/ngv_la_it_20050320_lampedusa_scoppia_19_marzo_05_.avi
3  www.gisti.org/doc/actions/2005/italie/complaint20-01-2005.pdf
4  www.guidasicilia.it/do/news/35616/limmigrazione-non-piu-un-problema-di-lampedusa
5  www.interno.it/mininterno/export/sites/default/it/sezioni/sala_stampa/notizie/immigrazione/0193_2009_05_14_gaeta_consegna_motovedette.html_1084908904.html
6  *The Times of Malta*, n.d. Where Have All the Immigrants Gone? Available at: www.timesofmalta.com/articles/view/20090628/local/where-have-all-the-immigrants-gone [Accessed 3 August, 2009]
7  Executive Committee for the High Commissioner's Programme, Standing Committee, Interception of Asylum-Seekers and Refugees, International Framework and Recommendations for a Comprehensive Approach, 18th meeting, EC/50/SC/CRP.17, 9 June 2000.
8  Gomez-Pena, Guillermo. 1993. *Warrior for Gringostroika: Essays, Performance Texts, and Poetry*. St. Paul, MN: Graywolf Press. p. 37.
9  In 1998, the United Nations Committee on the Elimination of Racial Discrimination (CERD) expressed concern about Libya's alleged "acts of discrimination against migrant workers on the basis of their national or ethnic origin." See www.unwatch.org/site/apps/nlnet/content2.aspx?c=bdKKISNqEmG&b=1313923&ct=8411733
10  www.repubblica.it/solidarieta/profughi/2012/06/19/news/livia_ermini-37510944/

# References

Agamben, G., 2000. *Means without End: Notes on Politics*. Minneapolis, MN: University of Minnesota Press.

Agamben, G., 2005. State of exception. Chicago, IL: University of Chicago Press.

Agnew, J., 1995. *Mastering Space: Hegemony, Territory and International Political Economy*. New York, NY: Routledge.

Anonymous, 2009, Immigrants Riot in Lampedusa Detention Centre. *France 24*. Available at: www.france24.com/en/20090218-illegal-immigrants-riot-italian-detention-centre-lampedusa [Accessed 5 November 2009]

Arendt, H., 1973. *The Origins of Totalitarianism*. New York, NY: Harcourt Brace Jovanovich.

Attir, M., 2012. Illegal Migration in Libya after the Arab Spring. *Middle East Institute*. Available at: www.mei.edu/content/illegal-migration-libya-after-arab-spring [Accessed 7 September 2013]

Bigo, D. & Guild, E., 2005. *Controlling Frontiers: Free Movement Into and Within Europe*. Burlington, VT: Ashgate Publishing.

Burchell, G., Gordon, C. & Miller, P., Eds., 1991. *The Foucault Effect: Studies in Governmentality*. Chicago, IL: University of Chicago Press.

Castells, M., 2000. *The Rise of the Network Society (The Information Age: Economy, Society and Culture, Volume 1)*. 2nd ed. Oxford, UK: Wiley-Blackwell.

Caesar, Julius. 2006. *The Gallic War*. Translated by H. J. Edwards. Mineola, NY: Dover Publications.

Chambers, I., 2008. *Mediterranean Crossings: The Politics of an Interrupted Modernity*. Durham, NC: Duke University Press.

de Certeau, M., 2002. *The Practice of Everyday Life*. Berkeley, CA: University of California Press.

Dodman, B., 2006, 11 March. Europe – The Elusive "Door of Europe." *France 24*. Available at: www.france24.com/en/20110306-elusive-door-europe-lampedusa-italy-north-africa-immigration-europe/ [Accessed 17 October 2014]

Fernandes, J.L.A., 2007. *Challenging Euro-America's Politics of Identity: The Return of the Native*. New York, NY: Routledge.

Foucault, M., 1986. Of Other Spaces. *Diacritics*, 16(1), Spring, pp. 22–27.

Hau'Ofa, E., 2008. *We Are the Ocean: Selected Works*. Honolulu, HI: University of Hawaii Press.

Herzog, R., 2009. *Noi difendiamo l'Europa*. Audiodoc.it Production. Available at www.audiodoc.it [Accessed 3 June, 2010]

Human Rights Investigations, 2011. Libyan Rebel Ethnic Cleansing and Lynching of Black People. *Human Rights Investigations*. Available at: http://humanrightsinvestigations.org/2011/07/07/libya-ethnic-cleansing/ [Accessed 10 September 2014]

Isin, E. & Rygiel, K., 2007. Abject Spaces: Frontiers, Zones, Camps. In D. Elizabeth & C. Masters, eds. *The Logics of Biopower and the War on Terror : Living, Dying, Surviving*. London: Palgrave Macmillan, pp. 181–203.

Kristeva, J., 1994. *Strangers to Ourselves*. New York, NY: Columbia University Press.

Labor k3000, MigMap – Governing Migration. Exhibition *Project Migration* Available at: www.transitmigration.org/migmap/home_map2.html [Accessed 3 November 2009]

Lefebvre, H., 1992. *The Production of Space*. New York, NY: Wiley-Blackwell.

Levi, P., 1996. *Survival in Auschwitz*. New York, NY: Simon & Schuster.

Meo, N., 2011. Libya's Lost Immigrant Souls with Nowhere to Go. Available at: www.telegraph.co.uk/news/worldnews/africaandindianocean/libya/8739774/Libyas-lost-immigrant-souls-with-nowhere-to-go.html [Accessed 7 September 2014]

Opondo, S. O., 2011. Libya's "Black" Market Diplomacies: Opacity and Entanglement in the Face of Hope and Horror. *Globalizations*, 8(5), pp. 661–668.

Porsia, N., 2014. Libia, milizie contro i trafficanti: da Zuwara niente più barconi per l'Europa. *Redattore Sociale*. Available at: www.redattoresociale.it/Notiziario/Articolo/467255/Libia-milizie-contro-i-trafficanti-da-Zuwara-niente-piu-barconi-per-l-Europa [Accessed 10 September 2014]

Pugliese, J., 2010. *Transmediterranean: Diaspora, Histories, Geopolitical Spaces*. New York, NY: Peter Lang.

Rajaram, P. K. & Grundy-Warr, C., 2008. *Borderscapes: Hidden Geographies and Politics at Territory's Edge*. Minneapolis, MN: University of Minnesota Press.

Rancière, J., 2010. *Dissensus: On Politics and Aesthetics*. New York, NY: Bloomsbury Academic.

Reuters Italia, 2009. Respinti in Libia migranti presi in mare, Onu preoccupata.

Available at: http://it.reuters.com/article/topNews/idITMIE5460MB20090507?pageNumber=2&virtualBrandChannel=0 [Acccessed 5 june 2010].

Rinelli, L., 2012. European Alternatives – Global Health, Global Security. Available at: www.euroalter.com/2012/global-health-global-security [Accessed 10 September 2013]

Squire, N., 2009, 20 May. Concentration Camps for Immigrants Admission by Silvio Berlusconi. *The Telegraph*. Available at: www.telegraph.co.uk/news/worldnews/europe/italy/5355280/Concentration-camps-for-immigrants-admission-by-Silvio-Berlusconi.html [Accessed 7 October 2014]

# 5 Anglers of men

*The boat is a floating piece of space, a place without a place that exists by itself,*
*that is closed in on itself and at the same time is given over the infinity of the sea.*
*(Foucault 1986, p. 27)*

## 5.1 Legal borders

This chapter seeks to theorize the dynamics that emerge from the intimate relations
between contemporary African migrants, borders, and justice on single boats around
the island of Lampedusa. That is the stance I take on Foucault's famous description
of a boat as a heterotopic space in relation to matters of justice and human dignity
that people have to face when alone, out on the high seas. These are the same waters
on which Ulysses and Aeneas roamed for years; the Italian government has recently
erected new frontiers that traverse two distinct legal realms. At the international
level, on 6 May 2009, following a bilateral agreement with Libya that skipped over
parliamentarian debates (Lavenex 2006), the Italian government unilaterally inaugurated a new strategy for stemming the flow of African migrants and asylum seekers. It consisted of intercepting migrants in Mediterranean international waters and
sending them back to Libya. These actions stand in violation of Article 33 of the
1951 Refugee Convention, a convention that Libya has never endorsed.[1]

At the domestic level, with the introduction and subsequent enforcement of the
crime of aiding and abetting clandestine immigration (Article 110 of the criminal
code, Article 12 of Legislative Decree 286/98), the state criminalized de facto
any action aimed at rescuing boatloads of African migrants who may become
stranded in the Mediterranean Sea. Some individuals, fishers, and NGOs have
decided to act in violation of the law, while others, out of respect or fear of the
same law, have judged immigrant lives unworthy of rescue. In response to this
new legal paradigm, three trials were initiated in the same Court of Agrigento:
one in 2006 against the crew of the *Cap Anamur*, a German aid agency, and one in
2007 against seven Tunisian fishermen, both for aiding and abetting clandestine
immigration.

The third trial, in 2008, was initiated against Mr. Mariano Ruggiero, a fisher who forced a Somali back in the water as soon as he had reached Ruggiero's vessel in order to rescue himself and his friends, who were lost at sea. Sanwá was the name of this Somali man who left the Libyan coast on the night of 6 January 2008. There were about sixty people on the boat with him, Somalis and Nigerians. The women sat at the center of the boat to stay protected from the splash of the sea. That same morning, as the boat came out of Libyan waters, the vessel *Enza D* left from the port of Syracuse to go fishing south of Lampedusa. On the third night of sailing, the boat ran out of diesel. With little fuel left, they approached a vessel for help. That vessel was the *Enza D*. Arriving alongside the *Enza D*, the boat with African migrants turned off the engine, and the passengers began to ask for help in English. They repeated "diesel," waving the empty tank in the air. Suddenly, one of them stood up and gripped the edge of the boat. One of the sailors ran to help him. He held tight to the vessel with both hands until he was able to haul the tank aboard. Meanwhile, the captain had turned on the engines and was moving away from the boat before the other migrants could hop on. The man on board was Sanwá, lying on the ground, begging for help with not much strength left, while Captain Roger Marino ran nervously back and forth from the cabin at the stern. He kept shouting to his men, "Here we go all in trouble." A few minutes later, the sailors heard the splash in the water. A few desperate strokes and Sanwá disappeared in the sea, dragged down by the weight of his soaked clothes. The sailors did not want to believe what they had just seen. Some burst into tears; others went into hiding on deck. None of them had been able to stop the captain. Ruggiero surfaced after only a couple of hours. The fishing work could not wait – it had to be resumed. A year has passed since then, and Ruggiero's lawyers have requested a plea bargain. He is accused of murder aggravated with cruelty and wrongful death. Ruggiero has never admitted to killing Sanwá. He has said, however, that he feared that authorities would have seized the vessel and that he would have lost three or four days of work.

By analyzing the rulings of the tribunal of Agrigento, I will make an attempt to expose the rigid conceptions of borders and frontiers that naturalize the government's efforts to define the limits of territory as the necessary frame to domesticate alterity and hide the intrinsic violence of the bordering practices of exclusion. While discussing the rulings in relation to the three trials, I will consider how the micropolitics of justice are capable of shaping the contours of the discourse on migration. With this term, following Shapiro (2012, p. 266), I refer to a "process in which individuals are affected by legality/illegalities and employ different courses of action of what is just in contrast to macro politics of justice or the way states administer the law." Such encounters between the concepts of legality/illegality and individuals highlight the way the law affects alternative loci of enunciation that exist before the law, such as solidarity in the maritime context. I call this approach sympathetic (Chismar 1988) because it involves the direct participation of individuals in engaging the law and related institution. At the same time I draw on this method for reading other liminal spaces around the world, whether we come across torrid deserts, deep blue seas, or urban peripheries at the margins of contemporary metropolis.

However, more importantly, I am interested in analyzing how African migrations test the contours of legal obstacles set by the national government and provoke the judicial order to intervene and reset the frame of discourse around human dignity and justice. In so doing, the act of transgressing/traverse raises the tension between jurisprudence, legality, and the law. In other words, the micropolitics of justice do not only act according to an idea of what is in contrast to the state's administration of the law but, more critically, different courses of action taken by individuals and communities force the state to rethink the substantial line between legality and illegality in relation to the dignity of human life.

## 5.2   Legal framework

With regard to international legislation, it is broadly recognized that the focus must be on saving the lives of migrants in distress at sea. This is a long-standing maritime tradition as well as an obligation enshrined in international law. This principle is based on two international Conventions: the United Nations Convention on the Law of the Sea and the International Convention for the Safety of Life at Sea.

Article 98(1) of the 1982 United Nations Convention on the Law of the Sea[2] provides that:

> Every State shall require the master of a ship flying its flag, in so far as he can do so without serious danger to the ship, the crew or the passengers: (a) to render assistance to any person found at sea in danger of being lost; (b) to proceed with all possible speed to the rescue of persons in distress, if informed of their need of assistance, in so far as such action may reasonably be expected of him.

In a similar provision, Regulation 33(1) of the 1974 International Convention for the Safety of Life at Sea[3] (SOLAS Convention) provides also that:

> The master of a ship at sea which is in a position to be able to provide assistance, on receiving information from any source that persons are in distress at sea, is bound to proceed with all speed to their assistance, if possible informing them or the search and rescue service that the ship is doing so.

Not only are the obligations of individuals outlined in these conventions; they also outline and define the obligations of states. For example, the 1979 International Convention on Maritime Search and Rescue[4] (SAR Convention) obliges state parties to

> ensure that assistance be provided to any person in distress at sea . . . regardless of the nationality or status of such a person or the circumstances in which that person is found (Chapter 2.1.10) and to . . . provide for their initial medical or other needs, and deliver them to a place of safety (Chapter 1.3.2).

However, the interpretation of these conventions, which goes beyond the scope of this book, must be considered in relation to the state responsible for the migrants found at sea, with particular regard to the distinction between rescues at sea and abetting undocumented immigration. The thin line that separates the two events represents the space of politics, or the frontier, in which the border emerges, especially if we consider the anxiety of the European nation-states over the increase of African migration on the southern borders of Europe over the last few years. Regarding the fear of invasion by sea, it is worth noting that migration experts take into consideration the importance of technologies of transportation in enhancing human mobility, but often they fail to recognize the impact of sophisticated technologies of detection and interception deployed in the Mediterranean Sea in counting the number of migrants approaching Europe and the world population's growth.

Notwithstanding the reality, and the partiality, of these numbers, it is a given that only a tiny minority – between 10% and 13% – of undocumented migrants arrive in Europe by traversing the Mediterranean (Dünnwald 2011). Still, despite the increasing dangers and mounting death tolls among African migrants, the situations that migrants face crossing the Mediterranean have been spectacularized extensively by the media and used by politicians for mere propaganda. I have previously extensively discussed the significance of the spectacularization and militarization of the Mediterranean Sea in relation to the idea of the externalization of African migration. Because of the visual impact of boats crowded with desperate migrants lost at sea, and recently coupled with the risk of the arrival of the Ebola virus, politicians have considered the containment of African arrivals on the Italian southern shores an absolute priority. Burton-Jeangros, a sociology professor at the University of Geneva, quotes a recent *New York Times* article: "objectively, the risks created by Ebola in Europe are very small, but there is an uncertainty that creates fear" (Higgins 2014). As an example of this panic:

> In Alcorcón, a town on the outskirts of Madrid where a Spanish nurse lived until she contracted Ebola virus while treating a sick priest, local businesses reported this week that their revenues had plummeted as customers stayed away. Among those hit by the scare was a hair salon where the nurse, María Teresa Romero Ramos, had gone for a waxing before she tested positive.
>
> (Ibid.)

This is the paradox of our contemporary condition where we live connected more than ever; however, we keep isolating and bordering our lives for fear of the unknown.

Along these lines, the government's practice of charging "good Samaritans" who have saved lives at sea with the crime of "abetting undocumented immigration" deters these humanitarian rescues and ultimately is a form of border control. Italian law stating the relevant penalties for this offense appears in Article 12 of Legislative Decree 286/1998. Four years after this statute was enacted, the infamous Bossi-Fini Law, Law 189 of 30 July 2002, made Article 12 penalties more severe by emphasizing "the character of law enforcement and public safety . . . partly reversing the vision of solidarity in an exclusively repressive" approach (Italian Supreme Court, Criminal Section III, Judgment n. 3162/03 in Zaccaria 2004). Following the Bossi-Fini revisions, unless the facts show a more serious offense, a person performing acts designed to procure the entry of a foreigner into Italy can be prosecuted for "abetting undocumented immigration." An Article 12 offense is considered a "common" crime – that is, one of which anyone can be an "active subject." In other words, his or her job or qualifications do not matter. Furthermore, the conduct criminalized can be almost anything – a typical free-form conduct – meaning that one can be apprehended by the authorities even if the actual illegal entry did not take place. In fact, all that is necessary for the act to be considered a crime is for the accused to initiate an activity that potentially is able to achieve a foreigner's arrival on Italian soil. However, the offense does require intent, which means that these acts must be consciously and voluntarily committed.

On the other hand, if intent is present, then the act can be defined as an offense of "danger" that does not require any actual "damages" in order for punishment to be imposed. Abetting undocumented immigration is just an emblematic offense characterized by anticipated consummation, which then does not allow the configuration of the attempt. In other words, an individual cannot be charged with "attempting" to abet undocumented immigration: noticeably, the intention, the *forma mentis*, is crucial – either the person wants to facilitate the entrance of people or not. The law outlines the crime in question as an instantaneous offense. An Article 12 indictment can remain subordinated should the act constitute "a more serious offense." As a matter of fact, standard detention can last up to three years, but if the act involved smuggling five or more people, exploiting minors, or prostitution, then one can be incarcerated for a period of up to fifteen years.

Nevertheless, a specific exemption from criminal liability is granted in the event that assistance is given to migrants in need: humanitarian aid and assistance provided to these people does not constitute a criminal offense. This is the space of politics within which people are interacting with borders of migration control and attempt to mold them. It is clear, then, that fishing boats and merchant ships are dissuaded from providing assistance to migrants at sea, since they fear that they could be charged with facilitating illegal immigration. Without examining the matter in detail, which would require an in-depth legal analysis, it is worth mentioning two stories that have caused a tremendous outcry in Italy and abroad and which are paradigmatic of the conflict between the need to effectively fight against irregular migration and the primary obligation to rescue people in need.

## 5.3   Anglers of men

The first is the *Cap Anamur* case, for which the accused was acquitted by the Agrigento Court on 7 October 2009. According to the historical reconstruction at the trial, a boat named *Cap Anamur*, flying a German flag and belonging to a humanitarian organization, had rescued thirty-seven shipwrecked irregular immigrants in the Sicily Channel who declared that they had escaped from Sudan because of the civil war. After taking on board the African migrants in international waters, the *Cap Anamur* was deemed to have passed in Maltese territorial waters without any passengers disembarking there. Then, the boat set sail for Sicily, but with only seventeen miles left to go to dock at Porto Empedocle, Italian authorities refused the ship entry to national territorial waters. A dispute therefore arose as to the competencies and responsibilities of the Maltese, Italian, and German states – Italy being the coast state, Germany being the state with whose flag the boat was sailing, and Malta being the first state in which the boat had arrived with the asylum seekers aboard.

As a matter of fact, as it emerged at the trial, the *Cap Anamur* had visited the port of Malta on two occasions before and after the rescue. In particular, Captain Schmidt, on 25 June, five days after the rescue, did not inform the Maltese authorities of the presence of the thirty-seven migrants aboard when the boat was docked for mechanical repairs. What is more, the Italian authorities believed that Captain Schmidt had informed them that the rescue had taken place on 30 June instead of 20 June in order to obtain permission to enter the harbor. Finally, three weeks later, Italy granted the permit of entry into Porto Empedocle, and the following day disembarkation was authorized. The captain and crew were accused of abetting irregular migration and were arrested, while the shipwrecked people were sent to a reception center. The following day, the captain and crew were released, as the competent court did not confirm the restrictive measures against them.

The second case involved seven Tunisian fishermen who were arrested at Lampedusa and had their boats seized in August 2007. They claimed to have saved the lives of forty-four migrants (including eleven women and two children) from rough seas thirty miles south of Lampedusa, but the captains of two fishing boats and their five crew members were charged with abetting illegal immigration and in November 2009 were sentenced to three-and-a-half years of detention. Ironically, they received the Gold Civil Medal from the German Federation for Human Rights just one month after their sentencing. As a matter of fact, the captains of the two Tunisian fishing boats, Abdelbasset Zenzeri and Abdelkarim Bayoudh, had contacted the maritime rescue coordination center asking for medical assistance for one of the two children aboard. Upon making a medical visit aboard the boat, the authorities determined that the health condition of the migrants was not critical, therefore making it possible for them to claim that the humanitarian basis of the exemption from liability did not apply. Based on these claims, the Court of Agrigento authorized the provisional arrest of the captains and crew, noting that there was adequate evidence of guilt in their conduct in relation to the crime of abetting illegal immigration. For the first time, then, the law of the land – that is, the nation-state with its defined territory and population – ruled against the law of sea. The law of the land would invite these brave captains to leave persons lost at sea to their fate, most certainly death; many accepted the invitation, as illustrated by the stories that follow where, fearing for the loss of their boat, their freedom, and their right to live, captains failed to rescue immigrants stranded at sea even when it was within their means to do so.

These two cases are particularly interesting in view of the fact that, on one hand, they bring up the issue of the legality of their conduct in relation to the scope and the *ratio*, which is the logic, behind the introduction of the criminal offense of abetting irregular immigration. On the other hand, they question the limit of the exemption from criminal liability for humanitarian reasons, which from time to time different governments try to render historically contingent – that is, dependent upon a specific regime of visibility and invisibility (Rancière 2006). In addition to the action of governments and their executive power, the valuation of migrant lives, whether they are worth being rescued or considered just bare life (Agamben 1998) that can be abandoned at will, is dependent on a complex discourse of migration control. For instance, the media and politicians were particularly keen on and effective at mounting a sense of insecurity and panic at the idea of immigrants invading the general public during the period of the two trials. Based on the spectacular performance of the media and local politicians, "legitimate" citizenships of Italy were invited to participate in a discourse that constantly raised questions about the intent and means of the rescue. This included questions such as: were they actually mere operations of rescue at sea, or were the constitutive elements of a crime present? Did the rescuers merely intend to provide assistance, or were they determined to take the shipwrecked migrants on board for other reasons?

In addition, the element of profit, among other reasons, was decisive for the arrest of the *Cap Anamur*'s crew. As a matter of fact, the reasoning of the decision, which validated the initial arrest of the captain and the officials of the *Cap Anamur*, contains a reference to the notion of profit. Although they were certainly not *passeurs* – that is, professional smugglers – and were therefore not motivated by economic interests, the constitutive element of the crime of smuggling subsisted. According to the prosecutor, the crew wanted to get the most out of the media coverage and publicity in favor of the organization. On the contrary, as emerged during the trial and as we can read in the motivations of the panel of judges, the *Cap Anamur* did not invite journalists and photographers to the boat but have instead themselves deduced the importance of the issue while on board. However, even if the *Cap Anamur* had uploaded photos and news about the rescue of African migrants, according to the court, this is completely irrelevant once the conduct is cleared of criminal illegality. In fact, whatever the finality the defendants may have wanted to achieve in terms of media visibility, the conduct is criminally irrelevant.

As to the extent of the exemption for humanitarian reasons, the decision issued in relation to the provisional arrest agreed with the public prosecutor's position: the captain and the officials of the *Cap Anamur* on one hand willingly and unlawfully introduced the thirty-seven migrants into Italian territorial waters in breach of the Italian law on migration. On the other hand, according to the accusation the persons involved were neither real asylum seekers, nor were they in critical status needing prompt assistance. As a consequence, they were not entitled to claim exemption from liability.

The judgment rendered by the third section of the Court of Appeal of Palermo in the case of the Tunisian fishers aboard the boats *Mohamed Hedi* and *Mortadha* took a more "open" approach. The court ruled against the decision issued by the Tribunal of Agrigento in the first grade, which condemned and invalidated the provisional arrest of the rescuers. According to the Court of Appeal, the circumstances grounding that order in relation to the conduct of the fishers were not sufficient to establish that they had acted for the purpose of facilitating illegal immigration. In particular, the fact that neither nets nor fish were found on the boat by Italian authorities was not considered appropriate evidence. Similarly, in relation to the exemption from criminal liability, the fact that the doctors who visited the shipwrecked migrants on board did not judge that their lives were in danger was not sufficient to exclude the fact that the fishers acted in good faith. During the trials, it has also been pointed out obligations to cooperate in rescue operations at sea, which require proper actions that have nothing to do with facilitating undocumented migration, or violating the measures set by the law against irregular migrants. The fishers were fully absolved because the act of rescuing does not represent a crime as they have it carried out in consideration of what perceived as a state of necessity/emergency.

## 5.4   Micropolitics of justice

*How do you recognize that the person who is mouthing a voice in front of you is discussing matters of justice rather than expressing his or her private pain? Politics is in fact about that preliminary question: who has the power to decide about this?*

*(Rancière 2005)*

According to Rancière, then, in order to dislodge the matter of these stories from the assessment of righteousness, justice can only be formulated as a question. It is a matter of discerning legal expressions within power relations, of sketching their relation to the idea of "the proper" itself, and of adding up words to the common sphere, without waiting for the proper formulation expressed by those in a position of power to decide. The significant judgments on both cases drew wide interest considering the media coverage and the tension they generated. The rulings were pronounced in 2009 and 2011, and both absolved the defendants from the charge of abetting undocumented immigration, but with some relevant differences. Whereas in the case of the *Cap Anamur*, in 2009, the defendants were absolved "because the fact does not constitute a crime," according to Article 530 of the Italian Criminal Code, the Tribunal of Palermo acquitted the seven Tunisian fishermen of abetting undocumented immigration but found the two captains guilty of resisting the Italian coast guards who had attempted to stop them. It is worth noting that during the trial, important newspapers like *Il Giornale* and *Der Spiegel* sustained the public prosecutor's accusation that the two boats ignored the Italian Coast Guard's order to stop and return to a Tunisian port. At the trial, it was discovered that the Italian Coast Guard made numerous attempts to intercept the two Tunisian boats and escort them out of territorial waters, as it was "an American Cup for illegals."[5] As a matter of fact, the boats did not return given the bad weather conditions and the survivors aboard who needed urgent medical attention.

This border practice is in violation of all of the international conventions that recognize the right to ask for asylum even in extraterritorial waters and a dangerous practice that provoked a collision between the *Sybille* and the Italian Coast Guard during the shipwreck of seventy Albanians in 1997.[6] The practice of interrupting the flow of migrants across the Mediterranean Sea border has become more frequent lately and, until a few months ago, these interceptions were made in collaboration with Libyan coast guards. Even if a complete analysis is beyond the scope of this chapter (see Chapter 3), it is important to note that these practices of interception tend to focus on national security concerns and, for this reason, it is difficult to reconcile them with human rights treaty obligations.[7] Indeed interception and rescue share little common ground. What they do have in common is the management of time in terms of promptness of intervention or, on the contrary, abandonment and delays in intervention. The capacity of managing time – to divide it or to extend it to the infinity of death – is a matter of politics. It is a delimitation and systematization that simultaneously determine and shape the border as a form of experience and the community around it.

With regard to the *Cap Anamur*'s case, the motivations that have now been disclosed finally provide a definitive clarification of the circumstances that, in the initial police reports, were contradictory at times and tended to blame those responsible for the *Cap Anamur* for both the communication delays and the state of emergency experienced on the ship. Also, the decision was taken in light of the subsequent statements made in court by the top leadership of the Ministry of the Interior. In reality, the delay was a consequence of the fact that the interior ministers of Germany and Italy had failed to find an agreement on the request for entry and asylum filed by the survivors. The story of the judicial case, with the participation of all parties, established that the denials interposed for weeks at the entrance of the *Cap Anamur* territorial waters were devoid of any legal foundation. Instead, they were the product of political decisions made by the then–Minister of the Interior, Mr. Pisanu, and later agreed upon at a European summit with Germany and Britain in Sheffield. The same political decisions were then translated into orders for the suspension of permit protection for humanitarian assistance granted to twenty-one refugees after their landing in Sicily and later into the mass expulsion of the survivors (save two) despite the precedent provided by different courts and an appeal pending at the European Court of Human Rights.

While it is significant that both rulings absolved the defendants from the accusation of abetting undocumented immigration, public opinion still holds, especially among fishers, that those who rescue others stranded at sea choose to do so with the risk of having their boats and fishing tools confiscated for years. They will then face public trials with enormous legal expenses, with the consequence of compromising the destinies of their families. After all, according to Plato workers or artisans or fishermen cannot intervene in the decisions that affect the community because they do not have time. We return then to the question: when is there a border? There is a border when fishers cannot save the life of a drowning African migrant because of the years it takes to undergo a trial or the cost of having the boat confiscated while, as always, "work will not wait" (Rancière 2006, p. 13). The two cases mentioned here act as a deterrent for those who may be in a position to rescue migrants in international waters, and therefore they constitute the moment of the border. Many migrants have provided evidence that ships and fishing boats ignored their requests for help and sometimes did not even alert the closest port or the authorities. Sometimes migrants are left to die at sea, simply ignored, and become bare life without someone being held responsible for their deaths. And sometimes things are even worse.

The same Court of Agrigento that hosted the aforementioned hearings was in charge of ruling on the accusation of homicide against Mr Mariano I have recounted the details at the beginning of this chapter. The conditions under which Ruggiero acted can be summarized this way: "what other notion could he have of the world, if around him, the word 'just' had always been suffocated by violence and the wind of the world had merely changed the word into a stagnant, putrid reality?" (Leonardo Sciascia, *The Day of the Owl*, 1961, in Shapiro 2012, p. 481).

Against this background, then, the spectacle of the African migrants' invasion has been performed, and the fascination of the national audience with it must be understood as a form of desensitization and depoliticization of the public sphere. On one hand, military operations of European states to intercept African migrants are considered "humanitarian"; however, on the other hand, violent outbursts of pure evil are reduced to mere individual deviations instead of linking the two events together as expressions of the same logic, only at two distinct levels.

The individual practices of rescuing or killing, once implemented or just acted out, attain their own lives and indicate a choice to follow, therefore alternately closing down or opening up new possibilities of political community. Fundamentally, they fashion innovative contours of the frontier and shape the space of the political as they perform because "the genesis of a space of this kind also presupposes a practice, images, symbols, and . . . of localized social relationships" (Lefebvre 1992, p. 245) like those between Tunisian anglers and African migrants. In other words, the idea around which this chapter is built relies on a conception of territory that is constantly modified, contested, restructured both according to the actions of individuals and to the institutional setting. It is, then, the fundamental space where the concept of people finds its own perennial origins beyond the "normality of national citizen-subject" (Balibar & Hahn 2002, p. 78). When this normality becomes internalized and becomes essentially the only identity, it is also the border to be internalized as it moves with the individual. As Balibar and Hahn put it, "borders cease to be purely external realities. They become also . . . what Fichte . . . magnificently termed inner borders [*inner grenzen*]; that is to say, *invisible borders*, situated everywhere and nowhere" (Ibid.).

## 5.5   Conclusions

The imagination is as essential as indifference for the construction and operability of the border. The imagination of invasion from Africa produces anxiety, which conversely allows for the militarization of the frontier and of individuals. This is true for the Mediterranean Sea as much as for various European metropolises. The anxiety is experienced as a feeling that lurks on the streets but never takes shape and is located everywhere and nowhere. Anxiety causes political immobility, which manifests itself as a wall of indifference that is a border in itself. Still, the border is contingent on power practices whose perennial fluctuations make the border seem natural and inevitable (Williams 2006, Chapter 2). It is important to shake this assertion and demonstrate the border's reliance on a complex interconnection of historical contingencies and, consequently, to reveal its violence and, at the same time, its precariousness. The idea of the fixity of the border reinforces the discourse of Fortress Europe as a socio-political body under a permanent state of siege that instigates violent panic reactions (Gebrewold-Tochalo 2007). Privileging an ahistorical perspective, synchronic approaches interpret conflicts in Africa, for instance, as disconnected to politics and colonial histories and instead translate them as security issues that menace an imagined secure political space of Europe. A discourse of securitization and risk analysis conceals the real functions of frontiers and borders to filter out certain individuals while crystallizing the imagery of the nation-state (Balibar 2014) as the only place in which "authentic politics"(Walker 1992) is possible.

This is the logic behind the government's approach of accusing fishermen of human trafficking when they are found to have assisted distressed migrants at sea or the Italian government's latest practice of intercepting migrants/asylum seekers in international waters to disrupt their trajectories. These practices, once implemented or just acted out, attain their own lives and indicate an alternative direction to follow, therefore alternately closing down or opening up new possibilities of political community. As these boat stories highlight, any individual can assume the responsibility of setting up a dialogue with another, to have a say on who is in and who is out, to break the wall of silence and invisibility intrinsic to any externalization practice. Relying only on police (Rancière 2006) at a distance, we run the risk of becoming anesthetized and indifferent when people silently disappear within the space of exception because

> one of the paradoxes of the state of exception lies in the fact that in the state of exception, it is impossible to distinguish transgression of the law from execution of the law, such that what violates a rule and what conforms to it coincide without any remainder.
>
> (Agamben 1998, p. 57)

It is indispensable, then, to rediscover the substance of the borderscape, at the edge of the externalization of migration control, inside as well as outside the geographical features of Europe, closer to Africa. That is a space of negotiations, confrontations, and recognitions of diversities without which there exists no polis and no politics but only a pencil-drawn silhouette of the European citizen, cut off from bureaucracy.

## Notes

1   The Jamahiriya has signed neither the 1951 Geneva Convention nor the 1967 Protocol and continues to consider asylum seekers as foreigners without any particular distinction. Still, the United Nations High Commissioner for Refugees (UNHCR) opened an office in Tripoli in 1991 and works with Libyan authorities. Libya also signed the Convention of Refugee Problems in Africa, which was adopted by the Organization for African Unity in 1969.
2   www.un.org/depts/los/convention_agreements/convention_overview_convention.htm
3   www.imo.org/About/Conventions/ListOfConventions/Pages/International-Convention-for-the-Safety-of-Life-at-Sea-%28SOLAS%29,-1974.aspx
4   www.imo.org/About/Conventions/ListOfConventions/Pages/International-Convention-on-Maritime-Search-and-Rescue-%28SAR%29.aspx
5   www.guidasicilia.it/ita/main/news/print.jsp?IDNews=27608
6   www.repubblica.it/online/fatti/vedetta/rinvio/rinvio.html
7   These practices were defined by the International Organization for Migration [IOM] as one of the most effective measures to enforce states' domestic migration laws and policies in United Nations (UN) Document EC/GC/01/11, 31 May 2001.

## References

Agamben, G., 1998. *Homo Sacer: Sovereign Power and Bare Life*. Stanford, CA: Stanford University Press.
Balibar, É., 2014. *Equaliberty: Political Essays*. Durham, NC: Duke University Press Books.
Balibar, E. & Hahn, D., 2002. *Politics and the Other Scene*. Londo, UK: Verso.
Chismar, D., 1988. Empathy and Sympathy: The Important Difference. *Journal of Value Inquiry*, 22(4), pp. 257–266.
Dünnwald, S., 2011. On Migration and Security: Europe Managing Migration from Sub-Saharan Africa. *Cadernos de Estudos Africanos*, 22, pp. 103–128.
Foucault, M., 1986. Of Other Spaces. *Diacritics*, 16(1), Spring, pp. 22–27.
Gebrewold-Tochalo, B., 2007. *Africa and Fortress Europe: Threats and Opportunities*. Aldershot, UK: Ashgate Publishing.
Higgins, A., 2014. In Europe, Fear of Ebola Exceeds the Actual Risks. *The New York Times*. Available at: www.nytimes.com/2014/10/18/world/europe/in-europe-fear-of-ebola-far-outweighs-the-true-risks.html [Accessed 22 December 2014]
Lavenex, S., 2006. Shifting Up and Out: The Foreign Policy of European Immigration Control. *West European Politics*, 29(2), pp. 329–350.
Lefebvre, H., 1992. *The Production of Space*. New York: Wiley-Blackwell.
Rancière, J., 2005. The Politics of Aesthetics. *ARTicles*. Available at: http://roundtable.kein.org/node/463 [Accessed 5 November 2014]
Rancière, J., 2006. *The Politics of Aesthetics*. London, UK: Continuum.
Shapiro, M. J., 2012. The Micropolitics of Justice: Language, Sense and Space. *Law, Culture and the Humanities*, 8(3), pp. 466–484.
Walker, R.B.J., 1992. *Inside/Outside: International Relations as Political Theory*. Cambridge, UK: Cambridge University Press.
Williams, J., 2006. *The Ethics of Territorial Borders: Drawing Lines in the Shifting Sand*. Houndmills, UK: Palgrave Macmillan.
Zaccaria, Pierpaolo. 2004. Il delitto di favoreggiamento dell'immigrazione clandestina alla luce della L.189/02. *Altalex*. www.altalex.com/documents/altalex/news/2010/07/23/il-delitto-di-favoreggiamento-dell-immigrazione-clandestina-alla-luce-della-l-189-02. [Accessed 6 March 2010].

# 6    The virtual door

*Οὐ καί ἡ τέχνη, ἧν δ᾽ἐγώ, ἐπί τούτῳ πέφυκεν, ἐπί τῷ τό συμφέρον ἑκάστῳ ζητεῖν τε καὶ ἐκπορίζειν; Ἐπὶ τούτῳ, ἔφη.*

*And isn't the art [techné] naturally directed toward seeking and providing for the advantage of each? Yes, that is what it is directed toward.*

Plato, The Republic, Book I, 341d

## 6.1    Arming the border: toward a technécology of migration control

In 2008, the European Commission outlined to the European Parliament, the Council, the European Economic and Social Committee, and the Committee of the Regions a technical framework for setting up a "European border surveillance system" (EUROSUR) to enhance the capabilities of member states to control the Mediterranean southern limits of Europe. The EUROSUR system is structured around three elements: (i) interlinking and streamlining existing national surveillance systems, (ii) common tools and applications for border surveillance at the European Union (EU) level, and (iii) creating "a common monitoring and information sharing environment for the EU maritime domain."[1]

EUROSUR is backed by a plethora of security research projects – Standards for Border Security Enhancement (STABORSEC); PASR; OPERAMAR; the WIMA2 project on Wide Maritime Area Airborne Surveillance; and EFFISEC, a €16 million project on Efficient Integrated Security Checkpoints – whose common idea is to enhance the interoperability between technologies of surveillance and patrolling. There is an adage among security personnel: "you cannot control what you do not patrol." Maritime and land border security must be conceived, then, as a fully integrated mechanism, under the supervision of the Frontex agency in the case of Europe, because commercial and tourist transportation systems are intertwined inextricably with the security and migration control infrastructure. Discussing the case of Lampedusa, we have realized the juxtaposition of distinctive layers, those related to the tourist industry with those more pertinent to the capture and detention of undocumented migrants. Here, instead we emphasize how the security and stability of trading routes are the main concerns in relation to the securitization of the frontier when commercial routes inevitably cross migrants' trajectories. At that moment, human beings and commodities become one.

One fundamental predicament of today's global relations is exactly the exacerbated tension between the management of free trading and human migration surveillance. The tension originated once the neoliberal model of economic development put countries where the capitalist system of production is at very different degrees of development into competition with each other (Neilson & Stubbs 2011). Structurally, this gap produces both unemployment in countries of older industrialization and the proletarianization of the population in the south of the world. The vicious liminality of these uneven levels left millions of men, women, and children fleeing from their countries on the road of exile, even if they are perfectly aware that the risk of dying before arriving in Europe is significantly soaring as a consequence of the securitization of the frontier. To imagine that the risk of incarceration, torture, and death can deter them from moving is only a symptom of a striking naïveté.

From the period of the Industrial Revolution in Europe, the expanding commercial trade of imperialism had to disentangle from the development of the state bureaucratic apparatus, which was designed to control populations, at home as well in the colonies, as the reserve – fiscal, military, and industrial – of emerging nations. Therefore, along with the technology of production, such as the steam engine, new technologies of population controls were implemented: first and foremost the passport, but also visa regulations, consulates as outposts of the state, and bilateral agreements that extended the reach of any given state within other states. Commercial expansion and human mobility management never ceased to interlace until today, when capitalism and the state apparatus have arranged a neoliberal design in which technological devices are indispensable ornaments. According to Guild and Bigo, today, to "analyze the forms of policing at a distance only as remote control public policy . . . is nevertheless insufficient . . . it does not address the central relations between order, border, and identity" (2003, p. 258). Similarly, Hardt and Negri state that "the passage to Empire emerges from the twilight of modern sovereignty. In contrast to imperialism, Empire establishes no territorial center of power and does not rely on fixed boundaries or barriers" (2001, p. xii). The rule of empire is thus decentered and deterritorialized, wrapping the entire planet in a net of multiple mobility controls that assert standards of extraterritorial management of human mobility. This network is, at the same time, global and increasingly common to distinctive areas of the world intended as critical nodes of interface, such as Palestine/Israel, Mexico/the US, and the Mediterranean Sea between Africa and Europe (Jones 2012).

Nevertheless, this conceptualization remains somehow flat and bidimensional. The twenty-first century, with September 11 as its incipit, saw the tridimensional renovation of such controls in width and depth with the growing role of sophisticated biometric technologies of surveillance that deepened scrutiny at the skin level and beyond. As with biological infections, controlling migrants' trajectories requires a coordinated and immediate response and the deployment of the latest technologies of surveillance and control at multiple levels. At the same time we should keep in mind that power relations at the moment of the border are always intricate and never unidirectional. A truly comprehensive analysis of the phenomenon of African migrations into Europe cannot avoid facing the changes that technological advancement has brought into it and asking what forces are implicated in this change. Border practices intended only as governments' tools of control do not account for the application of technologies that are overproduced in highly industrialized societies of Europe and re-employed by African migrants. We must acknowledge the circular dynamics of technological production and the insurrectional role of human migrations as two distinct but complementary aspects of globalization in the form of a mutually constitutive grand narrative that serves to dislocate the illusion but also the reasons behind a never-ending effort to set up a system of total control. The aim is to move on to delineate the ecology of human migrations at the border that serves to comprehend the spatial and temporal interrelationships between migrants and the economic, social, and political structure of control.

As Plato's epigraph reminds us, techné (art or craft) is functional for everyone according to his or her intentions and serves as a reminder to look into productive tensions generated at the border by the interaction between African migrants, European governments, and new technological devices. For instance, along with the development and increase of biometric controls, we witness the materialization of biometric fraud, where skin patches on thumbs and index fingers are removed and then regrafted onto the matching digits of the opposite hand. Hence, new technologies intended for control and migratory movements, like satellite phones or trucks, provide the means and sometimes the motivation for engaging border practices. Technological advancement, then, provides indispensable support along contemporary migrants' trajectories and, at the same time, accounts for the newest implementation of border control in response to more fragmented and elusive migrants' trajectories. Technologies that overflow from the West to the rest of the world – in this case, from Western Europe into Africa – are re-elaborated in their scope and *raison d'être* within an organic system of relation. I call this theoretical approach "technécology" to emphasize the interconnectivity between technological practices of migration control and migratory insurrectional movements to shed light on the complex interconnection between technological innovations and human migrations that generates a system of organic relations and spatial organization in an incessant process of territorialization and deterritorialization. Borders no longer exist only as defense lines or concrete walls. As explained previously in Chapter 3, borders exist in symbiosis with increased human mobility, emerging here and there, in a continuum of events and power relations, and subsist through individuals who are the vehicle of their existence.

## 6.2   From analogical to digital

As a matter of fact, even in its spatial multiplicity, if intended only as a static control device, the border resembles an analogical mechanism similar to Bentham's design of a prison, reread by Foucault (1995), where individuals are interned and eventually disciplined while always being under the undetectable gaze of the guardian. That vision implies an idea of arrest, correction, and individualization gathered in a specific place. The disciplinary society of the nineteenth century was analogical in nature, aimed at individualizing, fragmenting, and re-educating whole identities through schools, prisons, hospitals, and barracks within a well-planned city. This was, by definition, an anti-nomadic technology. "This is why it fixes, arrests and regulates movements; it clears up confusion; it dissipates compact groupings of individuals wandering about the country in unpredictable ways; it establishes calculated distributions" (Foucault 1995, p. 218).

Although extremely groundbreaking at that time, the idea of the Panopticon cannot encapsulate the transformations of migration control necessary to facilitate the high mobility of goods necessary for contemporary flows of capital and the identification of human beings – whereas previously with passports, we had "identities." Closer to the contemporary system of control within a capitalist structure of production is a further passage in which Foucault clarifies the only apparent failure of the prison. He states that the carceral system

> helps to establish an open illegality, irreducible at a certain level and secretly useful, at once refractory and docile; it isolates, outlines, brings out a form of illegality that seems to sum up symbolically all the others, but which makes it possible to leave in the shade those that one wishes to – or must – tolerate. This form is, strictly speaking, delinquency.
>
> (Foucault 1984, p. 231)

Therefore, when a human being crosses the border or dwells in it, what remains stuck on her skin is neither a name nor a nationality. She is illegal, Muslim, prostitute, temporary worker, black, alien resident, or *gambas manipuladora* (shrimps handler) (Biemann 2003), according to the settings of that border in a specific moment. This concept emerges clearly from critical visual scholar Ursula Biemann's video *Europlex* in which the author follows women going back and forth between Morocco and Europe to work in transnational zones in North Africa for the European market. Superimposing digital images and script over their traditional clothing, Biemann points out how the border practice let surface only one layer of any human being – that is, the one that is important in that particular moment. If, then, a border is not located at the border anymore, a Foucaldian approach is without a doubt instrumental to understanding the multiplicity of border practices, "to rediscover the connections, encounters, supports, blockages, play of forces, strategies and so on which at any given moment establish what subsequently counts as being self evident, universal and necessary" (Foucault *et al.* 1991, p. 172).

It can be argued that the border performs today as it did in the past: filtering the good from the bad, the welcomed from the unwanted. Within this general understanding, specific geographical locations are designed as points of entry/exit or gateways into specific political entities. Europe, accordingly, has 1,792 designated crossing points: 665 are in the air, 871 are across the sea, and 246 are over land crossing points (Anonymous 2008). To presume that these data represent the reality of the border is misleading for the reason that they simply cannot account for the ubiquity, multiplicity, and mobility (Balibar & Hahn 2002) of border practices today. The border performs simultaneously at different times and spaces, and a contrast with official designated entry locations of the past would perhaps allow for a better understanding of contemporary technological features of border practices.

Ellis Island is a clear example of a past gateway to the emerging society of North America where the biopolitical operation of filtering was performed. Migrants had to pass through those points that were at the same time points of arrival but also receptions. There was a real feeling to be at the edge of two societies, a point of passage from one social dimension into another. Andreas and Nadelmann (2008) examined the change in border technology at the turn of the twentieth century when industrialized regions of the world designed points of entrance where the implementation of new legislations of migration control interconnected with scientific and medical notions of health. Ellis Island was an iconic place in this sense, performing a powerful role in the imagination of migrants who ventured in crossing the Atlantic, lured by a marketed mirage of a land of promises.

This moment has been visually expressed in many novels and visual documents, among which the movie *Golden Door* (Crialese 2006) perhaps accounts for one of the most vivid re-enactments. The *Golden Door* recounts the odyssey of a Sicilian family that decides to leave the land where they belong to migrate to the new world of North America. It is not a coincidence that the most heartbreaking shot in the film is when the ship departs the port of Naples to embark on an epic journey toward the dreamland of America. The director, Mr. Crialese, raises his camera high above the masses so that they, those who leave, at the beginning indistinguishable in their commonality, are slowly torn apart as the ship leaves the dock. The void thus created is filled with agony, hope, and an intense silence, broken only when the foghorn goes off. The journey across the Atlantic Ocean lasts more than a week, and the movie goes on between the bowels of the liner where the third class of humanity struggles with dramatic bravery against claustrophobic conditions and a storm that leaves everyone almost dead.

The approach to Ellis Island is covered in fog, preventing the passengers and film viewers from seeing the New World. The reality of America would certainly at that point look different than the idyllic dimension of hospitality and acceptance inscribed on the Statue of Liberty. However, the focus here is on the specific space of the island as a site of selection that, for many years, has represented the quintessential nature of the border, condensed in a definite time and place in which to traverse and live. Immediately upon reaching the island, migrants are subjected to a series of tests, both medical and social, to assess their worthiness to go beyond the "Golden Door" and enter the New World of scientific and logical civilization. Here, at the border, the government of the new world reveals its biopolitical side, doing away with those having biological (both mental and physical) features that do not fit with the pre-ordered model.

The dialogue between the mother, Fortunata, and the customs officer is illuminating when she is asked to assemble geometrical shapes in a "logical" order.

When she questions the officer's right to define a worthy human being (a trait that, for her, belongs only to God), we hear the absurdity of a scientific delirium that defines biological defects as infectious for the purity of the New World's society. Her skepticism brings to light what generic narratives that celebrate the US as an open-armed sanctuary for everyone, obscure (Behdad 2005). Eventually, Fortunata returns to her world because there is no space for the magical and the illogical in the New World, a world that is headed toward a technological future. The rest of the family stays, and Salvatore and Lucy get married, fulfilling those requirements that draw the line between legality and illegality for any migrant, which is still the case even today.

## 6.3   Banopticon versus Panopticon

> *The EU had to use the most advanced technology to reach the highest level of security to stop visitors overstaying their welcome in Europe and to prevent terrorists from coming in.*
>
> *Mr. Franco Frattini, former European Commissioner responsible for justice, freedom, and security (BBC News 2008)*

The strong statement that serves as the incipit for this section clearly demonstrates how immigration and terrorism are increasingly linked within the public discourse of Western Europe, as in this period of its history. The two phenomena have grown spectacularly in the past several decades, translated as mass immigration and global terrorism as illustrated by the Madrid bombings and by the Van Gogh incident or, more recently, with the shooting at the office of the Charlie Hebdo satirical magazine in Paris and the breakdown of Libya. As a reaction to the transformation and multiplication of border practices, the spatial dimension of the border has changed. Institutions like Ellis Island have lost their practicality and have become historical attractions, simulacra of amnesiac societies that have become more democratic according to some, more Orwellian according to others. Gilles Deleuze's *Postscript on the Society of Control* (1992) emerges as a highly influential piece in explaining the shift from a disciplinary society of the nineteenth century, embodied by Ellis Island, to a contemporary society of control. With this in mind, Deleuze claims that disciplinary societies are turning into control societies, from an analogical system to a digital one, where power has become more fluid, abandoning structures of confinement in favor of fluctuating networks where the lines (borders) are blurred and where the inside is not so distinct from the outside. Deleuze argues that "whereas discipline set up a productive tension between masses and individuals, with control we witness a world of 'dividuals' whose context is not the mass or society, but proliferating databanks, profiles and markets" (Walters 2006, p. 191). In this direction, Didier Bigo (2008), taking inspiration from Foucault's concept of disciplinary societies, developed the concept of "Banopticon" to describe contemporary social practices of control, realized by the "routinization of the monitoring of groups on the move through technologies of surveillance" (Rajaram & Grundy-Warr 2008, p. 4). The

French scholar maintains that border practices of surveillance appear here and there, outside and inside, as in a Moebius strip (Bigo 2007). Bigo explains what he calls *banopticon* and how it differs from Bentham's *Panopticon*, reread by Foucault, when he states:

> The latter supposes that everyone in a given society is equally submitted to surveillance and control that there exists a physical proximity between watchers and the watched, as well as an awareness of being under scrutiny. The banopticon on the contrary, deals with the notion of exception, and the difference between surveillance for all but control of only a few.
>
> (Rajaram & Grundy-Warr 2008, p. 6)

The dystopia of diffuse control along the frontier, as well as inside and outside it, is made possible by the implementation of technologies of control and security. What appears to differ is the simultaneity of border practice in different places at the same time and how the same technologies are equally utilized to assist necessities of war, health, and business together.[2] This is the case of the uprising of opposition forces in Libya in 2011 against Gaddafi's regime. On 23 March 2011, NATO forces assumed command over the arms embargo and declared a maritime surveillance area to control all the information flowing in and out of Libya, relying on

> a complex assemblage of remote sensing technology so to detect stress hidden within maritime traffic. It includes AIS [Automatic Identification System] vessel tracking system which emits signals to coastal radio stations with information, as speed identity and position of commercial vessels. . . . NATO also relied on synthetic apparatuses of radio imagery which emits radar signals from satellites snapping the surface of the Earth according to their orbit. The return of large vessels appears as bright pixels on the sea's dark surface. Through such technologies, the sea's liquid waves are supplemented by a constant pulsating sea of electromagnetic waves.
>
> (Heller & Pezzani 2014)

While, then, it is reasonable to claim that the border functions as a filter, today the border, in its technological reconfiguration, is extremely permeable and mobile. Similar to a firewall, it differentiates between low and high speed, it fights viruses and freezes Trojan horses (but, at the same time, it exists because of them). It materializes here and there. As a matter of fact, there are points of interceptions, convergences, and crises that manifest themselves on the geographical territory and appear sometimes and somewhere but whose trajectories are often dislocated from a tangible materiality. This is particularly true if we refer to the virtual gateways of Europe. Walters (2006) reminds us how the UK immigration service provides companies and their staff with detailed instructions to detect bodies that utilize the mechanical technology of the truck to enter the UK from continental Europe. What we might call the "securitization of the truck and its milieu" turns the truck and its entire route into a dispersed, mobile border (Walters 2006, p. 194). The border practice of control does not happen only before leaving France or when the truck disembarks in the UK, but it continues until the destination, at every gas station or at random checkpoints on the highway. Technologies have therefore rendered the EU externalization of migration control an integrated system with all components in communication with each other under the supervision of Frontex, a special agency created *ad hoc* for this scope.

## 6.4    Frontex

Privatization of migration control is a consequence and the cause of the overproduction of the technological means of migration control that overflow into North Africa. Drones are deployed over the desert, transmitting data back to remote receivers; unmanned aerial vehicles spot migrants crossing the desert in the nighttime, equipped with night vision and thermal cameras; technologies of *vision-ability* and reconnaissance order divide and master territories covering everything with a carpet of satellite and radio signals where migratory and digital geographies overlap like during the NATO surveillance operation mentioned previously. When we analyze practices of border control the inextricable interdependence between private and public spheres clearly surface between the numbers of stellar profits made by those winners of public competitions. It is also important to pay attention to a certain language that betrays a managerial matrix and that nowadays characterizes discourses of migration control. Therefore, interoperability, effectiveness, efficiency, and rate of risk are no longer concepts limited to financial speculations. Interoperability of multiple border control practices and management of mobility are key contemporary features of practices of border control that operate around and beyond the geopolitical limits of the state. The two concepts are not in contradiction with other because mobility cannot be halted. Instead, from the states' and corporations' point of view, human migration needs to be controlled, managed, and fragmented in different sections at distinctive paces in order to synchronize it with accelerated flows of capital and labor, able to meet security needs from European social and cultural spaces.

Practices of mobility management must then operate simultaneously everywhere by "using the connection between the speed of digitalized information, the capacities of computers to manage huge quantity of data and to share them under procedures on interoperability" (Masse & Lodge 2007, p. 10). The border, then, is constructed by different agencies at the regional, state, and municipal levels that share information and risk assessments. In this sense, risk management has become a characteristic of migration control intended as an opportunity for agencies to choose among different courses of action. Interestingly enough, these agencies exist as public institutions but operate as private actors and in terms of accountability, often "at the margins of civil society" (Masse & Lodge 2007, p. 11). The colossal deployment of European state forces at the southern frontier of Europe would not function well without coordination and integrated strategy. This function has been provided since 2005 by the European Agency for the

Management of Operational Cooperation at the External Borders of the Member States of the European Union – Frontex. We can define Frontex as the brand-new technology of migration control that functions as the umbrella for the single technological innovations deployed by the EU and single states to stem the flow. The Council Regulation 2007/2004 established the agency with headquarters in Warsaw. Since then, the agency has been active in stemming the migration flow from Africa, coordinating several joint operations of EU states, among which "Hera" (2008) in the Canary Islands, West Africa, was the most successful when measured in terms of the number of migrants diverted back (5,969) and €10 billion of the budget[3] invested.

From Frontex's official website,[4] we can read that its main tasks are:

*Risk analysis*: Monitor and analyze the day-to-day situation at the EU's external borders and optimize the allocation of resources.

*Coordination of operational cooperation between member states*: When needed, Frontex proposes joint operations at the Union's external land, sea, and air borders in which member states are invited to take part.

*Training*: Frontex assists member states in the development of common training standards for border guard authorities.

*Facilitating the attainment of research and development goals*: Frontex serves as a platform to bring together Europe's 400,000 border personnel and the world of industry to bridge the gap between technological advancement and the needs of the end user.

*Providing a rapid crisis-response capability available to all member states*: Frontex has created a pooled resource in the form of Rapid Border Intervention Teams (RABITs), bringing together specialist technical and human resources from across the EU.

*Assisting member states in joint return operations*:[5] When member states make the decision to return foreign nationals who have failed to leave voluntarily, Frontex assists those member state governments in coordinating their efforts to maximize efficiency and cost-effectiveness while also ensuring that respect for fundamental rights and the human dignity of returnees is maintained at every stage of the operation.

Frontex's origins can be traced back to the Commission Communication 2002 – *integrated management of the external border of the member states of the EU*. The legal framework that defines the general competences of Frontex does not help, though, to resolve the problem of coordination between member states and the agency that has been extensively analyzed elsewhere (Jorry 2007) (Baldaccini 2010). Often, the agency operates above European institutions with a very business-oriented approach in dealing with third-country governments. For instance, Sergio Carrera (Masse & Lodge 2007, p. 67) provides some critical reflections about the nature and legal basis of Frontex. The agency is supposedly a depoliticized organism, neither private nor public, which in fact has been greatly influenced by both the European Commission and the council while coordinating

European state forces in joint operations of migration control. Its hybrid nature manifests in an evident uncertainty in the demarcation of responsibility between member states and the agency in operational activities. Regulation 2007/2004 clearly establishes that "the responsibility for the control and surveillance of external borders lies with the Member States" but in reality, most of the operations of interception and expulsion are carried out according to the agency's risk analysis. Some scholars envisage a reduction of the states' autonomy (Baldaccini 2010) but also a decrease of responsibility. Who is responsible, for instance, for the death of a migrant during operations of interceptions carried out by a national coast guard with different officials from different states under the supervision of Frontex officials? According to Neal (2009), Frontex represents a shift from the previous intergovernmental approach to border surveillance to a supranational one. However, considering that a board of national border control high officials and two European commissions manage it, the reality is more complicated. Because the European states have reservations about creating a European border police (with what powers, what jurisdictions, what hierarchy?), there is a degree of ambiguity over the agency's role.

Still, single member states and EU institutions seem willing to assist and support Frontex as if it were their natural offspring, even when the agency has not been successful in coordinating EU member states with each other. According to the Human Rights Watch Report 2009:

> In 2008, Operation Nautilus focused on the flow of migration between North Africa and Italy and Malta but diverted no one back to North Africa. Its failure was attributed to the difference of opinion concerning the responsibility of migrants saved at sea.
>
> (Human Rights Watch 2009, p. 36)

What is more, Frontex's sea operations translated into no accountability or compliance with European and international legal obligations, with particular regard to the question of disembarkation and the possible violation of the principle of non-refoulment (Edwards & Ferstman 2010). The former executive director of Frontex, General Lakkinen, justifies the legality of operations of interception and forced return of migrant vessels when he states that:

> FRONTEX is a coordinator, and the thing that we are doing is to do and make an operational plan. . . . To do this, is to assure the safe return to the port of origin. *For this reason we go aboard* to verify that they have lifejackets, water, food, and enough fuel to return back, and *merely explain to them what the safest way to solve the problem is.* [emphasis added]
>
> (Herzog 2009)

Therefore, it is through a process of problematization that Frontex put into practice the apparatus of externalization. Foucault intends problematization as the idea that "transforms the difficulties and obstacles of practice into a general problem for which one proposes diverse political solutions" (Foucault 1984, p. 389 in Soguk 1999, p. 50). To problematize, then, means to read a practice (of migration) in a certain way, and this includes a necessary initial stage of (risk) analysis, secretive and undisclosed, of a particular situation during which certain activities are understood as "difficulties." In this particular situation, Frontex conceives the influx of immigrants into the EU, their trajectories, as a problem that includes a certain quantity of risk and that requires an adequate response. The problematization of migrants' trajectories requires a relentless individuation of emergency, a continuum of risk that from Africa leaks into the heart of Europe and that necessitates urgent and rapid actions. Ultimately, to attain a fully integrated border management, Frontex operates a territorialization of the frontier by installing borders intended as a coordinated plethora of technologies of control that occurs beyond and within geopolitical configurations and according to maps of evaluated emergencies.

## 6.5   Technologies of migration control

> *The body is simply a source of data.*
>
> *(Lyon 2001, p. 68)*

As articulated in the 2004 Hague Programme, measures to control crime and terrorism are linked to undocumented immigration, defined as "illegal," to the point that the very concept of war has been reframed beyond interstate dynamics. After the terrorist attacks on 9/11 in New York and on 3/11 in Madrid, terms such as *criminal*, *terrorist*, and *illegal immigrant*, once distinctive, now overlap, "establishing a continuum of security measures that effectively links visa application procedures and entry and exit procedures at external border crossing" (Lindahl 2009, p. 55). As stated in the programme:

> The citizens of Europe rightly expect the European Union, while guaranteeing respect for fundamental freedoms and rights, to take a more effective, joint approach to cross-border problems . . . the coordination and coherence between the internal and the external dimension has been growing in importance and needs to continue to be vigorously pursued.
>
> (Council of European Union 2004, p. 3)

The Hague Programme, in this sense, represents the central document that articulates in Europe the interconnection between security controls and migration management and clearly articulates the technological and digital transformation of the externalization of migration control at the European level. This transformation entails words and things that, even if with apparent different aims, play an important common role in maintaining an incessant (in)security continuum. Therefore, collection of personal biometric data, deployment of technologies of surveillance inside/outside/above the EU, patrolling, interception, intervention and expulsion before entry, media campaigns – all of this constitutes a continuum of (in)security measures that features the most advanced technological devices available.

As mentioned previously, Michel Foucault (2003) locates the emergence of the biopolitical form of state governance when the state's interest moved from territory to population. The family, school, barracks and prisons then constituted a system of discipline based on individuation, arrest and correction of any deviant behavior. However, technologies of body measurement and identification anticipated contemporary biometrics and are descendants of phrenology, physiognomic or anthropometry. Fingerprints, for instance, were once developed by the colonial British administration in India after the Mutiny (1857) to reinforce control and identification of a population that was otherwise undistinguishable (Cole 2002). Today, state governance is still very much interested in a population that, after the end of historical colonialism, became increasingly mobile beyond the frontiers of the empire. Once normally conceived as progress that would bring people together and foster inter-/intracultural understanding, the miniaturization of our habitat has come together with the proliferation of technologies of tracking. We can scamper free now across the gate attached to an invisible leash that runs deeper than our skin. Today, fingerprints operate together with iris scans, face recognition, DNA, and palm prints to amount to an incredible volume of data stored in digital databases available contemporarily at different access points. Biometrics and data collectors are still firmly inscribed within state logics of population control that split the body into a myriad of digital bits of identification.

When accessed at any nodal point of the network, these technologies materialize a digital template that will disclose clandestine identities without the corporeal presence of the subject. Along these lines, a multi-million euro border control project was launched in Spain at the end of April 2013 that sees drones, satellites, and aerostats deployed over the southern Mediterranean. It provides the EU "with an operational and technical framework that increases situational awareness and improves the reaction capability of authorities surveying the external borders of the EU."[6] The project of "collaborative evaluation of border surveillance technologies in maritime environment by pre-operational validation of innovative solutions" – shoehorned into the abbreviation CLOSEYE – is intended to reinforce the *Sistema Integrado de Vigilancia Exterior* (Integrated System for External Surveillance) SIVE project, which has been in operation since 2002. It makes use of radar and surveillance cameras scattered throughout the coastline to scan incoming vessels and intercept them if they are suspicious. The addition of satellite imagery, aerostats, and drones such as the Camcopter S-100 will significantly increase the powers of state authorities acting in the Mediterranean Sea.

It is clear, then, how biometric technologies and data collectors operate within a system of population management centered on the concepts of speed and mobility. It is not necessarily essential to arrest or correct anymore. It is important to understand how the implementation of these technologies relies on the assumption that biometric technologies will eventually gain the absolute truth of what one person is.

The security industry . . . has presented the border technologies of control in a open society, as the way to deal with this new context, and as solution to terrorism, drug trafficking, illegal immigration and movement of people, by reinforcing the technologies of tracing the flows . . . and monitoring the future of the course of action by profiling the next events and prevent them before they happen.

(Masse & Lodge 2007, p. 11)

The question of "What have you done?" has been replaced, then, by "What are you?" and this is more often "Who are you?" It is noteworthy that the visibility of a few migrants' bodies on radar and scanning equipment serves the scope to recover Western societies from the anxiety of the invisible and unknown. When clearly located on a night-vision radar screen, migrants' bodies appear as white dots that, like a virus when detected, run in every direction. The screen display transforms the corporeal elements of migrants running for their lives into data analogous to those signs that enclose them. The effect of this representation is one of ubiquity – it could be anywhere, even in our backyard – and suspension – the viewer keeps staring at the screen image – between real and virtual. Its visual representation is suggestive of a contested space whose impossible location produces anxiety in the viewer, which in turn is the *raison d'être* behind the image and the technology that produces it. The key element that characterizes biometrics and data collection, then, is not certainly arrest but the traceability of both goods and bodies after being input into an electronic database.

At the European level, the Schengen Information System (SIS) was the first European database developed for migration control purposes in 1995. The reason for its introduction emerged ten years before when the Schengen Convention was signed to eliminate the internal borders of Europe and facilitate the movement of labor guaranteed in the Treaty of Rome along with the free movement of goods, services and capital. The collapse of internal checkpoints as a consequence of the Schengen Treaty necessitated the registration of every good and person that was refused entry at the external checkpoints. It is necessary to understand that speed and traceability are the key elements behind the development of technologies of surveillance. It is not a coincidence that the development of SIS is strictly connected with the Schengen Area of free movement and marks the beginning of a new era of European migration policy characterized by the reinforcement of external borders. As a matter of fact, SIS was designed as a tool of intercommunications among different crossing points. With more eastern European countries joining the EU, SIS expanded into SISII and SISone4all in order to cope with the increase of goods and people crossing the borders of Europe. In the end, SIS turned out to be the biggest European database. Accordingly, in 2010, "SIS contains over thirty one million records, including more than one million records of persons" (Council of European Union, Document No. 6162/2010).

Next to SIS, EURODAC was designed to cope with asylum requests according to the Dublin Convention of 1991 that forbids multiple requests of asylum into different states (cynically defined as asylum shopping). As a matter of fact, the EURODAC database

> enables European Union (EU) countries to help identify asylum applicants and persons who have been apprehended in connection with an irregular crossing of an external border of the Union. By comparing fingerprints, EU countries can determine whether an asylum applicant or a foreign national found illegally present within an EU country has previously claimed asylum in another EU country or whether an asylum applicant entered the Union territory unlawfully.
>
> (Council Regulation, No. 2725/2000)

Currently, the EU relies on biometric data to record asylum seekers' fingerprints and, with the second generation of SIS, developed to register any entry into the Schengen Area, is equipped with biometric technology called the Automated Fingerprint Identification System, whose results are then stored in the Biometric Matching System (BMS). Lastly, the Visa Information System (VIS) has been designed to record all visa applications of third nationals (non-EU) and will make use of the same technological infrastructure as SIS for storage – namely, the BMS. To indicate the size and capability of the VIS alone, according to a proposal prepared by the European Commission, the VIS database will become one of the largest biometric databases in the world, storing close to 70 million sets of fingerprint for a period of five years so that the "matching capacity needs will rise linearly with the number of fingerprints in the database." (Commission, 2004/0287, p.45).

A particular problem emerges when we consider that fact that biometric reliability is not absolute. About 5% of mankind has no fingerprints or has fingerprints that are difficult to read with a machine (European Data Protection Supervisor, 2013). And, "according to the Dutch Minister of Internal Affairs (2005), the quality of the fingerprints of young children and elderly people are so bad that they can hardly be read by a machine" (Besters & Brom 2010, pp. 455-470). On the subject of children's rights, it is worth mentioning that the age limit of fourteen years to collect biometric data is openly in contrast with existing international law instruments – namely, the Convention of the Right of the Child of 1989. In this regard, the council has ignored concerns expressed by the European Parliament (Masse & Lodge 2007, p. 65). More importantly, with regard to centralized data storage, it seems that decisions are taken without too much political debate and without much distinction between anti-terrorism measures on one hand and migration control policy on the other.

With the development of larger and more inclusive databases, the endorsed government aims appear to render migration flows visible, giving a sense of total control and traceability. What is undetectable is a source of anxiety, at the personal and social level, and it is the reason behind technological innovations of surveillance. In fact, the possibilities to make migration flows visible are intrinsically connected and dependent on the possibilities offered by technological means (Besters & Brom 2010). The design of European migration control policies is more and more related to technological tools and the outcome of their implementations and, conversely, rendering the trajectories of migrants visible is strongly dependent on the effectiveness of technological advancements.

However, a complete visibility of migrants does not correspond necessarily to their social inclusion. After all, migrants who have passed through the border and survived are far from being politically and socially included. They acquire a condition characterized by a differential form of inclusion and *clandestinization*. They acquire a precarious status that perfectly fits a capitalist market's need for a labor reserve – often-delinquent non-persons (Lago 2009), not even denizens, to be used and thrown away (Kleenex workers). The effect is to externalize after detection, to ban or incarcerate those who do not fit within the visible space of the society and to keep them under control but still marginalized. Every European city features undocumented migrants who, once detected and included in databases, hide at night but surface when the sun rises as they gather at the busy corners of urban outskirts waiting for a chance to get a job. They are living a life wrapped into a Moebius strip, officially depoliticized by the anachronistic model of citizenship but at the same time completely immersed within capitalist power relations.

## 6.6 Technologies of migration

Despite the keen interest that Bigo's studies have generated in the understanding of the use of technologies for the political management of populations, scholars either focus on technologies of surveillance and control (Boswell 2007) or try to explain how human beings use technologies and knowledge related to them to migrate (Fortunati *et al*. 2013) from an anthropological point of view. This book has the ambition to consider the impact of technologies together with migrants' trajectories as elements of power relations that are mutually constitutive on the idea of borders. As I implement Foucault's suggestion to focus on practices, it is important to pay attention to practices of bordering as much as debordering. I have in mind a passage at the beginning of *Discipline and Punish* when Foucault admonishes us to

> not concentrate the study of the punitive mechanisms on their "repressive" aspect alone, on their "punishment" aspects alone, but situate them in a whole series of their possible positive effects, even if these seem marginal at first sight. As a consequence, regard punishment as a complex social function.
>
> (1995, p. 23)

In the final part of this chapter, then, I look into productive tensions generated by the interaction between migrants and new available technologies. New technologies, I maintain, provide the means and sometimes the motivation for engaging border practices intended both as practices of control and migratory movements. Technological development, in fact, provides the necessary support for the organization of migrant trajectories and at the same time accounts for the newest realization of border control in response to longer, more fragmented, and elusive migrants' trajectories. Taking this approach means studying how the over-production of contemporary technologies of border control impacts the meaning of European externalization of migration control in relation to African populations and societies.

Technologies of migration control (satellites/biometrics/radar) are, at the same time, the means and ends of the same process that involves labor and migration. Because of these technologies, migrants are detected and differently included within the host society in a position of vulnerability. Technologies of visibility are then essential to determine the structure of the working class but, at the same time, they became crucial economic factors of research and industrial development for receiving countries within a comprehensive technécology of migration control that focuses on the interconnectivity between technological practices of border control and migratory movement.

The overproduction of European technologies of control of African migrations inevitably makes these technologies available in the region and allows African migrants to move across inhospitable territories and reinforce existing social networks among the same migrants. In contrast, with the majority of academic analysis of the externalization of European migration control that gives the impression of total control over migration, I emphasize the symbiotic relationship that exists between technologies of migration control and occurrences of African migrations. These analyses cannot explain the ramifications of power relations at the moment of border control. Migrants must continuously be aware of migration control and even if the majority of them tend to avoid these encounters, it is fair to say that sometimes they voluntarily cross the lines of control because they want to get caught. They have knowledge of satellite maps that cover a certain area and being at one particular spot at one given moment then does represent an insurrectional move. For instance, migrants often sail along the route of patrol, hoping to be intercepted and saved from being left adrift in the ocean. At the same time, with regard to the Mediterranean Sea, state control agents avoid intervening and saving lives in order to render the migrants invisible.

Starting from the beginning of any given journey, a migrant leaves home because of a variety of reasons that cannot be reduced merely to economic push/pull factors. Equally, geopolitical characteristics of the area of origin are not sufficient for a comprehensive reading of migration. Without going into the intricacies of this debate, I would like to point out how technologies of visibility like TV, satellites, or the World Wide Web can trigger desires for change and can function as an important determining factor or migration. I am referring here to images of a prosperous Europe produced by a powerful network that wants to expand its audience and be broadcast directly into the houses of many cities in Africa. It is possible to read this phenomenon both as a legacy of colonial enterprises or, if you allow me, a globalized ramification of capitalist encounters: the same technology can be at once the source of migration and the tool to control it. Internet points also function as political spaces where it is possible to access useful connections and acquire knowledge of travel possibilities. It is not a coincidence that Europe has now enforced a new policy of asking for the

IDs and sojourn permits of those who wish to utilize computers to surf the Web at Internet points in order to capture as much information on undocumented migrants as possible.

As soon as the journey begins, and then at any given leg of the voyage, migrants must have secure access to financial capital to avoid getting stuck during transit, as in the case of incarceration in Libya. New technologies of satellite phones interlace with ancestral systems of personal trust to lend and send money across regions, like the hawala system that is common in East Africa (Rinelli & Opondo 2013). Thanks to the use of new technologies, migrants are now able to stay in contact with family members and friends at a relatively cheap cost. When the cost of a phone call is too much, migrants use the cell phone as a telegraph by making use of the beeps as Morse code without spending any money. What is more, trucks that are manufactured in Europe with reliable mechanical technology – Mercedes, Volvo – are employed by African governments to patrol the frontier as much as they have replaced camels to cross the desert. Nowadays, these technologies are necessary tools along the trans-Saharan routes. Bedouins must be skillful mechanics, able to intervene under extreme desert conditions, if they want to maintain a reliable and competitive service for migrants.

Even if migration routes rely on historic patterns like trans-Saharan caravan routes (Clezio 2010) and established social networks, nowadays migrants must operate from remote locations, and they have to be able to respond immediately and adapt to migration policy changes. This is a pattern that preoccupies the European institutions and has made Mr. Franco Frattini, the former European Commissioner responsible for justice, freedom, and security cry out that "we cannot have mafia, or traffickers or terrorists using better technology than our police" (BBC News 2008). For example, referring to Frontex actions, Operation Hera (the summer of 2006) has been considered the most effective operation implemented in the Mediterranean Basin so far, both in terms of the high number of interceptions and the resulting drop of migrants embarking from the coast of Morocco to cross the tiny Strait of Gibraltar to get into Spain. Nonetheless, it has been noted how, while "the number of irregular boat arrivals to the Canary Islands, Spanish territory off Africa's western coast, dropped by 74 percent from 2006 to 2008, meanwhile, in Italy, boat arrivals increased by 64 percent from 2006 to 2008" (Human Rights Watch 2009, p. 36). As a result, instances of deterritorialization due to the deployment of aggressive technologies of migration control correspond to a reterritorialization of the same territories due to the same technologies employed with opposite intent. Given that migration, as well as surveillance and control practice, is today structured along a fluid network of interoperability, any technologic event at any point in the network (closing or opening of opportunities) will be felt in any other node of the network in an organic relation of symbiosis or "technécology". In other words, migrations from Africa into Europe continue with high or low intensity partially in response/in relation to technological inputs from more economically advanced countries. Those stimulus, via media and marketing, however, are never questioned in the context of the supposed African migrants' invasion because the migrants' flood remain ultimately the *raison d'être* of the continual virtual control.

War, hyper-production, hyper-waste, hyper-media floods over the south and back to the north of the globe, generating human mobility, which conversely stimulates technologies of control in a vicious capitalist cycle. "There is no capitalism without migrations" (Mezzadra 2005, p. 186), and to comprehend the historical changes within the regime of migration control means to understand contemporary class arrangements and the new form of labor. There is a structural nexus that links the contemporary capitalist economy and transformations of migration patterns and related control policies in Europe. This technological transformation, according to Deleuze, "must be a mutation of capitalism" (1992, p. 6), and it is extremely dispersive. It is an intricate relationship between migration, labor, and new technologies of control and production.

> Man is no longer man enclosed, but man in debt. It is true that capitalism has retained as a constant the extreme poverty of three-quarters of humanity, too poor for debt, too numerous for confinement: control will not only have to deal with erosions of frontiers but with the explosions within shantytowns or ghettos.
>
> (Deleuze 1992, p. 6)

The contemporary de-regularization of the labor market together with the change of relations between the market and the state – less state intervention in providing social shelter to foreign and domestic workers – rendered undocumented migrants 'illegal', therefore invisible. It is neither economically nor socially suitable to create and sustain a complex public program to import workers linked to specific tasks and needs. It is preferable to let them be invisible and vulnerable. The market will take care of them, those without proper documentation, without a voice as J. Rancière mentioned many times in his books. Interestingly J. Rancière published *Disagreement* (1998) the same year of the revolt of the *sans papiers* (without papers) in France. Since then, the number of undocumented invisibles has grown in numbers to include both nationals of the EU as well as third-country nationals. In the midst of an enduring economic crisis, technologies of screening and detection are still envisioned as the perfect solution to solve economic and social inequality and delinquency. Discrimination does not only emerge in terms of the power of access to technology, but its use differs according to gender, race, and national codes.

> The representations of transnational subjects produced by global capitalism differ greatly. While discourses about residents of technology-consuming societies tend to efface specificities related to identity in favor of transnationally mobile consumers, those on the producing end become even more over-determined and restricted by gendered, sexualized, racialized, and nationalized representations.
>
> (Biemann 2001, p. 2)

To focus on a technological transformation of the border, then, is a matter of analyzing practices of bordering or rebordering and comprehending how the network nodes where the border operates are the space of politics in itself. I am thinking here again about the Internet café as a space of resistance through the Web and, at the same time, a space of control via monitoring and identification. The management of that portion of the unknown variable – that is, the management of risk – then constitutes the new aspect of the migration control policies of the EU and is calculated upon the degree of (in)visibility. The intent is not to render visible every single migrant's trajectory. The system of control allows them entry into society – a differential inclusion – after being tagged as a prostitute or illegal providing then for a permanent social stain: "to be visible means to be legally legitimized to exist, or, on the contrary, it means to be more exposed to the consequences of one's own juridical and social illegitimacy" (Brighenti 2009, p. 86). If we recognize that illegality and delinquency is a by-product of (today's) law, then technologies of migration control in reality are not aimed at eliminating the existence of "illegality" by rendering everyone visible and legitimized. They aim to contain the power of the mobility of migrant workers in terms of social and economic conditions.

Thus, awareness and perception of each one's own visibility is of great importance for marginalized subjects [abject]. Migrants must possess a knowledge and mapping of technologies of surveillance. For instance, the city centers in Europe are nowadays mapped out by undocumented migrants who choose which trajectory to take according to the location of the video surveillance cameras and the deployment of police forces in strategic locations. Technologies of surveillance can turn an entire autobahn or a subway station into a mobile border that is fluctuant and volatile because databases translate the flows into calculable, comparable data and produce percentages of risk that continuously change and adjust. However, at the same time, trucks can be tools to cross frontiers hiding beneath and between them, as happens on a daily basis at Calais to enter the UK. Consequently, technologies have transformed border practices into a more dynamic phenomenon, entirely dependent on the use of the same technologies both for control and for subversion. In other words, in relation to migrants' trajectories, border technologies resemble the way an anti-virus relates to a hacker: both exist in relation to each other for the reason that not all power relations flow in one direction.

## Notes

1   *Commission Communication on the Creation of a European Border Surveillance System (EUROSUR)*, COM (2008) 68, 13 February 2008. Available at: http://eur-lex. europa.eu/LexUriServ/LexUriServ.do?uri=COM:2008:0069:FIN:EN:PDF

2   On the use of technology for security practices, see Didier Bigo and Julian Jeandesboz, *Border Security, Technology and the Stockholm Programme*, INEX Policy Brief No. 3, CEPS, Brussels, November 2009. Here is Bigo's latest: www.ceps.eu/search/node/bigo

3   http://wiki.triastelematica.org/index.php/Frontex

4   www.frontex.europa.eu/origin_and_tasks/origin/

5   For the first time since it was launched in 2004, the Warsaw-based agency responsible for the EU's external borders has funded and organized its own charter flight to deport undocumented aliens. *Le Monde* reports that on 28 September, "in a deliberately low-key operation," fifty-six Georgian migrants arrested in Poland, France, Austria,

and Germany were flown from Warsaw to the Georgian capital of Tbilisi. In 2011, Frontex, which has been granted a budget of €676 million for the period 2008–2013, plans to organize and finance between thirty and forty charters to repatriate migrants who have illegally entered the EU. For Frontex's deputy director, the increased role of the European Union "will come as a relief to national governments who will no longer have to 'carry the burden' of negative public opinion, embarrassment and disapproval prompted by collective repatriation procedures." *Le Monde* also notes "another advantage" of grouped operations is that they benefit from the "added weight" of the EU, "which can exert more pressure than individual member states when negotiating with third countries on the return of their citizens." See www.presseurop.eu/en/content/ news-brief/352121-frontex-launches-first-expulsion-charter

6　www.closeye.eu/

## References

Andreas, P. & Nadelmann, E., 2008. *Policing the Globe: Criminalization and Crime Control in International Relations*. New York, NY: Oxford University Press.

Anonymous, 2008. EU Plans Biometric Border Checks. *BBC News*. Available at: http:// news.bbc.co.uk/2/hi/europe/7242386.stm (Accessed 27 April 2010)

Baldaccini, B., 2010. Extraterritorial Border Controls in the EU: The Role of Frontex in Operations at Sea. In V. Mitsilegas & B. Ryan, eds. *Extraterritorial Immigration Control Legal Challenges*, (pp.229–255). Leiden, the Netherlands: Martinus Nijhoff Publishers. Available at: http://public.eblib.com/choice/publicfullrecord.aspx?p=583763 [Accessed 4 February 2015]

Balibar, E. & Hahn, D., 2002. *Politics and the Other Scene*. Londo, UK: Verso.

BBC News, 2008. EU Plans Biometric Border Checks. *BBC*. Available at: http://news.bbc. co.uk/2/hi/europe/7242386.stm [Accessed 15 January 2014]

Behdad, A., 2005. *A Forgetful Nation: On Immigration and Cultural Identity in the United States*. Durham, NC: Duke University Press Books.

Besters, M. & Brom, F.W.A., 2010. Greedy Information Technology: The Digitalization of the European Migration Policy. *European Journal of Migration and Law*, 12(4), pp. 455–470.

Biemann, U., 2001. Performing the Border: On Gender, Transnational Bodies, and Technology. *geobodies.org*. Available at: www.geobodies.org/03_books_and_texts/texts/ [Accessed 24 March 2011]

Biemann, U., 2003. Europlex. Available at: www.resetdoc.org/story/00000001417 [Accessed 15 April 2011]

Bigo, D., 2007. Detention of Foreigners, States of Exception, and the Social Practices of Control of the Banopticon. In P. K. Rajaram & C. Grundy-Warr, eds. *Borderscapes*, (pp. 3–34). Minneapolis, MN: University of Minnesota Press.

Bigo, D., 2008. Globalized (In)Security: The Field and the Ban-Opticon. Available at: https://kclpure.kcl.ac.uk/portal/en/publications/globalized-insecurity-the-field-and-the-banopticon(910bbd8d-8b43–4d7d-8af9–9000779d8bac).html [Accessed 22 January 2015]

Boswell, C., 2007. Migration Control in Europe after 9/11: Explaining the Absence of Securitization. *JCMS: Journal of Common Market Studies*, 45(3), pp. 589–610.

Brighenti, A. M., 2009. *Territori migranti. Spazio e controllo della mobilità globale*. Verona, Italy: Ombre Corte.

Brom, F.W.A. & Besters, M., 2010, Greedy Information Technology: The Digitalization of the European Migration Policy. *European Journal of Migration and Law*, 12(4) pp. 1–24.

Clezio, J.M.G.L., 2010. *Desert*. Boston, MA: Verba Mundi Books.

Cole, S., 2002. *Suspect Identities: a History of Fingerprinting and Criminal Identification*. Cambridge, MA: Harvard University Press.

Council of the European Union, 2004. The Hague Programme: Strengthening Free-dom, Security and Justice in the European Union. Available at: http://ec.europa.eu/home-affairs/doc_centre/docs/hague_programme_en.pdf [Accessed 10 April 2009].

Council of the European Union, 2010. Document number 6162. Note to the SIS-TECH working party. Available at: www.statewatch.org/news/2010/feb/eu-council-sis-stats-6162-10.pdf [Accessed 16 November 2013]

Council Regulation, No 2725/2000 of 11 December 2000 concerning the establishment of 'Eurodac' for the comparison of fingerprints for the effective application of the Dublin Convention *Official Journal L 316, 15/12/2000 Available at:* http://eur-lex.europa.eu/LexUriServ/LexUriServ.do?uri=CELEX:32000R2725:EN:HTML [Accessed 18 September 2010]

Crialese, E., 2006. *Golden Door.* Available at: www.imdb.com/title/tt0465188/ [Accessed 11 April 2011]

Deleuze, G., 1992. Postscript on the Societies of Control. *MIT Press,* Fall 59, pp. 3–7.

Edwards, A. & Ferstman, C., 2010. *Human Security and Non-Citizens: Law, Policy and International Affairs.* Cambridge, UK: Cambridge University Press.

European Commission, 2004, Proposal for a Regulation of the European Parliament and of the Council concerning the Visa Information System (VIS) and the exchange of data between Member States on short stay-visas {SEC(2004) 1628} COD 2004/0287 Available at: http://eur-lex.europa.eu/legal-content/EN/NOT/?uri=CELEX:52004PC0835 [Accessed 6 July 2010]

European Data Protection Supervisor, 2010. 'Opinion of the European Data Protection Supervisor on the Proposal for a Regulation of the European Parliament and of the Council concerning the Visa Information System (VIS) and the exchange of data between Member States on short stay-visas'. Official Journal of the European Union, C 181, 23 July 2005. Available at: https://secure.edps.europa.eu/EDPSWEB/webdav/shared/Documents/Consultation/Opinions/2005/05-03-23_VIS_EN.pdf (Accessed 7 January 2012)

Fortunati, L., Pertierra, R. & Vincent, J., 2013. *Migration, Diaspora and Information Technology in Global Societies.* London, UK: Routledge.

Foucault, M., 1984. *The Foucault Reader.* New York, NY: Pantheon.

Foucault, M., 1995. *Discipline & Punish: The Birth of the Prison.* 2nd ed. New York, NY: Vintage.

Foucault, M., 2003. *"Society Must Be Defended": Lectures at the College de France, 1975–1976.* New York, NY: Picador.

Foucault, M., Burchell, G., Gordon, C. & Miller, P., 1991. *The Foucault Effect: Studies in Governmentality.* Chicago, IL: University of Chicago Press.

Guild, E. & Bigo, D., 2003. Le visa Schengen: expression d'une stratégie de « police » à distance. *Cultures & Conflicts,* 49(1), pp. 22–37.

Hardt, M. & Negri, A., 2001. *Empire.* Cambridge, MA: Harvard University Press.

Heller, C. & Pezzani, L., 2014. *Liquid Traces – The Left-to-Die Boat Case.* Available at: http://vimeo.com/89790770 [Accessed 4 November 2014]

Herzog, R., 2009. *Noi difendiamo l'Europa.* Rome, Italy: Audiodoc productions

Human Rights Watch, 2009. *Pushed Back, Pushed Around.* Available at: www.hrw.org/reports/2009/09/21/pushed-back-pushed-around-0 [Accessed 8 November 2011]

Jones, R., 2012. *Border Walls: Security and the War on Terror in the United States, India, and Israel.* New York, NY: Zed Books.

Jorry, H., 2007. Construction of a European Constitutional Model for the Management of Operational Coordination at the EU External Borders: Does the Frontex Agency take a decisive step forward?, CHALLENGE Research Paper n. 6, March 2007. Available at: www.libertysecurity.org/IMG/pdf_Construction_of_a_European_Institutional_

Model_for_Managing_Operational_Cooperation_at_the_EU_s_External_Borders.pdf [Accessed 9 January 2012]

Lago, A. D., 2009. *Non-Persons*. Vimodrone, Italy: IPOC di Pietro Condemi.

Lindahl, H., 2009. *A Right to Inclusion and Exclusion? Normative Fault Lines of the EU's Area of Freedom, Security and Justice*. London, UK: Bloomsbury Publishing.

Lyon, D., 2001. *Surveillance Society: Monitoring Everyday Life*. Buckingham, UK: Open University Press.

Masse, J.-P. & Lodge, J., Eds., 2007. *Are You Who You Say You Are? The EU and Biometric Borders*. Available at: www.libertysecurity.org/article1738.html [Accessed 4 April 2011]

Mezzadra, S., 2005. *Derecho de fuga: migraciones, ciudadanía y globalización*. Buenos Aires, Argentina: Traficantes de Sueños.

Neal, A. W., 2009. Securitization and Risk at the EU Border: The Origins of FRONTEX. *JCMS: Journal of Common Market Studies*, 47(2), pp. 333–356.

Neilson, D. & Stubbs, T., 2011. Relative Surplus Population and Uneven Development in the Neoliberal Era: Theory and Empirical Application. *Capital & Class*, 35(3), pp. 435–453.

Rajaram, P. K. & Grundy-Warr, C., 2008. *Borderscapes: Hidden Geographies and Politics at Territory's Edge*. Minneapolis, MN: University of Minnesota Press.

Rinelli, L. & Opondo, S. O., 2013. Affective Economies: Eastleigh's Metalogistics, Urban Anxieties and the Mapping of Diasporic City Life. *African and Black Diaspora: An International Journal*, 6(2), pp. 236–250.

Soguk, N., 1999. *States and Strangers: Refugees and Displacements of Statecraft*. Minneapolis, MN: University of Minnesota Press.

Walters, W., 2006. Border/Control. *European Journal of Social Theory*, 9(2), pp. 187–203.

# 7   The brick door

*If the name and the identity of something like the city still has a meaning, could it, when dealing with the related questions of hospitality and refuge, elevate itself above nation-states or at least free itself from them in order to become, to coin a phrase in a new and novel way, a free city? . . . Certain places (diplomatic or religious) to which one could retreat in order to escape from the threat of injustice.*
*(Derrida 2003, p.9)*

## 7.1   Movement, capture, and insurrectional migrant urban lives

Derrida's epigraph serves as a reminder of a concept that is not new but comes from the Bible. In the book of Numbers, God orders Moses to institute six "cities of refuge" or "asylum" for the "resident alien or temporary settler." This idea was taken into Christianity as the "sanctuary" provided by churches to secure immunity and survival for refugees and Rome, being the household of Catholicism and the city of a hundred churches, is the perfect candidate for this role. The end of the journey for African migrants does not mean the end of their perils because there is no city that does not completely adhere to the nation-state's general policies. In order to prevent the mobility of asylum seekers and migrants, state and non-state entities have employed spatializing practices predicated on the elasticity, fragmentation, and even virtualization of sites of capture and abandonment. These include *source reduction* techniques like the creation of regional protection areas (RPAs) and off-territory transit processing centers bent on keeping migrants and asylum seekers away by preventing their arrival at a country's territorial borders (Haddad 2007).

Nonetheless, as cities become home to a greater number of immigrants (Sassen 2001), urban and immigration policies necessarily overlap. As I previously discussed in Chapter 2, the dialectic of movement and capture characteristic of the border today involves both a logic of space and a temporal rhythm within which it becomes possible to police the movement of foreign bodies or to enhance the managerial aspects of humanitarian operations. The city has increasingly been presented as that which must be secured against the encroachment of refugee and migrant populations. Ironically, the protection of cities and nation-states from foreign presence has contributed to the normalization and proliferation of camp conditions within the city. Not only are we witnessing the mushrooming of detention camps in most cities of Europe,[1] but there has also been a proliferation of the "novel socio-spatial form of 'city-camps'" (Agier 2002, p. 320).

Informal and improvisational as it may seem, the city-camp is a spontaneous or institutionalized environment that emerges from the agglomeration of refugees and migrants for periods that "last far beyond the duration of the emergency" (Agier 2002, p. 320). The contestation of the camp logic becomes more urgent as the city/camp duality is concretized, normalized, or erased through technologies and techniques that "hinder the practice of claims-making" (Isin and Rygiel 2007, p.26).

As such, camps and city-camps become the site of a different form of capture as the permanence of the camp conditions becomes normalized through "developments" and corporate interests and further humanitarian management rather than providing a space for self-fashioning and claim-making. Given that camps have housed displaced people for more than a generation in some cases, it is not surprising that humanitarian and corporate interests merge in this space, as evidenced by the recent teaming up of the Swedish housewares giant IKEA and the United Nations (UN) for the purpose of designing more innovative tents for refugees. By simultaneously shaping households in the city while creating generic camps, IKEA becomes the quintessential *corpor[ate]ality* of the city-camp to come.

Instead of entering into a debate over the concept of citizenship and the right to the city, corporate and humanitarian interests intersect to design the "perfect camp," to build generic "cabinet homes" to be reproduced countless times in countless spaces, where refugees will be comfortably confined as long as it takes. Read otherwise, IKEA's attempt to make more durable, comfortable, and expensive camp houses, equipped with all the amenities a house in the city can possibly have, transforms the refugee camp into an omnitopic space dislocated from its surrounding environment. The modular form also enables the camp to be inserted into a continuum of IKEA-mediated images while its structural mutability transforms it into an editable construct.

The discourse of more comfortable and durable refugee tents makes it possible to keep refugees out of the city proper and its politics while facilitating more effective policing of refugee lives. As journalist Mac (Mcclelland 2014) irreverently asks with regard to the perfect camp and the kind of policing of refugee lives that it enables: "if a camp becomes a shelter not just for a few months but for year, a substitute – even a deterrent – to a real solution, how much does it matter how nice it is?"

This being the case, refugees and other immigrants have been involved in a number of tactical practices in an attempt to access cities and, once there, they have on numerous occasions asserted their right to the city through the creation of camp-cities. The right to the city, David Harvey tells us, "is one of the most precious yet most neglected of our human rights" (2008, p. 23). While often presented in terms of refugees' quest for a different economy, the claim to a right to the city, as I will illustrate in the following, "is far more than the individual liberty to access urban resources" (Ibid.). It is more than an economic concern. It is an isonomic claim that asserts the equality of rights of all urban inhabitants even where it involves translating city spaces into camp enclaves or populating the city with bodies designated for the camps.

As refugees, asylum seekers, and immigrants assert their right to have rights and their right to the city, they also enact a politics of movement and stasis that contests or transgresses humanitarian and administrative police regimes. Specifically, as I maintain in this chapter, to attend to the question of refugees today, one must critically engage the insurrectional practices and bodies that highlight and disturb the relationship between the camp and the city. Such a treatment of *citiness* and the logic of the camp does more than challenge the principle of the inscription of nativity and the trinity of state/nation/territory that the nation-state is based upon (Agamben 1998). It also goes beyond humanitarian concerns and the question of equivalence between the rights of citizens and the rights of stateless persons and seeks to open up the possibility of new forms of movement, inhabitance, self-fashioning, and claim-/place-making.

This chapter, then, examines insurrectional African migrants and refugee practices that highlight and disturb the legal and spatial relationship between institutionalized zones of capture and the city of Rome. While governmental and humanitarian agencies develop new techniques and technologies to manage refugee presence, asylum seekers and refugees continue to disturb the dominant logics of cities and camps through insurrectional acts that create spaces of possibility and ethical possibilities where another idea of belonging and cohabitation is possible. However, given the proliferation of camps and camp conditions and their interaction with everyday forms of urban life, what are some of the insurrectional acts that enable immigrants and recognized refugees, Arendt's humanity in excess (1973), to reorient our political and ethical sensibilities? What kind of political practices and subjects emerge within and between these spaces of capture, and what kinds of movement or settlement do they enact?

So much for the questions. Back to the documentary *Like a Man on Earth* (Segre & Yimer, 2008) that provides the leitmotiv of this book. The documentary opens with the camera gazing over the railway that leads to Termini, Rome's central station, and then it dives into the city to reach its periphery, migrants' destination. The stories that follow are insurrectional enactments that affirm refugees' and asylum seekers' right to the city while highlighting transformations in the logics and operations of the camps. They trace and disturb the laws and policing practices that seek to contain or limit access to the city by making it a zone of citizenship while designating detention centers that operate under the camp logic as the only proper space for the refugee and the asylum seeker. In effect, the events we analyze reveal the violence of control mechanisms while illustrating how insurrectional practices make immigrants' and refugees' lives in the city livable, their precariousness notwithstanding.

## 7.2   Into the city

Historically, immigrants and migrants tend to be concentrated in the most important urban areas in a receiving country. The filtering effect of urban borders, which alternately deflect, tolerate, or promote dwelling, conditions every urban person's existence. No migrant enters a neutral ideological context when arriving in the European Union (EU). Once migrants have crossed the frontier of the EU, they come to occupy a precarious place in the city that exists at the margins of integration. Depending on how external controls situate and catalogue migrants individually and collectively, they differently regulate how, and even whether, people are able to enter the EU's urban centers and call them "home" (Balibar 2003).

This chapter locates one of the new frontiers of Europe within a fundamental paradox of the city of Rome: an inexorable expansion of buildings together with a mounting rejection and marginalization of an emergent immigrant population that is vital to the city's expansion. Questions to be explored in this chapter will be related to the official discourse of multiculturalism set in motion by Rome's town hall and whether it pushes African migrants to the margins of the city, creating distinct places in the city's peripheries. Once at the margins, it is important to identify migrants' tactics of resistance and place-making that support individuals and their communities. It is important to focus on these tactics since they seem to lead to alternative urban imaginations beyond marginalization.

There are two reasons to study the city of Rome as the brick door in relation to the contemporary European policies of migration control. First, the route that goes from East and Central Africa toward Libya via the Sahara Desert has been, at least until the summer of 2011 and now again, the most trafficked and policed in North Africa and therefore the most dangerous. The main flow of migrants traveling from sub-Saharan Africa to Europe sails from the Libyan coast and arrives at the southern coast of Italy. Several scholars have recently made the case for the significance of studying the topic of migration to Italy and its relation to questions of space, time, control, power, and visibility (Parati 2005; Bullaro 2010). Rome represents the place where immigrants in Italy can most quickly find points of reference and social coordinates to build new ways of life.

What is more, as a long time ago at the apex of its grandeur, Rome's vocation is linked to that of the Mediterranean, which leads to the second reason. Not only is the Mediterranean the fulcrum of the European migration control – even though of a small percentage of migrants enter into the Schengen Area by the sea – but more importantly, the new urban plan for the city of Rome explicitly promotes the Mediterranean Sea as a harmonious space where different cultures coexist with Rome as its core. Unfortunately, the past 25 years of European and Italian border restrictions in Mediterranean contradict the above intent to foster the Basin of the Mediterranean as a melting pot of diverse cultures. The opposite is true, if we consider how the introduction of visa in 1991–1992 for North African migrants working in Europe have frozen migrants' journey into permanent settling, interrupting previous circular migration. More importantly while failing to curb undocumented immigration they achieved the opposite effect resulting in an increasing dependence of migrants on smugglers to cross borders thus intensifying cultural conflicts.

Several city administrations have taken on the difficult task of formulating a new urban plan for Rome, but only forty-five years after the last urban plan,[2] on 14 March 2008, the city council came to an agreement. The result is a compromise among groups of private landowners, developers and city hall officials to regulate the expansion of the city. Squeezed in the middle is a growing immigrant population that has been left out of the public debate. Officially, the plan aims to give a voice to the different sounds of the immigrant communities living in the city; in reality, I maintain, it renders their rhythm unintelligible and their essence never a possibility.

The introduction to the new plan is solemnly titled "Rome – Peace Capital of the Mediterranean: The New Urban Plan of Rome" (Morassut 2003). It is worth mentioning how the history of urban planning in Rome, and particularly in relation to the fascist ideology and colonial endeavor, should be problematized in the use of the Mediterranean as a mechanism that harmoniously regulates the residency of people in Rome's urban space. In the initial document, Roberto Morassut, town-planning councilor in 2003, describes a utopian city that is accessible to its inhabitants, filled with social opportunities, and modern without forgetting its historical heritage. But what exactly does this document entail? At first sight, the link between Rome and the Mediterranean recalls a distant past perhaps best encapsulated by the Roman imperial tag *mare nostrum* (our sea). As I have pointed out in Chapter 4, the characterization of the Mediterranean as *mare nostrum* [our sea] appears at the beginning of Caesar's *De bello gallico* (2006), indicating the self-belief of having already acquired full control over the Mediterranean – which conversely led to a change in Rome's foreign policy to now be oriented to the north toward the Atlantic. Lefevbre comprehended well this double nature of the eternal city, at the same time prone to the aesthetics and beauty in a transcultural environment, however built over the sketch of a military camp.

> On the one hand the orbis and the urbs, circular, with their extensions and implications (arch, vault); on the other hand the military camp with its strict grid and its two perpendicular axes, cardo and decumanus – a closed space, set apart and fortified.
>
> (1992, p. 245)

The idea of *mare nostrum* entailed together the variety of cultures that constituted Rome's uniqueness but also a complete military control over a sea that was considered by Roman emperors as a mere lake "already conceptualized as a homogenous space of confinement, possession, and colonization" (Pugliese 2010, p. 11). However, the Mediterranean Sea has never been reduced to a homogenous space, neither during the Roman occupation nor today when European policies of migration control attempt to purge it of foreign bodies as they traverse the few miles that separate Europe from Africa entering into Italian territory.[3] Coincidentally, *mare nostrum* is the code that was given to the "search and rescue" operation carried out by Italian authorities after the tragedy that occurred on 3 October 2013 on the shores of the island of Lampedusa. The operation, after only one year and more than 100,000 lives saved at sea, has recently been questioned and terminated because it is believed to encourage more immigration and is too costly (see Chapter 7 for details). Meanwhile on land, the conditions of detention centers for migrants remain dreadful and have caused rioting and destruction.

The overture of the urban plan is intended to highlight Rome's crucial role in promoting intercultural and interreligious dialogue featuring social cohesion, as "the richness of contemporary metropolis is over all associated with their standards of social quality" (Morassut 2003, p. 27). But how does the new plan supposedly promote social quality? First of all, it does so through environmental protection. It reserves 88,000 hectares of territory to green areas. Second, the protection and preservation of historical Rome is to be extended beyond the classic Roman ruins to include contemporary architecture that is located within the periphery. Third, and most important, the innovation that the urban plan envisions revolves around the concept of the polycentric city: there will be eighteen new urban nodes, or miniature cities, within the city, each with schools, hospitals, and administrative services. Lastly, Rome requires the "iron cure," which is the modernization and lengthening of the entire metropolitan rail system.

However, according to the Italian National Institute of Statistics (ISTAT), between 1995 and 2006, three billion cubic meters of cement were utilized to build two-million-and-a-half new houses, although the number of Italian families increased only by several thousand (Anonymous 2009). Rome already extends for 1,285 km$^2$ – Berlin is only 892 km$^2$ for example – and is the largest municipality in Europe because of the financial investments and money laundering in the estate business. As a matter of fact, despite a demographic decline of the city's population (Insolera 1993), the new urban plan of 2008 authorizes seventy million m$^3$ of new cement. In other words, the new plan anticipates, and again requires, urban growth. However, given the stagnant demographic growth of the Italian population and the constant exodus of the population of Rome from the city toward the villages or just abroad, immigrants must, in one way or another, be expected to be the final consumers of this profitable housing market. It is true that in the last fifteen years, immigrant communities have produced visible effects on the city of Rome. They comprise 12.4 % of the total population of the city, while the national average is around 8.2%. They accounted for 9.3% of the total population in 2008, while only 4.8% lived in Rome in 1998 (Menghi 2010, p. 167). In numbers, the segment with foreign citizenship in Rome on 31 December 2013 was equal to 353,785 persons[4] (compared to 201,633 in 2004 and 151,221 in 2000). Thus, immigrants have deeply changed and shaped the aspect and identity of Rome in multiple ways. Nonetheless, the new privately funded houses are hardly affordable or accessible for the majority of new immigrants. The rent paid by new immigrants is 30% to 50% higher than the average rent paid by Italians. Further, 85% of immigrants have signed unregistered rental contracts. About €1 billion in taxes have been dodged as a result of building policies that prey on, and marginalize, the immigrant population. Because of these political and economic factors, the majority of new immigrants do not reside within the municipality of Rome but, as I have suggested previously, the foreign inhabitants of the city are those who revitalized a moribund estate market even within the economic contraction. Immigrants are responsible for more than 10% of the buying and selling of real estate. However, this is the case for the Chinese, Romanian and Filipino communities for reasons that go beyond the scope of this book. When it comes to African migrants and refugees, they are marginalized and secluded within the city they inhabit. Even so, this does not mean that immigrants and refugees do not engage in and shape the city. Perhaps immigrants are those who properly live in the urban space, transforming it before and beyond city hall interventions as they engage in urban segregations. The urban border, as a matter of fact, appears only in the moment in which it has been crossed, "for the border is not a thing but, rather, the materialization of authority" (Chambers 2008, p. 6) that has been contested and subverted.

## 7.3   Reorienting the city

"Italy does not offer sufficient guarantees concerning reception facilities for asylum seekers," the European Court of Human Rights (ECHR) said in a ruling last November 2014 (Ansa 2014). In light of Italy's record of poor reception of migrants and refugees, those who are forced to remain in Italy and live in the city have to come up with tactics and strategies of survival, while those who attempt to settle in other EU states have to devise ways of avoiding arrest and/or returning to Italy. For instance, homeless Somali nationals have occupied the former Somali Embassy in Via dei Villini in Rome (Kassovitz 1995), located in the upmarket area of the city. By dwelling in an abandoned embassy – an extraterritorial diplomatic space – the Somali migrants intervene in the organization of urban political space and give it new meaning by bringing into the city the forms of life that are often abandoned, concealed, or captured in extraterritorial spaces of migration control. Unlike the anonymity produced by generic or "comfortable" camp conditions that attempt to fix where refugees should live and how they should do so, the creation of an urban camp makes the refugees visible and transforms frontier figures into liminal subjects who exist between citizenship and exile. In a self-made camp-like space in the city, the authorities have cyclically challenged their presence, but immigrants have always come back to claim their space until the authorities in 2011 succeeded in evacuating the building. Precarious and untidy as it may be, the diplomatic urban space of cohabitation that the Somali migrants occupied pointed to the possibility of pluralist urban existence that disturbs the dichotomy between illegitimate foreignness on one hand and legitimate urban life characterized by multiculturalism or complete integration on the other.

While the Somali occupation of the former Somali Embassy is an act of dissensus predicated on enhanced migrants' and refugees' presence and visibility, stories of bodily alterations by asylum seekers determined to erase their identities in order to prevent detection and return to Italy, or to protest the conditions under which they are held in detention or reception facilities, abound. Not only is their movement within Italy limited, but migrants are also subjected to biometric-enabled modes of capture through a centralized system for keeping and comparing the fingerprints of all asylum applicants in the EU. The EURODAC database enables EU states to prevent people from applying for asylum in more than one country – the so-called asylum shopping – while passing off responsibility for the asylum seekers to countries of first arrival like Italy in accordance with the Dublin

Agreement. Methods range from burning off one's fingerprints to using sandpaper to erase finger and palm prints to avoid detection by the EURODAC database. Similarly, refugees and asylum seekers have sewn their lips together (Anonymous 2013b) in order to protest against the prison-like conditions in migrant expulsion centers (Martin & Allen 2009). Here, to be silent rather than to speak emerges as a louder form of protest, while concealed identities and erasure enable those who the state scripts in very specific and limited ways to escape its technologies of capture. On the whole, these insurrectional practices highlight the possibilities of refugee existence beyond the camp and present the city or the right to the city (Harvey 2008) as one way of contesting the proliferation of camp conditions in the city.

As I have illustrated previously, the reconfiguration of the camp and the transformation of the city through refugee movements and settlement enable refugees to raise isonomic claims based on their right to have rights while enacting their right to the city and to a dignified life. Consider, for instance, the experience of more than 100 Eritrean refugees in Rome who a few years ago created a semi-structured urban environment within the city. Not too far from the subway station of Ponte Mammolo[5], they built shacks with tin-plated roofs and doors that during the day stay shut. The heat and cold are hard to bear; hence, the refugees fabricated a more solid masonry building as the recreational area at the center of the settlement. They consider it "the bar/restaurant area" and have painted the walls pink. You may spot a Koran and a Bible on a shelf "because here we are all brothers," Sanal says. "It does not really matter if you are Christian or Muslim" (Anonymous 2013a). They indeed share the same space and the burden of it. Every person who is employed supports five or six others, and those who are unemployed cook and take care of the communal areas. The majority of refugees find seasonal employment as fruit and tomato pickers in the south of Italy to come back in winter at the end of the warm season. In a very simple way, these individuals, then, have organized their own existence, between labor and dwellings and their social relations, despite or making use of the multiple boundaries that come between them and the host societies in order to create a new transversal social space of *camp-villes* between the refugee camp and the city.

With time, within spaces like Ponte Mammolo, new social assemblages and new cultural syntheses are created that, in many ways, stand for claims of social and political inclusion and resistance. Out of necessity and proximity, dwellers devise new models of reciprocal support, new forms of aggregation that render material and tangible their inherent hope for change and access to the city. As a matter of fact, these movements and struggles over migration challenge nation-centric readings of the project of citizenship, rights, and community while providing novel spatial coordinates from which one can articulate or enact political subjectivities. From this point of view, both mobility and settlement become the basis for overcoming bare life by reaffirming the dignity and agency of refugees without romanticizing them. Through attentiveness to the heterogeneity of camp conditions today and the insurrectional practices that contest or appropriate it, it becomes possible to carry out a critique of the post-colonial and global present by pointing to the specter of colonial encampment and its mechanisms of control within the urban setting. Beyond historical critique, the presence or absence of refugee camps in some states and migrants' assertion of their right to move or settle highlights the south-north assemblages of power characterized by European externalization of migration control as revealed by the arrangements between Gaddafi's Libya and the EU or Israel and Uganda. Ultimately, the agency of refugees and their insurrectional political acts reveal how the camp is being transformed into a proto-urban space and the city into a potential space of encampment and capture. The refugee, as an in-between figure, then, becomes the marker of a notorious double absence that disrupts by simply moving or settling in a space (Sayad 2004). In these moments of rupture, refugees' claim to the right to the city and a dignified life presents the possibility of a new form of cohabitation and ideas of community beyond citizenship.

Once the African migrant becomes visible in the urbanscape, once she has navigated the surface of the Mediterranean Sea, she comes to be incorporated, more often than not, as a multicultural ingredient that serves to promote the image of a tolerant and multiethnic city. The latter has to be contextualized within the strict relation between the market and urban society. Multiculturalism has a major leverage for generating future growth and attracting investment capital and consumers. This phenomenon illustrates a growing relationship between neoliberalism and cosmopolitanism, whereby Rome competes with the other great capitals of Europe, like Paris and London, in their social make-up. It is worth noting here, although briefly, that Rome has only recently approached the discourse of multiculturalism and is doing so in a superficial way. The tardiness of government policies is not necessarily linked to the ethnic composition of its society, which does not share the post-colonial flows of Paris and London. Instead, it has to do more with the fact that Italian society has not come to terms yet with its colonial past, the idea of race, and its contemporary role as a country of immigration.

## 7.4   Orchestrated harmony

Nowadays, the immigrant, when detectable, stands as a classic example of a fetish where multiculturalism and the celebration/construction of difference are the natural outcomes of a managerial approach to the city. As Deleuze and Guattari have noted, "the dividing line is not between inside and outside but rather is internal to simultaneous signifying chains and successive subjective choices" (1987, p. 178). This implies a fulcrum, a homogenizing principle at its core, a white wall on which to design a rainbow cloth. The idea behind the document that introduces the urban plan is that Rome, with its monuments and (imperial) history, plays this role. In this sense, the slogan "Rome – Peace Capital of the Mediterranean" of the new urban plan signifies a homogeneous space, without conflicts, in which therefore the city's market can flourish and different voices can be distinctly heard. Peace, intended as the absence of conflict, is then the necessary chamber to generate harmony. But where can harmony be found other than in an orchestra?

The documentary *L'Orchestra di Piazza Vittorio* (Vittorio Square's Orchestra) (Ferrente 2009) takes place in the district around Rome's main train station, and

I consider this celebrated project a classical example of the organized systematization of culture within the city. Today, immigrants – mostly Chinese, Filipinos, and Bangladeshi whose activities revolve around a square, Vittorio Emanuele II Square – largely populate the area around the central station. The square is, as it has always been since its origins, a hub for various cultures, sounds, and odors from all corners of the world (Lakhous 2006), even though Chinese shops colonize the entire area.

> He is listening to the noise of the train in the throat of the journey. The noise is as regular as the lines. Over this, irregularly, rising to crescendos and falling away, are the noises of what the train is passing: the field murmur, brick walls pound fists on metal, a station throws gravel against the windows. When the terminus first arrives, it does so in silence.
>
> (Berger 1989, p. 68)

This *piazza*, its essence, inspired musician Mario Tronco and filmmaker Agostino Ferrente to reunite some of the most extraordinary performers among immigrants, each one unique in origin, instrument and musical experience, in an orchestra that plays world music all over the globe. In 2006, a documentary that tells the story of how the project took shape was released; since then, it has been screened in many festivals around the world and has won several awards. Watching the documentary, we walk in a sort of harmonious melting pot that fits perfectly with the official discourse of Rome as a multicultural place presented with the new urban plan. While the story revolves around the project to revitalize and save an old theatre, the Apollo Theatre, from being transformed into a bingo hall, we get the impression that immigrants exist simply to provide some color to this political mission; they never participate directly in the group's meetings, nor are they involved in conversations with the town hall representatives. They remain isolated from the political possibility of this endeavor. They are left aside to do what they are good at doing: playing music.

The two central characters, both Italians and both quite established within the art community, seem to enjoy the practice of fishing for new artists in the area around the square. An attentive reading of these scenes reveals an instinctive hesitancy, incomprehension and sometimes hostility, toward the two Italians. At the beginning of the documentary, when the two Italians enter different shops to look for artists, whether a singer or a player of tablas, they do it by intruding into others' spaces with a sort of nosiness and naïveté, "only dimly aware of a certain unease in the air" (Pink Floyd 1977).

Even when the documentary offers glimpses of the real life of some of these musicians while they struggle to survive in the city of Rome, the Italian organizers are preoccupied with accomplishing their musical and political project. They panic, for example, because the date of the concert is approaching fast and the Indian player is sent back to India for visa issues, or after several requests for help made by Raul, the Argentinean drummer, because he is going to be evicted from the garage where he lives. The documentary does not rest enough upon the city's urban policies and high rent costs and the consequent marginalization connected with these municipal issues. It seems as though immigrants exist outside of global capitalist social relations and their corollaries of nationalism and racism.

Overall, the documentary does not engage in a dialogue with immigrants who essentially are the orchestra because setting a dialogue would highlight those tensions that occur generally within the "organization of difference as a qualitatively homogeneous fetish."(Sharma 2006). In the same way, the discourse of multiculturalism presented within the urban plan of Rome does not imply a separation between immigrants. Instead, the celebration of difference, both within the orchestra as well as between the lines of the urban plan, celebrates sameness within a generic alterity. The fundamental separation exists within hierarchical differences that are aimed at "reducing complex and overlapping relations" (Hardt and Negri 2001).

It suggests the preservation of a firm core around which legal and economic status and place meaning revolve, as the planets do around their sun. As Fernandes brilliantly put it:

> The West is cosmopolitan only insofar as it understands its culture as the final step in a historical movement. Hence, Western cosmopolitanism does not celebrate globalization as flows that breed differences but seeks to discipline the proliferation of differences through colonial-inspired racial and spatial hierarchies.
>
> (2007, p. 99)

In the end, a well-liked project such as the *L'Orchestra di Piazza Vittorio*, both despite and because of its politically correct multicultural language, not only fails to question the dominant political organization and creation of differences but also vacates the urban from other ideas of communities and reinforces the homogenization of immigrants' unique experiences of the urban. Instead, true relationships within the urban occur when they are disconnected from the planned idea of difference and are connected to space through practice. Home comes to be defined, then, through experience rather than imposed places and identities. As Cresswell put it, "the geographical ordering of society is founded on a multitude of acts of boundary making – of territorialization – whose ambiguity is to simultaneously open up the possibilities of transgression."[6] By concentrating on the marginal, we achieve a novel perspective on the role they play in defining the central or the normal and dominant. At the margins of the city, it is possible to encounter processes of transculturation that, instead of being transcendent, rely on continuous negotiation. Processes of transculturation are indeed linked to subjectification that happens through imaginative reconfigurations of the political in a perennial movement of subjectivity.

Disillusioned with official discourses of multiculturalism, from its epicenter of the town hall, I move my research toward the discursively external part of the city: the periphery. There, in the southeastern area of Rome, I ultimately recognize the interconnections between Europe's emerging southern border and the urban space of Rome. Like a border, the urban structure does not change spontaneously. Nor does a single powerful agent, such as the state, determine it. The urbanscape changes in ways that are related to forms of inclusion/exclusion that occur through modalities of externalization or, in the case of the cityscape, of *peripheralization.*

## 7.5   Central periphery

We move, then, southeast, toward the liminal part of Rome where, following Pier Paolo Pasolini – a critical foreign lover and attentive observer of the Roman society – the city meets fields. This marginal portion of the city is a vital axis for the entire city and for all south-living immigrants outside the municipality of Rome who arrive in the morning at the Anagnina bus station to find a job. It is the desire to get into the urban dimension, to be part of the legitimized *polis* that drives the newcomers here, much like the desire that drove Pasolini's *Mamma Roma* (1962) and his son, following an entire generation of Italian migrants fifty years ago.

At the beginning of the documentary *Like a Man on Earth* (2008), a close-up aligns with Dagmari's profile, resting, deeply lost in his thoughts. In the background, gray benches outline the Anagnina bus station, the southeast doorstep of Rome and, until only a short time ago, the unmistakable threshold of the urbanscape. It is not a coincidence that this station sets the initial tone for Dag's documentary about his journey from the Horn of Africa to Rome. We sense that Dag, an Ethiopian refugee, has finally reached Europe and the city of Rome after an agonizing odyssey. The Anagnina bus station is emblematic of the understanding of Rome's peculiarities in relation to the new urban plan. Today, the wide open space of the station is a crucial hub for trade and information sharing among migrant workers who come to the city from the countryside. As I have pointed out ahead, immigrants not necessarily live in this area because they can not afford the high cost of rent within the city compared with areas few kilometers away. The renting market, together with immigration laws, works to keep immigrants disconnected from the city without having to renounce a cheap workforce. What is more, the station functions as the southeast door to the city because it welcomes the long-distance bus routes that connect the small villages and towns south of and along the coast of Rome. These towns are being occupied by newly arrived immigrants who have revitalized them, abandoned by the previous generations of Italians, and have boosted, if not basically created from scratch, a renting market that was otherwise sterile, especially along the coastline during the winter seasons.

Basically, Romans do not utilize these long routes as means of transportation, and almost all of the commuters are of foreign origins. When these buses arrive at Anagnina Station to drop into the underground metropolitan network, immigrants sit at the margins, genuine strangers to the city, looking for a good bargain or some useful information, before scattering along the ring that surrounds the eternal city. Every day, the space of the bus station blooms with vendors of every kind of object. They mostly come from the former Soviet bloc and the new state of the EU but also come from Africa and South Asia. It is a self-sustained, spontaneous market, still at the beginning of its existence and without the official endorsement of the municipal authority. This is a transient space, for and by nomads who none-theless are increasingly involved in organizing a series of social, economic, and cultural activities. They dwell in this space that belongs to them as they intervene in the "distribution of the sensible" (Rancière 2006) of the political space that otherwise has been sterilized and evacuated. These are border figures who exist between citizenship and exile, in a camp space beyond the dichotomy of legitimi-zation and illegitimization, between multiculturalism and complete integration.

Instead of representing a pathological syndrome that can be cut out, the "out-siders" personify an indication/warning of the central paradox of a new urban policy for Rome that permits no alternative to liberal multicultural hegemony. There is a widespread consensus among Italians that the urban condition needs to be taken seriously, that a managerially illuminated multicultural approach from above should be implemented in cities like Rome or Milan to avoid the otherwise inevitable social calamity (see Paris' banlieus in 2005 and 2007). As Rancière put it (1998), consensus far from representing absence of conflict or peace indicates a subterranean permanent violence intrinsic to any form of social purification and political evacuation. The mechanism of externalization related to migration control is indeed an example of consensus wherever it may occur far from the government's geographical location or within the metropolitan areas of Europe. However, it would be erroneous to configure the idea of consensus as a hegemonic and homogenous space, a plaque, where political life occurs separate from naked life. In this space of purity, we will all be living dominated by an overwhelming power "entrapped in the complementarity of bare life and exception" (Rancière 2011, p. 11). Instead, proper politics are all about perforating this space, to pro-duce breaks of elocution, which before was only heard as mere noise: that is what the documentary achieved. As Rancière repeatedly put it:

> Political argumentation is at one and the same time, the demonstration of a possible world, in which the argument could count as an argument, one that is addressed by a subject qualified to argue, over an identified object, to an addressee who is required to see the object and to hear the argument that he "normally" has no reason either to see or to hear. It is the construction of a paradoxical world that puts together two separate worlds.
>
> (2010, p. 39)

## 7.6 Selam Palace

It is possible to come across/enter a paradoxical world a few miles from the Anag-nina bus station, where the second University of Rome Campus "Tor Vergata" is scattered in a vast, desolate, industrial area. The neighborhood also quarters a huge mall complex and the comforting blue profile of IKEA, plus several ex-factories, now clothing and home furniture outlets that, every day, attract thousands of dis-tracted consumers. One of the university buildings, the former faculty of humani-ties, is a twelve-store blue glass building. Here, without electricity or heating, lives a community of 1,200 refugees from the Horn of Africa, among which there are

*Figure 7.1.* Selam Palace
Photograph by Lorenzo Rinelli

300 women and seventy children (Del Grande, 2007). Some of them were born during the exodus through the Sahara Desert and then across the Mediterranean Sea. These are those who survived the strenuous journey, crossed many borders, and became refugees at the port of Lampedusa but inexorably crashed against the indifference of the post-political contemporary Europe. After being transferred into identification centers in Sicily, they were set free and, like many others before, they caught the first train to Rome without any help or directions.

Here within the peripheries of the metropolis is the very last frontier of Europe: its most internal one and probably the most difficult to decipher. In December 2005, with the support of Action (www.actiondiritti.net/), the building was occupied but, almost immediately, the refugees were cleared out. It is worth noting here that the occupation of Selam Palace is the offspring of a previous long-term occupation in Rome called Hotel Africa. Once 400 people were moved out, they separated; 250 occupied Selam Palace, while other families moved incessantly around the city in order to find a stable and secure residence. They constantly move into and occupy empty buildings and structures that are left rotten and unu-tilized, symbols of the decay and overconsumption of the European society, of the Western society whose urbanscape gets shaped by financial speculations more than the real housing needs of the inhabitants. Like contemporary urban nomads, African migrants and refugees take advantage of the cracks within the city and by doing so, they intervene in the general distribution of the urban space and redraw the line between modes of living in the city and forms of visibility.

Unmistakably, as I mentioned previously, the Italian authorities cleared out the building to reaffirm a certain order of the city where everyone should occupy a specific place as predetermined. Notwithstanding the orderly intent, authorities found nothing better than to leave people under a tent in a poor attempt, as Žižek would put it, "to gentrify the properly traumatic dimension of the political" (2006, p. 72). In response to this act, African refugees reterritorialized the position of speech by staging protests so loud that authorities were forced to let them stay in the last two floors of the building. After that, city hall signed a rent contract with the society that owns the building and in the meantime tried to find solutions to accommodate the refugees. These solutions were usually always temporary and, according to the refugees, simply inadequate, so they refused to move to some another place in the city that they had not checked out for themselves. They decided to settle within Selam Palace, a space of refuge they have built to protect themselves from a city that they say never accepted them. Of course, they complain about the size of the tiny rooms to share with other 5 or 6 people together with services. There are only 55 bathrooms, one toilet every 19 persons and 1 shower every 33.

What is more important, many of the African refugees would like the Italian authorities to erase their biometric data from the EURODAC database (see Chapter 5). According to the Dublin Regulation (2003/343/CE), the state responsible for examining asylum requests is the one through which the asylum seekers first enter into the EU. Once a person is recognized as a refugee, that person cannot apply to another state where he or she may have better chances of success and living conditions. The aim of this regulation, which replaces the original Dublin Convention (1990), is to prevent multiple asylum applications to more than one country. The image of hordes of moving 'asylum shoppers' heading north toward better life conditions provided for the consensus around this legislation which eventually strengthened the role of buffer zones for those state that geographically confine with 'problematic' countries. It is beyond the scope of this analysis to discuss the inescapable consequences of this reform on the lives of asylum seekers who, more and more, are subject to policies of interception, forced rejection, and expulsion. Here, it is important to note that once asylum seekers enter Europe, other forms of externalization intervene. Particularly for this case, the process of externalization operates through the combination of legislation of migration control together with the new urban plan for the city, the residency law, and its rental market. At the beginning of the occupation, African refugees declared Selam Palace as their residence, but when the occupation was declared illegal also, the residence became void. Since then, people in Selam Palace were forced to declare virtual residency in national institutions protecting refugees like the Jesuit Refugees Center located in the historical centre of the city. As a consequence, Selam's dwellers could not make use of social services, schools and hospitals in the close vicinity of the building because residence location matters. Whether they want to go to a doctor or to send their children to maternity school they have to embark in a daily strenuous journey to traverse the whole city to reach a hospital or kindergarten located in the historical center. The rejection of their elective residence translates in the rejection by the city many African refugees complain about. The police act of regulating residency embodies the urban border that refugees question to regain their human dignity. In the last few years inhabitants of the Selam Palace have tried to accommodate and compromise with the bureaucratic logic of counting and regulating residency by the national institutions without success.

Nevertheless, African refugees and migrants know very well how crucial it is to obtain residency. In case they have a spouse abroad, immigrants must present a residence permit to send any money home. Finally, the law establishes a fee of €200 every time a residence permit is released or renewed. This law also denies the fundamental human right to live with one's own family if the house does not satisfy the hygienic standards set by local regulations. Additionally, in the case of negative results from the health commission, the permit of residence will be refused. Without residence, it is impossible to access any public services like nursery school or first aid, which are usually provided by city services. So much for the polycentric city! It is obvious how important access to an adequate habitat is. However, having considered the rental market and social discrimination, this law increases the condition of marginalization for immigrants favoring the diffusion of slums and precarious dwellings.

Musé, one of the residents, complains that "to find a house in Rome is a massive challenge considering the renting rates. And more, when they [the landlords] hear that you are a foreigner they say that they do not rent anymore" (Anonymous n.d.). According to the SUNIA [Sindacato Unitario Nazionale Inquilini ed Assegnatari] (Anonymous 2009), a national union for residents, rents for immigrants are 30% to 50% higher than for Italians, while the offers of houses for rent surged 130%–145% in 1999–2008. Also according to SUNIA, Rome has the highest cost of rent in Italy, which has caused the exodus of the population from the city toward the outside, as I have discussed previously. However, African immigrants and refugees are forced to rent apartments often without a contract or any legal protection. What is more, real estate agencies do not want to deal with immigrants because Italian property owners do not trust them or prefer to deal with them on a condition of quasi-legality. The result is a situation of peripheralization at the margins of urban society in which the majority live in conditions of overcrowding and often unsuitable housing. This marginalization is the product of a virtual anxiety and indifference for those who share the same territory with Italians but who are not considered worthy of trust, even if their presence is crucial for the survival of the city. Once the majority of immigrants share their habitats with more than one other family, most likely, the apartment will not fulfill the hygienic and safety standards set by the law. Apart from bureaucratic violations, it is not rare for overcrowding to lead to tragedies. In January 2007, an apartment caught on fire, and Mary Begum and her son, Hasib, lost their lives. They lived with Mary's husband, another son, and eight other immigrants from Bangladesh. This also happened within the building at the Tor Vergata Campus, as mentioned previously. Reflected on the glass facade of that building, the silhouette of the urbanscape that once defined the imaginary of the city is immortalized by the last scene of Pasolini's "Mamma Roma" (1962). Against that glass is reflected the absurdity that emerges at the interstice of two worlds. The city only exists reflected on the outside. It is extremely close but at the same time definitely inaccessible.

## 7.7  Falling

Today, Rome's strategies are largely based on the outsourcing of all the services of immigrants' initial assistance from civic and religious organizations, which developed in the 1980s when city hall largely ignored the presence of immigrants. As a result, without much assistance from public authorities, in the last twenty years, criminal and neofascist/anti-immigration organizations have infiltrated the system of immigrant and refugee reception, taking control of funds and contracts whose magnitude and ramification has been revealed only recently with dozens of arrests and a hundred people under investigation. For instance,

> in an intercepted phone call, suspect Salvatore Buzzi was quoted saying that "drug trafficking earns less." Other evidence suggests that Rome's mafia has largely given up on trafficking in drugs and has instead embraced the more profitable "immigration business," according to investigators.
>
> (Noack 2014)

Regarding the brick door of Rome, we merely assist in the undisciplined expansion of the city. It is complicated to translate the intricate correlation between the market and urban policy for the city of Rome, but I may summarize it as a permanent condition of exception where financial speculators and developers can prosper. The immigrants who constitute the mobile future resource for the housing market today occupy the new periphery like Italian immigrants and native inhabitants of the proper Rome were once ejected from the center by the fascist regime toward the newly built peripheries known as *borgate*. Italo Insolera explained that this term was first used in 1924 to indicate Acilia, a site 15 km south outside the city of Rome in a zone infested by malaria where people previously living in the city center were relocated: "It is hardly a burg: a portion of the city in the middle of the countryside, which neither one nor the other" (Insolera 1993, p. 144). Nevertheless, despite the similarities, there is a fundamental difference with the urban policy of the past fascist regime. Today, the city administration is not interested in enforcing a strict regulatory plan to guide urban expansion. The externalization of migration control operates within the city of Rome throughout a national legislation that renders it compulsory to have a residence in order to have a permit to stay therefore pushing to the margins, externalizing those without a place to stay. As a result, this social and political condition splits the immigrant persona in two: at the same time they are vital workers for the expanding housing market and concrete victims of the same market speculations that flourish thanks to immigrants' marginalization. Migrants have found themselves relegated to the margins of a society that simply exploits them or ignores them, rendering their presence invisible.

Cynicism and indifference constitute the political dirt that the contemporary urban borders are built with. This resonates with the story of Nabruka that opens this book. The so-called lenience typical of Rome that is exemplified in the typical expression in Roman slang "*Nun me ne po' frega' de meno*" ("I couldn't care less") is indicative of a certain attitude of leaving the person next to us to her destiny. We leave to the task of selecting and filtering out those who do not belong to the state, and we leave it to private corporations to make use of those bodies that have been filtered in. The authorities are in charge of controlling the virtual anxiety of the invasion. Centers for detention for irregular migrants and asylum seekers are nowadays a common feature of the European urbanscape and Rome is no exception. Imagination is as essential as indifference for the functionality of the border control. The imagination of invasion from the south produces virtual anxiety, which conversely allows for the militarization of the border. This is true for the Mediterranean Sea as much as for the city, as I have pointed out throughout this book. By virtual, I mean that the anxiety is experienced fully as a feeling that lurks in ambush on the streets but takes shape almost never and nowhere. This anxiety provokes political immobility, which manifests itself as a wall of indifference within the city regarding the marginalization and suffering of African migrants which, together with a mounting unemployment rate, creates an explosive situation. The result is that "the depressed outskirts of Italian cities are ticking time bombs; far from the eyes of well-heeled vacationers perambulating the Colosseum, the country's fuse is sputtering short" (Severgnini 2014). *What else is new?* People may wonder, as urban unrest is nothing new. The novelty, I maintain, remains within the way we are dealing with this current social tension in a city which we affirm belongs to and represents us. The reality is that we have quit living in the city because we prefer to remain sheltered inside a cultural and political arrangement that supplies us with logic explanation of causes and effects behind the phenomenon of immigration without going through personal experience. We know nothing of our town and even less of migration and migrants who often are the actual dwellers of the city which, we, the so-called proper citizen nationals envision. We move within a city with the frenetic clumsiness of someone who has lost contact with gravity and is falling in the void.

> Heard about the guy who fell off a skyscraper? On his way down past each floor, he kept saying to reassure himself: So far so good . . . so far so good . . . so far so good. How you fall doesn't matter. It's how you land!
>
> (Kassovitz 1995)

## Notes

1   Since 2002, Migreurop has attempted to identify places of detention for migrants and asylum seekers, of which there is no official census, in order to make their existence in Europe visible. See www.migreurop.org/article2537.html?lang=fr

2   Rome, as the capital of the Italian state, has had five other urban plans: 1873, 1883, 1909, 1931, and 1962, but only one – that of 1909 – has been adopted by the city council. The urban history of Rome confirms its peculiarity in terms of the transparency of planning mechanisms (Insolera 1993).

3   Former Minister of the Interior Roberto Maroni said migrants who have landed on the island of Lampedusa threaten the institutional and social structures of Europe (Anon 2011).

4   www.urbistat.it/AdminStat/it/it/demografia/stranieri/roma/58091/4

5   As the book is in production, in the middle of May 2015, the camp at Ponte Mammolo in Rome has been destroyed by city authorities without advice and without providing Eritrean dwellers with a place to stay.

6   In 1962, Pier Paolo Pasolini realized *Mamma Roma* as a complex critique of the urban development of Rome (Rhodes 2007). Its central character, played by a superb Anna Magnani, is a prostitute who dreams to leave behind her life on the streets and bring her son with her to acquire their new home *coi signori* (among gentlemen) in one of the new buildings of the expanding southeast periphery of Rome.

# References

Agamben, G., 1998. *Homo Sacer: Sovereign Power and Bare Life*. Stanford, CA: Stanford University Press.

Agier, M., 2002. Between War and City towards an Urban Anthropology of Refugee Camps. *Ethnography*, 3(3), pp. 317–341.

Anonymous, 2009, La casa in briciole. *megachip.globalist.it*. Available at: http://megachip.globalist.it/Detail_News_Display?ID=58472&typeb=0 [Accessed 13 December 2014]

Anonymous, 2009. Casa, il Sunia: È emergenza affitti – Corriere della Sera. Available at: www.corriere.it/economia/09_febbraio_10/affitti_allarme_sunia_c4429edc-f76a-11dd-8e36–00144f02aabc.shtml [Accessed 13 December 2010]

Anonymous, 2011. Italy Warns Europe over Migrants. *BBC*. Available at: www.bbc.co.uk/news/world-europe-12461866 [Accessed 16 February 2011]

Anonymous, 2013a. Dalla dittatura alla baraccopoli: il destino dei 100 eritrei di Ponte Mammolo. *Redattore Sociale*. Available at: www.redattoresociale.it/Notiziario/Articolo/441736/Dalla-dittatura-alla-baraccopoli-il-destino-dei-100-eritrei-di-Ponte-Mammolo [Accessed 25 May 2014]

Anonymous, 2013b. Immigrant Detainees in Rome Sew Lips Shut to Protest Conditions. *Euronews*. Available at: www.euronews.com/2013/12/23/immigrant-detainees-in-rome-sew-lips-shut-to-protest-conditions/ [Accessed January 15, 2014]

Ansa, 2014. Italy Rapped over Reception for Refugees – English. *ANSA.it*. Available at: www.ansa.it/english/news/politics/2014/11/04/italy-rapped-over-reception-for-refugees_ec2d573b-edb8–475a-84e0-de1726ed9bd0.html [Accessed 13 December 2014]

Arendt, H., 1973. *The Origins of Totalitarianism*. New York, NY: Harcourt Brace Jovanovich.

Balibar, E., 2003. *We, the People of Europe? Reflections on Transnational Citizenship*. Princeton, NJ: Princeton University Press.

Berger, J., 1989. *A Seventh Man*. Harmondsworth, UK: Penguin Books

Bullaro, G. R., 2010. *From Terrone to Extracomunitario: New Manifestations of Racism in Contemporary Italian Cinema: Shifting Demographics and Changing Images in a Multi-Cultural Globalized Society*. Leicester, UK: Troubador Publishing Ltd.

Caesar, Julius. 2006. *The Gallic War*. Translated by H. J. Edwards. Mineola, NY: Dover Publications.

Chambers, I., 2008. *Mediterranean Crossings: The Politics of an Interrupted Modernity*. Durham, NC: Duke University Press.

Deleuze, G. & Guattari, F., 1987. *A Thousand Plateaus*. Minneapolis, MN: University of Minnesota Press.

Derrida, J., 2003. *On Cosmopolitanism and Forgiveness*. Hackensack, NJ: Routledge.

Ferrente, A., 2009. *L'Orchestra di Piazza Vittorio*. Magnolia Home Entertainment.

Del Grande, G., 2007, Fortress Europe: In fuga dall'Eritrea: il deserto, il mare e i ghetti di Roma. Available at: http://fortresseurope.blogspot.com/2005/12/in-fuga-da-tripoli-verso-i-ghetti-della.html [Accessed 25 February 2011]

Haddad, Emma. 2007. Danger Happens at the Border. In *Borderscapes*, edited by Prem Kumar Rajaram and Carl Grundy-Warr, 119–36. Minneapolis, MN: University of Minnesota Press.

Hardt, Michael, and Antonio Negri. 2001. *Empire*. Cambridge, MA: Harvard University Press.

Harvey, D., 2008. The Right to the City. *New Left Review*, 53, pp. 23–40.

Insolera, I., 1993. *Roma moderna: Un secolo di storia urbanistica, 1870–1970*. Rome, Italy: Einaudi.

Isin, Engin, and Kim Rygiel. 2007. Abject Spaces: Frontiers, Zones, Camps. In E. Dauphinee and C. Masters, (eds.), *Logics of Biopower and the War on Terror* (pp. 181–203). London, UK: Palgrave Macmillan.

Kassovitz, M., 1995. *La Haine*. Available at: www.imdb.com/title/tt0113247/ [Accessed 13 December 2010]

Lakhous, A., 2006. *Scontro Di Civilta' per UN Ascensore a Piazza Vittorio*. New York, NY: Europa Editions.

Lefebvre, H., 1992. *The Production of Space*. London, UK: Wiley-Blackwell.

Martin, A. & Allen, P., 2009. Asylum Seekers Burning off Fingerprints to Conceal IDs. *Daily Mail (London)*. Available at: www.highbeam.com/doc/1G1-206009874.html [Accessed 20 April 2014]

Mcclelland, Mac. 2014. How to Build a Perfect Refugee Camp. *The New York Times*, February 13. Available at: www.nytimes.com/2014/02/16/magazine/how-to-build-a-perfect-refugee-camp.html [Accessed 20 April 2015]

Menghi, B., 2010. I residenti stranieri nel comune di Roma 2009. Available at: www.google.com/url?sa=t&rct=j&q=&esrc=s&source=web&cd=2&ved=0CDEQFjAB&url=http%3A%2F%2Fwww.comune.roma.it%2FPCR%2Fresources%2Fcms%2Fdocuments%2FI_residenti_stranieri_nel_Comune_di_Roma_2009.pdf&ei=a1dpT9WzKKSXiAKL09z9BA&usg=AFQjCNHOkARRn-8S_Hbw1_G4sPcC50WMqg [Accessed 21 March 2010]

Morassut, R., 2003. Roma Capitale di Pace del Mediterraneo. Available at: http://static.repubblica.it/roma/piano_regolatore/presentazione.pdf [Accessed 16 February 2011]

Noack, R., 2014. For Rome's Mafia, More Refugees Means More Money. *The Washington Post*. Available at: www.washingtonpost.com/blogs/worldviews/wp/2014/12/04/for-romes-mafia-more-refugees-means-more-money/ [Accessed 13 December 2014]

Parati, G., 2005. *Migration Italy: The Art of Talking Back in a Destination Culture*. Toronto, ON: University of Toronto Press.

Pasolini, P., 1962. *Mamma Roma*. Available at: www.imdb.com/title/tt0056215/ [Accessed 1 March 2011]

Pink Floyd, 1977. *Animals*. Parlophone.

Pugliese, J., 2010. *Transmediterranean: Diaspora, Histories, Geopolitical Spaces*. New York, NY: Peter Lang.

Rancière, J., 1998. *Disagreement: Politics and Philosophy*. Minneapolis, MN: University of Minnesota Press.

Rancière, J., 2006. *The Politics of Aesthetics*. London, UK: Continuum.

Rancière, J., 2010. *Dissensus: On Politics and Aesthetics*. London, UK: Bloomsbury Academic.

Rancière, J., 2011. The Thinking of Dissensus: Politics and Aesthetics. In *Reading Rancière*, pp. 1–17. London: Continuum.

Rhodes, J. D., 2007. *Stupendous, Miserable City: Pasolini's Rome*. Minneapolis, MN: University of Minnesota Press.

Sassen, S., 2001. *The Global City: New York, London, Tokyo*. 2nd ed. Princeton, NJ: Princeton University Press.

Sayad, A., 2004. *The Suffering of the Immigrant*. Cambridge, UK: Polity Press.

Segre, A. & Yimer, D., 2008. *Like a Man on Earth*. Available at: http://likeamanonearth.blogspot.com/ [Accessed 21 September 2011]

Severgnini, B., 2014. Is Rome Burning? *The New York Times*. Available at: www.nytimes.com/2014/11/25/opinion/beppe-severgnini-is-rome-slowly-burning.html [Accessed 13 December 2014]

Sharma, Nandita. 2006. Home Economics: Nationalism and the Making of "Migrant Workers" in Canada. Toronto, ON: University of Toronto Press.

# 8    Lampedusa reloaded

*I began wondering if we did not still need such founding works today, ones that would use a similar dialectics of rerouting (détournement), asserting for example, political strength but, simultaneously, the rhizome of a multiple relationship with the Other and basing every community's reasons for existence on a modern form of the sacred which would be all in all, a Poetics of Relation.*

*(Glissant 1997, p. 16)*

## 8.1    Detour

The epigraph from Édouard Glissant's *Poetics of Relation* with which this concluding chapter begins reminds us that the founding texts of European and African civilizations – the Bible, the Aeneid, the Chansons de Geste, the Egyptian Book of the Dead – are inherently prophetic in announcing the failure of each community, afterward deemed to be reborn through a vital errantry. *Errance* for Glissant does not translate in an aimless wandering, or in a circular form of nomadism, or any form of conquering exploration. The word infers a note of the sacred, a necessary change of direction – a *détournement* – experienced by individuals who are drawn into a journey by self-discovery. The term moves beyond the pursuit and triumphs of rootedness despite the religious and political use to which these stories will have then been put (Glissant & Wing 1997, p. 15).

Nevertheless, this book fell short of being a eulogy to the idea of African migration into Europe but certainly moved away from mainstream approaches that lead either to assistance for migrants or rebuttal. In too many instances, this book has highlighted the suffering and difficulties of African migrants as they journey through the desert and the sea. The point here instead is that African migrations cannot be seen either as an emergency or analyzed only through the lens of an econometric calculus of push/pull factors "in which economists and especially econometricians discuss the problems of migration in complimentary or antithetical terms of benefits and costs" (Sayad 2004, p. 77). Both approaches regard African migration as an accident that casually happens but which holds neither reference nor correlation with the geopolitics of nation-states. More importantly, such a methodological approach has led to the pervasiveness of policies over politics, management of emergencies over encounters and confrontations, widening the gap between communities of people and a pervasive network of institutions. In its place, this chapter brings into view a series of processes, problems, and instances that form the substrata to elaborate a theoretical approach – different from integration or expulsion – that takes into consideration the political subjectivity of undocumented African migrants and its consequences for the European community.

Lacking legal authorization to dwell in Europe, African migrants without proper papers have traditionally been treated as passive objects, dependent on a network of human smuggling operatives, regulatory measures, and the state's security apparatus. Recently, scholars have begun to challenge this approach (Nair 2012; Butler 2011), stressing the kind of political agency that undocumented migrants and refugees may produce to question the arrangement of global politics. However, is it even possible for undocumented migrants to be effective political actors if they are excluded not only from formal channels of politics but also society due to the threat of deportation?

Throughout this book, I have conceptualized the very act of African migration into Europe as a true act of politics mingled with historical issues of colonialism to contemporary geopolitical instances. For that reason, I intend to conceptually dislodge the question of whether African migrants without proper documentation may or may not operate politically without the help of activists holding citizenship. On the contrary, I maintain that European/national/local political struggles that are always confronted with the need to translate their different aims across many different spaces and instances find their preeminent translator within the border struggles of undocumented migrants. In the contemporary globalized world, the problem of continuity in the organization of a collective opposition to neoliberal capitalism and militarization of frontiers cannot be addressed without confronting that opposition with the practice of border struggles, which are often caused by the same institutional framework. By focusing on the material conditions that generate the tensions at the border, a political space opened up in Lampedusa within which new kinds of political subjects operate beyond the logic of citizenship and conventional methods of political organization. As Butler suggests:

> To rethink the space of appearance in order to understand the power and effect of public demonstrations for our time, we will need to understand the bodily dimensions of action, what the body requires, and what the body can do, especially when we must think about bodies together, what holds them there, their conditions of persistence and of power.
>
> (Butler 2011)

Where do bodies gather together? Where do relations entangle? The island of Lampedusa indeed represents such a critical node, along the global axes between north and south, where rhizomic relations are hosting new dialectics of rerouting to a different idea of community "based on a modern idea of the sacred" (Glissant & Wing 1997, p. 16). The *LampedusaInFestiva* event that has been on this island for a few years has provided the rich background for the fabrication of such relations.

In fact, the island of Lampedusa has reached a symbolic status, both as the camp and the door of Europe, with the power to attract and catalyze different subjects, active on different struggles, whether with or without proper documentation.

> There are also [. . .] real places - places that do exist and that are formed in the very founding of society - which are something like counter-sites, a kind of effectively enacted utopia in which the real sites, all the other real sites that can be found within the culture, are simultaneously represented, contested and inverted.
>
> (Foucault 1986, p.24)

Lampedusa, being a tiny island in front of Africa, can be one of those places envisioned in Foucault's idea. As described in Chapter 3, scrolling through reviews of the most attractive tourist destinations in the Mediterranean and around the world, Lampedusa ranks high, with its turquoise waters and white sandy beaches. At the same time, the island has become the center of the European and Italian policies of migration control, as the route that links Morocco and Spain was closed off ten years ago (Dines *et al.* 2015). Later, Lampedusa acquired greater visibility because of a decade-long detrimental political relationship with Gaddafi to stem the flow of African migrants, which was followed by the current cruel civil war that projected Lampedusa to the forefront of the global war on terrorism.[1]

Lampedusa is all of this and much more – like a counter-site that has been generated by the confluence of endless attention and energy. Paolo Cutitta, referring to the theatrical piece of "Die Schutzbefohlenen" by Elfriede Jelinek, wrote some time ago that Lampedusa went from being the stage for the spectacle of migration control in the Mediterranean to being an actual show represented in theaters around Europe. Lampedusa is a symbol and the space where African migrants, European tourists, national institutions, and locals simultaneously share the state of being contemporary, sometimes colliding toward new directions.

Meanwhile, the touristic show must go on, and Lampedusa has found that the sinister allure of its dark side could represent an alternative type of attraction. As I mentioned in Chapter 4, how the border functions has to do with what is said and what is seen or concealed. This is very much true in reference to the boats used by African migrants and seized by Italian authorities. The boats had to be hidden away or destroyed, and those left had to be eliminated. For example, compared to a few years ago when the wrecks of migrants' boats were hidden from vacationers who were kept away from the reality of washed-up bodies nearby, today those same wrecks are on display where everyone can see them. While morbid and recreational activities seldom go together, on this tiny Mediterranean island, tourists from all over Europe keep coming down to these sandy beaches not in spite of but because of the deaths that take place there. An unlikely postcard from Lampedusa would feature green turtles diving between shipwrecks and cadavers. If Pugliese located in Lampedusa an "aporetic coexistence of the penal/holiday Island" (2010, p. 271) in which the two sides never touch each other, today the two aspects not only coexist but nourish and replenish each other.

*Figure 8.1.*
Photograph by Lorenzo Rinelli[2]

## 8.2    An island of relation

> *The tale of errantry is the tale of Relation.*
>
> *(Glissant 1997, p. 18)*

Filmmaker Dagmawi Yimer has returned several times to the island since he landed on this tiny rock in 2006 as an undocumented migrant. We met the first time in 2009 when we discussed his experience in Italy and the beginning of his promising career with the realization of *Like a Man on Earth*, the leitmotiv of this book. In 2010, he shot *Soltanto il mare* (*Nothing But the Sea*), an expression of affection for the island that saved his life. For the first time, a movie made by an African migrant set the dialogue between two parts that are often seen separated: migrants and locals. Dagmawi's movie draws attention to that rhizome of relations that constitutes the *raison d'être*, the essence of Lampedusa. In a discussion, I asked the filmmaker about the risk that the island would turn into a sort of Alcatraz where vacationers could go and authenticate what they have been watching daily on the news. Yimer responded:

> The more time I spend here [Lampedusa], the more I understand that I know nothing about this island. In my opinion, Lampedusa is more serene now than before. That was the time of the great fear of the invasion [2011]. For example, previously, the boats were in the middle of the island, hidden. Someone started a fire and the boats were gone. Before, they used to hide the boats. Lampedusa must act with intelligence. I think the island should not change its

nature. Locals have other problems [lack of schools and hospitals]. It is not to use immigration to market the island but to comprehend that it is something bigger than the island, not as a handicap but a point of leverage. Lampedusa is unique even because of that. The island is more peaceful because locals have noticed that vacationers come here. They feared no one would come anymore. Also, thanks to the Pope, many arrived in 2013.

(interview recorded by the author on 29 September 2014, Lampedusa)

In July 2013, Pope Francis chose Lampedusa for his first pastoral visit outside the Vatican since his election in March 2013 (BBC News 2013). In choosing Lampedusa, he drove the world's media attention to this tiny island and the destiny of African migrants and the local population. The Pope emphasized the shared responsibility we have toward other human beings as our brothers and sisters whose grievances we must feel and share in this globalized world we inhabit. "Where is your brother?" His blood cries out to me, says the Lord. This is not a question directed to others; it is a question directed to me, to you, to each of us" (Anonymous 2013). The Pope's consideration calls for a sympathetic approach (see Chapter 5) (Chismar 1988) because it involves the direct participation of individuals in engaging the law and related institutions when it comes to rescuing the Other. It also interrogates Lampedusa as much as other liminal spaces around the world, whether we come across torrid deserts, deep blue seas, or urban peripheries at the margins of contemporary metropolis.

The aesthetic aspect of the event is also significant. Due to the large attendance, the local soccer field in Lampedusa served as the venue for the Pope's religious service. Behind the Pope, as the camera spanned over the altar, the world caught a glimpse of several wrecked boats that had been used by migrants to reach the island. This wreckage, acting as a symbol of the precarious arrival of migrants to the island, had previously been hidden in the cemetery of boats in the middle of the island and kept in custody as proof of crime, so that no one could make any use of them (see Chapter 4). The boats were stored away from view in a calculated act to exclude the symbol of African migrations across the Mediterranean and the illegal trade of people smuggling, with the fight against such criminal activity being strategically chosen by European and national institutions to enable them to wrap the militarization of the frontier with a legitimizing humanitarian flag. Now those boats were on the screens of millions of global viewers. Something had changed within "the spectacle of migrant illegality" (De Genova 2013b) that had been constantly generating fear, rejection, and therefore invisibility of the corporeal presence of migrants. For the duration of the Pope's Mass, news and viewers registered the presence of the boats, which came to frame the presence of migrants on the island and encapsulated the nature of the frontier. It is not within the scope of this chapter to emphasize how the spectacle of the border supplies the scene for migrants' exclusion (see De Genova 2013b). Rather quite the opposite. For the duration of the Pope's Mass, the boats were the new frame of the spectacle within which the presence of migrants baptized the island in its nature of a frontier.

Before imparting my blessing to you I want to thank you once again; you people of Lampedusa, for the example of love, charity and hospitality that you have set us and are still setting us. The Bishop said that Lampedusa is a beacon. May this example be a beacon that shines throughout the world, so that people will have the courage to welcome those in search of a better life.

(Anonymous 2013)

It is possible, then, to envision the island of Lampedusa as the magnet and the symbol for political mobilization at the international level among African migrants struggling with borders, together with activists operating on migration issues, hence creating a space of relation, exchange, and encounter where everything is possible.

## 8.3   Enter Triton

*The thinking of errantry conceives of totality but willingly renounces any claims of sum it up or possess it.*

*(Glissant & Wing 1997, p. 21)*

On 3 and 11 October 2013, two of the worst shipwrecks in the recent history of African migration through the Mediterranean occurred just a half mile off the coast of the island of Lampedusa, taking the lives of over 600 people.[3] Since then, the island has been the beacon envisioned by the Pope, not only of European attention but, more significantly, of political creativity. Following the tragedy, the Italian government promptly granted citizenship post mortem to the deceased while the survivors risked being incriminated for illegal immigration. As Pablo Ordaz stated in his article: "The dead, however, will remain. Unable to be identified, they have been awarded a coffin, a number and a piece of land in cemeteries of Sicily to rest, now with the European nationality for which they risked their lives."(2013). Ordaz reported that the authorities initially refused to help local fishers in their efforts to rescue people. He reminds us how the Italian authorities actually have the right to stop people who want to rescue migrants at sea since "complicity with illegal migration," as has been extensively discussed in Chapter 5, could constitute the crime of abetting irregular immigration.

Thus, "what place is given to life, death, and the human body? How are they inscribed in the order of power?" (Mbembe 2003, p. 12). Achille Mbembe's questions stridently resonate in relation to the absurdity of a post mortem citizenship. It is evident how this event reveals the inconsistency of the contemporary European structure: its simultaneous normative idealism supposedly anchored to universal human rights principles coupled with the enduring selective dehumanizing practices of colonization and eradication. I am referring here to aggressive business practices in Africa, from oil boring to land grabbing and overfishing, which pair with restrictive and selective visa policies and corruption that date back to the end of European colonialism.

Reflecting upon the *ex morte* citizenship, we are perhaps led to believe that the whole notion of sovereignty subsists in the right to kill and to let die certain human beings, selected on the basis of race/gender/class/geopolitical subdivisions. Needless to say, with this premise, we could tend to accept that the territorial state owns unconditionally that overwhelming power. However, often African migrants defeat the limits of the contemporary European state, perforating that territory which, in mainstream IR theory, still defines sovereignty, therefore subverting and appropriating the idea of sovereignty by violating or transgressing its limits. But more importantly, they do so by seizing the idea of death and with it the peril of death from which politics emerges.

Because of these tragic events, Lampedusa then became once more the stage where European and national institutions could accommodate violent contradictions, celebrating their courage and perils while shutting the door to those alive. Migrants' deaths, according to Hein de Haas (2013), have been caused by the introduction in the last twenty years of visa requirements by European states and the consequential impossibility for African migrants to obtain a visa coupled with the increasing militarization of the frontiers between Africa and Europe. To celebrate a posthumous citizenship for those who were always refused legal acceptance into the European community is violent irony turned tragic. The incessant occurrence of shipwrecks proves the state of affairs after twenty years of "stemming the flow of a delusional African migrant 'invasion'" (de Haas, 2013) Increasing border controls on the western route and then across the entire Sahara Desert has not brought to a halt but rather "*diverted* trans-Saharan and trans-Mediterranean migration routes" (Ibid.). This is one instance of "rerouting," as mentioned in Glissant's opening epigraph that shows the failure of the European community because the militarization of the border has forced migrants and refugees to travel along routes that are more dangerous and has made them dependent on smugglers who facilitate border crossings. However, a new route for the European community has been set. In fact, as much as the militarization of the Sahara and Mediterranean has generated a network of alliances and multiple relationships among migrants heading north, the tragic event of the beginning of October 2013 marked a sharp turning point regarding the discourse of migration from Africa to Europe around the island of Lampedusa.

Confronted by a massive media crusade of humanitarian anguish, the Italian government launched the operation *Mare Nostrum*, a policy of rescuing people lost at sea beyond territorial waters. Oddly enough, Italian authorities chose the same Latin expression that I discussed in Chapter 7 regarding the new urban plan for Rome. I have underlined how problematic it is to use the Roman imperial tag to denominate a rescue operation in the Mediterranean. Back in the Roman Empire, the idea of *Mare Nostrum* entailed totality of control over a sea that ironically was considered by Roman emperors as a mere lake already conceptualized as a homogenous space of confinement, possession, and colonization. The code then recalls, at best, a hierarchy between the rescuer and the victim. The rescuer is also a military persona who keeps policing the frontier while rescuing migrants adrift, as indicated unmistakably on the Italian Ministry of Defense Web page, stating that the operation consisted of "an empowerment of the Migration Flows Control (CFM) activities carried out within the Italian Navy operation *Constant Vigilance*."[4]

Notwithstanding the various criticisms, the mission was primarily to save lives and represented a substantial improvement compared to the previous policy of stemming the flow. Unfortunately, in November 2014, one year later, the *Mare Nostrum* operation came to an end due to both economic and policy issues. It has been said that it was too expensive – €9.5 million for *Mare Nostrum* versus €3 million for Triton – and, more importantly, it encouraged further immigration. According to the Navy's website:

> During the last 364 days of relentless activity in all weather conditions, the units of the Italian Navy have engaged in 421 operations and rescued 150,810 migrants; 5 mother ships have been seized and 330 alleged smugglers have been brought to justice. These results have been achieved by 900 sailors engaged any single day, 32 naval units and 2 submarines taking shifts in over 45,000 hours of active operations.[5]

The operation *Mare Nostrum*, it is worth noting, was entirely financed by the Italian state. Therefore, Italy pressured the European Union (EU) to launch a new mission sharing in costs and responsibilities. One year later, the Task Force for the Mediterranean, chaired by the European Commission, finally led in November 2014 to the launch of Triton, the new joint operation of Frontex in the Mediterranean whose cost had to be equally supported by the Union.

Triton's mandate is limited to the patrol of the Schengen Area border, including an extant 30 miles of territorial waters, yet unlike *Mare Nostrum* it has no humanitarian component for the search and rescue of migrants. While *Mare Nostrum* has been operating in much closer geographic proximity to the north African coast, Triton essentially remains a monitoring operation of the Schengen Area border within a 30-mile limit. In addition, as discussed in Chapter 6, the sole rationale behind the creation of Frontex was the strengthening of border security by ensuring the coordination of member states' efforts for effective common management of external borders.

## 8.4    The Charter of Lampedusa

*The space of appearance comes into being wherever men are together in the manner of speech and action, and therefore predates and precedes all formal constitution of the public realm and the various forms of government, that is, the various forms in which the public realm can be organized.*

*(Arendt 1998, p. 199)*

According to Arendt, then, timing appears to be crucial in terms of political activism as much as the space where action takes form. The two elements, as indicated in her epigraph from "The Human Condition," cannot be separated. Following the tragedy of October 2013, a group composed mainly of Italian nationals decided to gather at the end of January 2014 in Lampedusa for a few days to write the Charter of Lampedusa. It is clear from the preamble that those who drafted the document did not seek approval from any institutions, nor intend to follow a normative path.

The Charter is not intended as a draft law, legislative proposal or as a petition to governments. All the groups and individuals who undersign the Charter of Lampedusa commit to putting it into practice and to defending its principles through our endeavors, in the ways, languages and actions that each of us considers relevant, whether or not the Charter obtains recognition by current state and/or supra-state institutions.[6]

The intent in this case is to anticipate and exceed the subdivision and allocation of persons already made by the state and European institutions within the discourse of migration through the Mediterranean. The EU's – therefore, "the member states'" – position is one of citizenship without community, while the progressive position, which people like Derrida, Balibar, and Mezzadra advocate, only to mention a few, envisage is one of the possibilities of community without citizenship. However, the realities of "neo-racism" (Balibar 2001) and the dynamics and pragmatics of migrancy and migration control call for both a different way of organizing and, if possible, a different analytic. And this is where the Charter comes in. The very idea of the public with regard to the space of politics is being disputed here, with the political intent of the Charter aiming to extricate the discourse of migration out from the false quarrel between public/state – institutions and agencies – and private – fishers, migrants and activists. What is private pours out into the public realm and becomes common because the real tragedy over the past twenty years of migration between Africa and Europe has been to systematically avoid confrontations and discussions and, most of all, to refuse to take responsibility, leaving policies to take the place of politics: "It makes of ethics and politics a technology" (Derrida 1992, p. 45). In other words, the last twenty years of externalization of migration control in Europe has meant the transition from an idea of a community of people toward a community of institutions relying on a complex apparatus. The opposite heading, not just another, if we reflect upon Derrida's warnings against the return in Europe of a centralizing hegemony on one hand and the multiplication of borders on the other.

The very public character of the political space, not only with regard to immigration, has been occupied, and then deserted, in order to generate a vacuum that is the space of exception. There is an urgent need to recuperate the idea of human relation. Only a redefinition of the idea of the border as a moment of confrontation and disagreement that is never fixed and stable can reduce the fracture between politics and policies. At that point, politics is no longer defined as the exclusive business of the public sphere as institutions define it. Lampedusa has been defined as the door of Europe, and the crucial debate is about when/why it shuts down and who is doing it. That is why the Charter affirms *the freedom of everybody to resist these whole policies and, as well as in their specific operating mechanisms, such as the institutions of containment and/or detention centers, of borders, acted through stay permits linked to work contracts.* The limits and contradictions of the migration discourse in the Mediterranean are exposed, and the link between the spectacle of the border and the legitimacy of the current migration management can be severed.

Of course, there are reasons to be suspicious and critical of such an idealized political move. As a matter of fact, promoters and subscribers of the Charter are, more often than not, Italian nationals and from the Northern Hemisphere. This simple observation brings up the dilemma of how to make sense of those who are not part of this political action, those who remain outside, especially when they constitute the subjects that the Charter is seeking to address. Notwithstanding the respectable intentions of the project, there is a risk of reifying the same old problem of the exclusion of the space of appearance for migrants that reminds one of Spivak's famous dilemma: "Can the Subaltern Speak?" (1996). In that seminal essay, Spivak worried that even the most benevolent effort to give silenced others a voice merely repeats the very silencing it aims to combat. After all, European colonialists often thought of themselves as well intentioned.

This is a crucial node because, as I have highlighted in reference to Arendt's epigraph, we cannot separate the space of appearance from the space of politics, and to be deprived of the space of appearance or visibility is to be deprived of reality, which the virtual space of the Web, where the Charter operates, can only widen. The whole project attempts to predate political institutions that codify rules and monopolize the position of sentinel for the existence of those rights in the name of those who have not been deprived of them. Whenever the Charter of Lampedusa lists a set of specific freedoms – freedom to stay, of choice, and certainly of movement – and detailed rights – the right to work, the right to receive education, and the right to social and political participation, the right to health care – the whole project stumbles upon the initial theoretical impasse of "The Human Condition." Migrants, refugees, and asylum seekers are excluded from such a space as much as slaves, foreigners and barbarians were cast out of the Greek polis that Arendt initially celebrated. Is this, then, the only way the plurality can take form? Are migrants, then, socially and politically dead, waiting for entitled citizens to breathe life into them?

It is worth remembering how, later, Arendt, in "The Decline of the Nation-State and the End of the Rights of the Man" (Arendt 1973), turned her attention to the fate of the stateless and refugees when she famously emphasized the right of those people to have rights above and before everything else. The right to have rights, as a matter of fact, does not depend upon any particular organization for its legitimacy and continuation. The philosopher felt the need, then (1973, p. 284), to point out the inadequacy of treaties and institutions to deal with people moving across lands and institutions. Acknowledging the significance of Arendt's work on the question of stateless populations deprived of any civil and civic rights, Etienne Balibar notes that Arendt performs a double inversion of political philosophy by reinstalling "right in the middle of debates about citizenship and political regimes." (2001, p. 17). Her move thus sets the stage for a "new foundation for the public sphere, where collective political *action* (or praxis) takes place, and not only the management of population movements and policing of social conflicts" (Ibid.). However, the Charter captures Arendt's essential insight when, in Article II3F, the author states that:

> Every person, regardless of their citizenship and legal, social or economic status, if they so wish, must be able to fully take part in their public and social

environment, and have full access to the places where this participation happens to be, including electoral and representative processes of democratic institutions on local, national and supranational levels.

The whole amount of European *acquis*, the entire list of human rights treaties and the national law and constitutions are significant only within the discourse of the right to have rights – that is, the right to and act in any community like an active subject. Hence, we return to the initial questions: what is necessary because the political action takes form? And who is entitled to be part of the action and to speak?

## 8.5 Militarization and resistance

The way we answer these questions is critical. If we follow the mainstream approach of establishing the political space, undocumented migrants and stateless individuals are excluded. In order to explore different paths following promising detours, I have chosen to focus on the political and cultural project of *LampedusainFestival*. The event was set up six years ago by the local group Askavusa[7] – which means bare feet in the Sicilian dialect to indicate raw interaction with the land – to be a festival of "communities, migrations, struggles, responsible tourism, and sea stories."[8] I participated and helped with the organization of the last event at the end of September 2014, with the aim to support the political project but also to weigh the impact of migrants in terms of political participation and creativity in dialogue with European activists and local Lampedusans.

As I anticipated, Lampedusa has ceased to be plainly a dichotomous space, as defined some time ago by Joseph Pugliese, struggling between being a holiday isle and a penal colony. The contemporary image/identity of this island is much more complex. A few years ago, Pugliese, drawing on Foucault's idea of crisis heterotopias, described the island as a space where migrants who crossed the sea are deemed to "[remain] invisible to First-World subjects despite being directly in their line of sight" (2009, p. 674). To support his vision of Lampedusa, Pugliese recalls the time when rebellious southerners at the end of the nineteenth century fought against the violent unification and colonization of the whole peninsula by an army under the guidance of the Kingdom of Savoy. When captured, the rebels were generally exiled to Lampedusa.

According to the Australian scholar, Lampedusa has now simply "morphed into another form of island gulag with a contemporary immigration detention prison" (2009, p. 667). Without dismissing the significant historical and cultural analysis provided in his work – which I have mentioned in Chapter 4 with reference to the previous status of Lampedusa – the impetus of Pugliese's choice to apply the idea of crisis heterotopias to contemporary Lampedusa derives from a conventional and problematic conception of the border as an impermeable, permanent space of exception. Such a theoretical approach runs the risk of reifying the isolation of migrants and drastically undermining their political agency (Mezzadra & Neilson 2013; Balibar & Hahn 2002). Although Pugliese borrows from Foucault to articulate his conception of Lampedusa, it seems that Agamben's conception of *bare life* would be more appropriate here, with all the risks involved. With the aggressive multiplication, virtualization, and intensification of the camp logic today, there is an urgent need to critically engage the conditions of encampment or capture and the multiple practices through which migrants, refugees, and asylum seekers escape or contest these techniques of policing and provisioning.

> This, of course, is not to romanticize migrants as a presumptive revolutionary subject, but rather to discern in migrant practices and struggles an instance of what Foucault's contemporaries, the Situationists (Debord, Vaneigem), theorized as "the revolution of everyday life."
>
> (De Genova 2013a)

From this point of view, mobility, settlement, and participation become the basis for overcoming *bare life* by reaffirming the dignity and agency of migrants and refugees without romanticizing their capacity for agency. Through attentiveness to the heterogeneity of the camp effect today and the insurrectional practices that contest or appropriate it, it becomes possible to carry out a productive critique of the post-colonial and global present (Soguk 2014). At the moment we are seriously elaborating on Foucauldian terms, we must intend the frontier as a battleground where "multiple devices of subjection are confronted with practices of subjectification" (Mezzadra & Neilson 2013, p. 252). Take, for instance, the racially motivated violent clashes that took place between 7 and 9 January 2010 in Rosarno, a small city of Calabria, a region in the deep south of Italy. Rosarno lies in a fertile land that has always been at the forefront of the war against *'Ndrangheta* – a Mafia-type criminal organization based in Calabria. The clashes, initiated after the wounding of two African immigrants by unknown individuals with an air rifle, later turned into an urban revolt that saw opposing forces, locals and immigrants.

> Following the first incident, more than 100 immigrants rampaged through the town on Thursday night, smashing car windows with steel bars, setting rubbish bins and cars on fire, and clashing with police in riot gear. Some 2,000 immigrants demonstrated in front of the town hall yesterday to protest.
>
> (Hooper 2010)

*The Economist* later defined the violence migrants had to face as "an ethnic clearance of Balkan swiftness, nastiness and comprehensiveness" (Anonymous 2010). Following Foucault, it is important to analyze power relations that operate in the area, dispossessing and exploiting individuals up to the point when individuals reach a moment of excess that constitutes their political subjectification. The local *'Ndrangheta* dominates the fruit and vegetable businesses in the area. Therefore, it controls the migrants working as fruit pickers. Migrants revolting against exploitation and camp-life conditions generate a force that penetrates and intersects local questions of mobility, labor and civil justice. Eventually, several migrants obtained legal permits to stay because of their struggle and their capacity to raise their voices against one of the most powerful criminal organizations in the world. "It is precisely when one enacts the rights that one does not have that one becomes a political subject" (Isin & Rygiel 2007, p. 189). The energy and "time they have not" (Ranciere & Reid 2012) as labor power then is translated in political consciousness and inspired local initiatives along the same lines, because "It is precisely when one enacts the rights that one does not have that one becomes a political subject" (Isin & Rygiel 2007, p.189). At that precise moment, I suggest, that the border emerges, whenever practices of control enter in relation, or rather collide with migrants' obstinate trajectories. In this way, the new frontier between Africa and Europe is to be located around points of interaction between the implementation of policies of migration control and acts of flows, that is, at the juncture of multiple discourses of migration and political struggle.

> Borders have lives of their own. They move, shift, metamorphose, edge, retract, emerge tall and powerful or retreat into the shadows exhausted, or even grow irrelevant.
>
> (Soguk 2007, p. 283)

When borders materialize, then, they localize in time and space the acts of power and resistance, which conversely mold new emerging and shifting frontiers. Borders are spaces, in the Foucaldian language, where it is difficult to locate power on one distinct point and resistance on another.

Thus, undoubtedly, it is important to look back at the colonial encampment and its mechanisms of control but without missing the role of derritorialization at the core of the disjunctive global cultural economy, as Appadurai years ago foresaw (Appadurai 1990). At the same time, it is crucial to pay attention to the consequential reterritorialization operated by migrants as a form of response. Turning our attention to Lampedusa, beyond historical critique, the presence of camp conditions and migrants' assertion of their right to move or settle highlight the south-north assemblages of power characterized by the externalization of migration control as revealed by the arrangements between Gaddafi's Libya and Italy until 2011 and the increasing militarization of the Mediterranean (Biemann & Holmes 2006). Simply put, border struggles are not simply fought at the border because what is fought at the moment of the border has repercussions and resonances that transcend the moment and locality of the border. This space/time cannot be separated from the act that generates it, and of that act it is important to highlight the role of migrants subject in participating in the dialectic of inclusion and exclusion, and in marking the spatio-temporal dimension of borders and frontiers.

Returning to the venue of *LampedusaInFestival*: a festival of migrations, indeed, where the focus is the errantry of human beings who have encountered, in one way or another, the shores of Lampedusa. A few African migrants returned to the island, and others went there for the first time to see what Lampedusa is today, for its magnetism as a political node, where locals walk *askavusa* (barefoot) on these rocks in the middle of the Mediterranean. What is more, the event brings together activists from different parts of Europe. While many more projects created by Africans were presented, not many African migrants could actually take part in the event due to a lack of proper documentation that limited their mobility because they still live on the border somewhere in Europe. That, to me, prompted not only organizational and logistical questions but also, more importantly, questions of translation and subjectivity. In particular, to what extent do they rely upon the support of activists that hold citizenship? And, if so, does this undermine the extent to which those undocumented migrants may themselves be said to have agency? Lacking legal permission to reside and move around their host country, undocumented migrants have traditionally been treated as passive objects subject to a network of human smuggling operatives, paternalistic orientalism on the part of activists, regulatory measures, and the state's security apparatus.

Is it even possible for irregular migrants to be effective political actors if they are excluded not only from formal channels of politics but also society due to the threat of deportation upon becoming publicly visible? Not only do I sustain that border struggles carry out by migrants are as intense as the managing and regulatory measures, but I argue that national and local political struggles, which are always confronted with the need to translate their different aims across many different spaces and instances, find within border struggles of undocumented migrants their preeminent translator.

A clear example is the link between the struggle against the militarization of the Mediterranean and the resistance of the NoMuos movement in Sicily against the construction of the Mobile User Objective System (MUOS), the most powerful system of military remote telecommunication on the planet. MUOS decodes the satellite information and translates it to a cellular service provider using the UHF SATCOM radio system and geosynchronous (GEO) satellites to guarantee communications coverage for US troops, even in disadvantageous environments. On 9 August 2014, hundreds of protesters gathered in front of the military base in Niscemi, where one of the MUOS ground stations is under construction, resulting in a clash with Italian police. According to the angry mob, the antennas will be the cause of significant electromagnetic pollution, dangerous not only for the inhabitants of the town but also for the animals of the natural reserve around the base. These concerns are certainly beyond the scope of my work in this book and certainly far from my knowledge to be able to discuss the scientific claims presented by both sides.[9] Instead, my aim here is to consider the role of Lampedusans with African migrants for the NoMuos movement in light of the ongoing recent history of militarization of the Maghreb and the Mediterranean Basin (Bensaâd, 2006). If Sicilians and Lampedusans were the precursors in protesting against the US and NATO militarization of these lands, beginning with the Cold War and then as the outpost of the War on Terror, then today migrants and refugees who claim their right to have rights join them. Their presence clashes with the mushrooming of antennas and radars across the region aimed at monitoring every human movement and migration. As a matter of fact, trans-Saharan and trans-Mediterranean itineraries rely on the opacity and dangerousness of these spaces. Errantry in the globalized and monitored world we inhabit pairs more often than not with clandestinity, which the MUOS apparatus that is the offspring of the militarization of the region and expression of a worldwide system of military communication aims to contain. Migrants and refugees from Africa and the Middle East embody the issue of dislocation and errancy caused by the multiplication of conflicts and warfare, while their subversive trajectories unsettle the territorial notion of well-being and hegemonic aspects of belonging, giving new vigor and inspirations to local struggles.

At the festival, another interesting partnership was made with the NoTav movement for the protection of the environment in mountain communities in the Alps between Italy and France, whose well-being is being threatened by the implementation of a high-speed train project. This train project that will link Lyon and Turin, labeled *Treno Alta Velocita* (TAV), has been under construction since 2011, but the plan to build the train has been hotly contested for almost two decades (). The reason for the contestation is a large disparity between the goals of the plan and the concerns of the people (Povoledo 2014). The TAV project is meant to provide a new outlet for surplus capital absorption, while local communities are concerned about the effects on the environment and so have begun occupying spaces to halt construction. How does this translate into African migrants' border struggles? It is enough to glance at the issue of land grabbing in Africa and technological innovations motivated by old modernist pulses which have transformed cultivated territories "into a destination for businessman and adventurers from the other half of the planet" (Liberti 2013, p. 5), driving out local African farmers who now sell their corporal force at the corners of every European city.

However, paperless migrants and even refugees that escape the Dublin Regulation are constrained by, if not denied, their social and political mobility. They run risks that are primarily corporeal, that of incarceration and deportation. "Are they the de-animated 'givens' of political life, mere life or bare life? Are we to say that those who are excluded are simply unreal, or that they have no being at all – the socially dead, the spectral?" 2011). Butler asks. The answer can only be negative based on the accounts listed previously because "if we claim that the destitute are outside of the sphere of politics – reduced to depoliticized forms of being, then we implicitly accept that the dominant ways of establishing the political are right" (Ibid.). Let's consider, for instance, another group who participated in the *LampedusaInFestival* – Lampedusa in Hamburg – a group mostly formed by African refugees and migrants that is very active not only in Hamburg but that is also well known in other cities of Europe.

> Some of them are living in housing-projects, but most of the 300 persons belonging to the group are homeless and still have no opportunity to make a living. For them the protest-tent at the Steindamm remains the most important place for meetings, exchange of information and organizing.[10]

Often, their logo and banners feature the bold statement: We are here to stay! They claim, then, a right to the city that is more than an economic concern. It is an isonomic claim that asserts the equality of rights of all urban inhabitants, and it involves translating city spaces into tents or camps or populating the city with bodies designated otherwise for the refugee camps or detention centers.

However, do they always need the help and support of legal citizens to achieve their political ends? Migrants' and refugees' means to achieve their ends are typically corporeal as much as the risks they run when they traverse economic, social and political frontiers. Abdelmalek Sayad taught us that the body of the migrants articulates what verbal expression cannot say, what he defines as "the organic importance of the body" (Sayad 2004, p. 213). By taking to the streets in Rosarno or occupying a space in Lampedusa, where Eritreans gathered for days in front of the main church, migrants use the visibility of their bodies, their physical presence, to weigh their claim. Therefore the answer is yes, they do need help. They need support because the body can be incarcerated, deported, ejected, and to deny it means to have little grasps of border struggles and politics in general, since "for politics to take place the body must appear." (Butler 2011). However, for the same reason they translate their power into local activists' project who adopt their tactics and share similar border struggles.

## 8.6   The planks of the boats of Lampedusa blossom

*But we need to figure out whether or not there are succulencies of Relation in other parts of the World (and already at work in an underground manner) that will suddenly open up other avenues and soon help to correct whatever simplifying, ethnocentric exclusions may have arisen from such a perspective.*

*(Glissant 1997, p. 21)*

What do they make and un-make when they meet? What are the stakes of such an encounter insofar as thinking and being-in-common is concerned? What or who is erased, reproduced or created? An interesting correlation and dynamic emerge at the *LampedusaInFestival* between the projects and experiences of different groups. I recall for instance how representatives of the 'Cucula' refugee company for Crafts and Design made an interesting intervention at the festival. The name originates from the Hausa language in western central Africa to indicate the action of "doing something together" as well as "taking care of each other."[11] Cucucla is an association, a workshop and an educational program for and together with refugees in Berlin. The refugees in charge of the project could not be present in Lampedusa because of the fact that they had entered the Schengen Area through Lampedusa, and according to the Dublin convention, they could only apply for asylum in Italy. Instead, after some time they left Italy and moved to Germany. There they met three inspired young Germans, two designers and an educator who, regarding the debate about the situation of refugees in Germany, had a more pragmatic, more immediate and action-oriented approach. Their aim and object was to achieve something "together with" the refugees and not simply "for them."

Inspired by the teachings of designer Enzo Mari,[12] a renowned modernist artist who is politically engaged but is also a brilliant furniture designer, they decided to build furniture with refugees and finance related educational programs. Refugees, in turn, learned new skills and enhanced their self-esteem, instead of being "administrated" and assisted. The refugees' idea was to send to Lampedusa their

German co-workers to gather planks from those same boats who carried them to Europe across the Mediterranean and with that to build pieces of furniture. They pursued the idea. After launching their pilot project and by using the boats' wood, Cucula Company thus acquired a solid foundation thanks to an impressive lucrative crowd funding and succeeded to give refugees access to stable employment, education, and most importantly, self-determination.

In the past as much as today, African artists and migrants have collaborated with the festival. For instance, writer Ubax Cristina Ali Farah and musician Mohamed Ba vocalized their border struggles in opposition to the contemporary institutional 'distribution of the sensible'(Ranciere 1998) by virtue of posing a challenge, reassembling the allocation of space in corporeal terms. What is at stake when such encounters take place? Definitely there is a risk that the social and political hierarchy, 'the distribution of the sensible' mentioned above, between full citizens and denizens is replicated all through the border struggle. While conversing with filmmaker Dagmawi Yimer, I expressed my own reservations to which he pointed out his own vision and praxis:

> Personally, I have always struggled to be autonomous and through the film, I am succeeding. I always had still need of support because you do not delegate a job so intense only to the immigrant. It is like launching a campaign against violence on women without including men. It is losing before starting. There is a need for cooperation, but we must give more attention to the thinking of the immigrant who must be a subject and not an object. He/she has to take it. It is a colonial understanding that in Italy is not there yet. But this is changing. There are characters that are becoming well known. The thing that fascinates me is the fact that I am observing that the representation of immigrants is not relegated to the left wing parties but there are migrant figures close to the right. There appears a shift from the idea of race towards the political ideology, even if I do not share the ideas on the right. This discourse may contradict that of migration but these migrants have the freedom to express themselves and they speak the same language of the Italian right-wing politicians.
>
> (interview by the author recorded on 29 September, 2013, Lampedusa)

Therefore, it is a matter of careful translation, of continuous negotiations and inevitable misunderstandings among parties, that capital and state are deemed to be untranslatable. It is worth remembering that this was the logic of plantations in Hawaii (Takaki 1984) and elsewhere in the Caribbean, Australia, and South America, to create a multiethnic work force that could not become organized owing to coming from different cultures – a pyramidal structure along racial lines with a multitude of slaves/workers of diverse origins – Africans and Europeans in the Caribbean and Asians and Europeans in the Pacific – from the top down, the pallid skin color of the northern Europeans fading away down to the bottom. This enclosed space, an economically efficient concentration camp, opened the world market for plantation managers and corporate agencies such as Dole, Castle and Cooke, C. Brewer and Company. But despite planters' tight control and the supposed incommunicability among so many diverse idioms, 'the always multi-lingual and frequently multiracial tangle created inextricable knots within the web of filiations, thereby breaking the clear linear order to which Western thought had imparted such brilliance.'(Glissant 1997, 71). Pidgin and creoles are the imme-diate linguistic responses to the tight rules and regulations imposed on slaves and workers; a sort of code that along with food made the underlying inventive political terrain for a new hybrid culture, not a sum of different idioms but a new rhizome in translation, always in relation and struggle.

Here in Lampedusa, I see the chance to generate a political subject adequate enough to meet the challenges of multiple ubiquitous borders, contemporary dislo-cations and the state of citizenship laws, but also a political subject able to handle the turmoil and storm of the contemporary financescape (Appadurai 1990). How-ever, as Glissant states, if the rhizome stands firm against the idea of the single homogenizing root, we must also note that it maintains the idea of rootedness, hence of a fertile ground, where it can open up and spread. We must begin with that.

## Notes

1  For information regarding the impact of the current civil war on migration between Europe and Libya, as well as past Libyan immigration statistics, see the report written in June 2013 by the MPC team on the basis of the CARIM South database and publica-tions, www.migrationpolicycentre.eu/docs/migration_profiles/Libya.pdf [Accessed 23 November 2014].

2  I have named this photographic composition "The Blue Door," as it features an Afro-European woman crossing the threshold of Lampedusa to evoke the idea of the border as a passage that has marked the entire book. In the foreground, the "Getaway to Europe," a sculpture by Mimmo Paladino (2008) is located at the extreme southern point of Lampedusa, representing the European entry point for African migrants.

3  For information and statistics, see Gabriele del Grande's blog, which keeps a record of the deaths at the frontiers of Europe since 1988. See http://fortresseurope.blogspot.com/p/la-strage.html

4  www.marina.difesa.it/EN/operations/Pagine/MareNostrum.aspx

5  www.marina.difesa.it/EN/operations/Pagine/MareNostrum.aspx

6  www.lacartadilampedusa.org/preamble.html

7  As indicated in the website of the Museum of Migrations at www.museodellemigrazioni.com/about-askavusa.html, [Accessed 22 September 2014]:

Askavusa is a cultural association based in Lampedusa founded in 2009 following demonstrations against the creation of a new Centre for Identification and Expul-sion (CIE) on the island. The purpose of the Association is to promote anti-racism and multiculturalism especially in relation to the arrival of boat migrants on the island. Among the several activities promoted Askavusa we should mention the LampedusaInFestival (www.lampedusainfestival.com, last access October 2014), a yearly cinematic festival that promotes a counter-hegemonic discourse around the regimes of patrolling and securitisation promoted by EU policies. Another interesting initiative of Askavusa still working as a form of resistance to the 'anonymisation' of boat migrants is Porto M, a space where objects recovered by the activists of Askavusa from the boats of migrants are collected and dis-played. The intent is to protect the memory those objects represent and especially to reinstate a new life in them. More information about the Porto M project can be found at: www.askavusa.wordpress.com/con-gli-oggetti.

8  www.lampedusainfestival.com/bando.html
9  For further information read: Matteo Emanuelli, 'MUOS Ground Station in Sicily Raises Protests and Concerns', *Space Safety Magazine*, www.spacesafetymagazine.com/space-on-earth/everyday-life/anti-muos-protest/ [accessed 4 January 2015].
10  www.lampedusa-in-hamburg.org/
11  www.cucula.org/en/
12  Enzo Mari became well known in the 1970s for his concept of "autoprogettazione." By the word *autoprogettazione*, Mari means an exercise to be carried out individually to improve one's personal understanding of the sincerity behind the project and to build furniture.

# References

Anonymous, 2010. Southern Misery. *The Economist*. Available at: www.economist.com/node/15271071 [Accessed 3 January 2015]

Anonymous, 2013. Homily of Holy Father Francis.

Appadurai, A., 1990. Disjuncture and Difference in the Global Cultural Economy. *Theory, Culture & Society*, 7(2), pp. 295–310.

Arendt, H., 1973. *The Origins of Totalitarianism*. New York, NY: Harcourt Brace Jovanovich.

Arendt, H., 1998. *The Human Condition*. Chicago, IL: University of Chicago Press.

Balibar, E., 2001. Outlines of a Topography of Cruelty: Citizenship and Civility in the Era of Global Violence. *Constellations*, 8(1), pp. 15–29.

Balibar, E. & Hahn, D., 2002. *Politics and the Other Scene*. London, UK: Verso.

BBC News, 2013. Pope Francis Visits Migrant Island. *BBC News*. Available at: www.bbc.com/news/world-europe-23224010 [Accessed 30 December 2014]

Bensaâd A., 2006. The Militarization of Migration Frontiers in the Mediterranean. In Biemann, U. & Holmes, B., eds. *The Maghreb Connection: Movements of Life across North Africa*. Barcelona, Spain: Actar.

Butler, J., 2011. Bodies in Alliance and the Politics of the Street. Available at: www.eipcp.net/transversal/1011/butler/en [Accessed 10 December 2014]

Chismar, D., 1988. Empathy and Sympathy: The Important Difference. *Journal of Value Inquiry*, 22(4), pp. 257–266.

Foucault, M., 1986. Of Other Spaces. *Diacritics*, 16(1), pp. 22–27.

Foucault, M., 2003. *"Society Must Be Defended": Lectures at the College de France, 1975–1976*. New York, NY: Picador.

De Genova, N., 2013a. Foucault, Migrations, Borders. *Materiali Foucaltiani*, II(3), pp. 153–177.

De Genova, N., 2013b. Spectacles of Migrant "Illegality": The Scene of Exclusion, the Obscene of Inclusion. *Ethnic and Racial Studies*, 36(7), pp. 1180–1198.

Derrida, J., 1992. *The Other Heading: Reflections on Today's Europe*. Bloomington, IN: Indiana University Press.

Dines, N., Montagna, N. & Ruggiero, V., 2015. Thinking Lampedusa: Border Construction, the Spectacle of Bare Life and the Productivity of Migrants. *Ethnic and Racial Studies*, 38(3), pp. 430–445.

Emanuelli, M., 'MUOS Ground Station in Sicily Raises Protests and Concerns', *Space Safety Magazine*, Available at: www.spacesafetymagazine.com/space-on-earth/everyday-life/anti-muos-protest/ [Accessed 4 January 2015].

Glissant, É., 1997. *Poetics of Relation*. Ann Arbor, MI: University of Michigan Press.

Haas, H. D., 2013. Hein de Haas: Smuggling Is a Reaction to Border Controls, Not the Cause of Migration. Available at: http://heindehaas.blogspot.com/2013/10/smuggling-is-reaction-to-border.html [Accessed 1 January 2015]

Hooper, J., 2010. Racial Violence Continues in Italy as Four Migrant Workers Wounded in Shootings. *The Guardian*. Available at: www.theguardian.com/world/2010/jan/08/standoff-italy-four-africans-wounded [Accessed 3 November 2014]

Isin, E. & Rygiel, K., 2007. Abject Spaces: Frontiers, Zones, Camps. In C. Masters & E. Dauphinee eds. *Logics of Biopower and the War on Terror* (pp. 181–203). New York, NY: Palgrave Macmillan.

Liberti, S., 2013. *Land Grabbing: Journeys in the New Colonialism*. London, UK: Verso.

Mattei, U., 2013. Protecting the Commons: Water, Culture, and Nature: The Commons Movement in the Italian Struggle against Neoliberal Governance. *South Atlantic Quarterly*, 112(2), pp. 366–376.

Mbembe, A., 2003. Necropolitics. *Public Culture*, 15(1), pp. 11–40.

Mezzadra, S. & Neilson, B., 2013. *Border as Method, or, the Multiplication of Labor*. Durham, NC: Duke University Press Books.

Nair, P., 2012. The Body Politic of Dissent: The Paperless and the Indignant. *Citizenship Studies*, 16(5–6), pp. 783–792.

Povoledo, E., 2014. Italy Divided Over Rail Line Meant to Unite. *The New York Times*. Available at: www.nytimes.com/2014/03/18/world/europe/italy-divided-over-rail-line-meant-to-unite.html [Accessed 4 January 2015]

Pugliese, J., 2009. Crisis Heterotopias and Border Zones of the Dead. *Continuum*, 23(5), pp. 663–679.

Pugliese, J., 2010. *Transmediterranean: Diaspora, Histories, Geopolitical Spaces*. New York, NY: Peter Lang.

Sayad, A., 2004. *The Suffering of the Immigrant*. London, UK: Polity.

Soguk, N., 2007. Border's Capture: Insurrectional Politics, Border-Crossing Humans, and the New Political. In *Borderscapes: Hidden Geographies and Politics at Territory's Edge*. Minneapolis, MN: University of Minnesota Press. Available at: www.jstor.org/stable/10.5749/j.ctttsn8c [Accessed 17 January 2015]

Soguk, N., 2014. Radical, Local, Global: From International Relations to Insurrectional Relations. In *The Sage Handbook of Globalization*, p. 1088. Thousand Oaks, CA: Sage.

Spivak, G. C., 1996. *The Spivak Reader: Selected Works of Gayatri Chakravorty Spivak*. London, UK: Psychology Press.

Takaki, R. T., 1984. *Pau Hana: Plantation Life and Labor in Hawaii, 1835–1920*. Honolulu, HI: University of Hawaii Press.

# Afterword

Spectres, Migrants and the Negotiation of Life

Sam Okoth Opondo

## I

"The migrant has no face, status or story[1]", so begins a recent Guardian OpEd piece by the novelist Hanif Kureishi. According, to Kureishi, the 'figure' of the migrant 'has not only migrated from one country to another, he has migrated from reality to the collective imagination where he has been transformed into a terrible fiction.' Rather than invite hospitable responses and compassion, this uninvited 'guest', a ghost figure, if you like, has been transformed into 'something resembling an alien. He is an example of the undead, who will invade, colonise and contaminate, a figure we can never quite digest or vomit.' Kureishi goes on to remind us that the popular European discourses on migration are best read in terms of their hauntological character. That is, the "uncanny, semi-fictional figures" of the migrant is both " a familiar, insidious figure, and a new edition of an old idea expressed with refreshed and forceful rhetoric." Not only is the familiar figure of the migrant a symptom of the material conditions of 'our times', migrants lives, deaths and contemporary responses to migration are best read in terms of what they tells us about the present and its entanglement with the past. Spatially rendered, migrant presence also tells us about Europe and its entanglement with other places and lives that it would rather disavow, exorcise and externalize.

Like Kureishi's article, Lorenzo Rinelli's *African migrants and Europe: negotiating the ultimate frontier* is an invitation to reflect on the current condition of migrants in Europe, the idea of Europe and the horrific border/order that characterizes European practices of the externalization of migration control. It also highlights the numerous strategies, tactics and modes of movement employed by migrants that reveal and disturb the European police apparatus. Within such a formation, the border becomes something less ossified and fixed. As the 'negotiations and encounters' characteristic of African migrations' increase, an apparatus that pushes Europe's migration control practices to spaces beyond continental Europe while simultaneously creating detention spaces, forms of capture and suspension within European cities and the surrounding waters emerges. Within these spaces of truth production, migrants are subjected to technologies of control and capture that deter their arrival or pathologize their presence in Europe. From biometrics and satellites for surveillance purposes to naval man hunting devices and forms of urban design within the city, migration control has become part of the everyday European imaginary and the virtual and actual spaces to which it extends itself. Not only do these practices shape and modify territories, they create and call up specters that are manifested in the border struggles of African migrants as well as the apparatus that creates zones of precarity and capture where the lives of African migrants are exposed to unmournable death and erasure. A zone of consensus, which Kureishi tells us, makes it impossible:

> [...] to speak up for the immigrant or, more importantly, hear him speak for himself, since everyone, including the most reasonable and sensitive, has made up their mind that the immigrant is everywhere now, and he is too much of a problem.

It is this consensus that Rinelli's book refuses to participate in since 'there is nothing more coercive and stupid than consensus, and it is through consensus that inequality is concealed.' By reversing the lens of a state discourse and migration control regime that sees a threat out there, Rinelli invites us to 'see differently' as we walk through a series of 'doors' and passages where encounters take place. Doors where traps are laid and sometimes lives saved. As one moves through the 'brick door' of the city, the 'sand door' in the Sahara desert or the 'blue door' in Lampedusa, the border becomes a dialectical formation that is best read and treated as a space of negotiation and negation. A space that is being produced beyond the European nation-state in spaces like Tripoli as well as within European metropolitan spaces such as the city of Rome. Ultimately, the 'sand door' invites us to read the Sahara desert as both a migration route and an enormous camp thus provoking attentiveness to migrant lives and deaths beyond those that happen at Europe's blue door (Lampedusa). The reading of desert and coastal 'sand-spaces' together provides a lens (the glass-sand relationship being more than accidental) through which ethical and political responses extend beyond what is often thought of as Europe's border. The ecological map that Rinelli provides raises numerous questions. Not only does it point to the outsourcing of migration control from Europe to Africa, it also calls upon us to ask what else is being outsourced and the effects of such outsourcing practices. Are these doors the symbols of 'our' times and if so, what stories do they tell? Which stories do they disallow as they regulate or enable passage to Europe? How does displacement within African states as a result of the workings of capitalist enclosure, war and intervention provide the impetus for migration to other parts of Africa and to Europe? These narrative and maps reveal metonymic character of the deaths in the Mediterranean sea given that they tell us a lot about the violence going on in Europe as well as in other parts of the world. In our folly, we tell the stories of death in one space and not the other. As Rinelli illustrates, these doors revolve and fold into each other, deaths and precarious lives are produced and distributed unequally through border practices. For instance, the Italian government has been actively involved in the interception and return of migrants to Libya. A state that does not recognize the existence of refugees or legal principles of *non-refoulment* while criminalizing the practice of rescuing African migrants stranded at sea by reducing a complex maritime gesture to the crime of aiding and abetting clandestine immigration. Ironically, the production of death coincides with the production of a time of citizenship as evinced by the practice of granting African migrants citizenship not upon arrival in Europe, but upon their death at sea. By granting the migrant *ex-morte* citizenship, the relationship between citizenship, birth, life and territory is disturbed. The trinity is undone by a necropolitical practice that makes arriving in Europe dangerous and co-habitation there close to impossible. However, migration persists. The migrant insists and in his/her insistence the story of borders, nation-states, Europe- Africa distinctions, cosmopolitanisms, 'hospitality' and the legal apparatus that enable them comes into question. In this insistence lies an element of hope. A hope that 'we' can move and live otherwise.

## II

Where Marx and Engels saw the spectre of communism as a haunting figure that brought together a holy European alliance, we might want to ask what kind of haunting the figure of migrant symbolizes such that a European alliance comes together to address the migration question – militarily, legally and through public discourse. Are they spectres of colonialism, neoliberal capitalism? Are the migrants spectres of the crafting practices that underline the need to create a coherent idea of Europe with its corresponding border practices, necropolitical engagements and spaces of exception? Of the numerous stories of resilience, resistance and capture in Rinelli's book, 1 want to focus on two people that seem to haunt the text and in their haunting provides an ethical, methodological and political shift in the way the narrative of *African migrants and Europe* proceeds.

Beginning with the tragic story of Nabruka Mimuni, the 44-year-old Tunisian woman who was found hanged in her cell at the Ponte Galeria CIE in Rome, Rinelli invites us to reflect on the meanings of home, the form and sites of present day externalization of migration control practices and with them the location of borders. Most significantly, his attentiveness to Nabruka's death and the attempt to break from the misnaming that takes place in the media and the popular imaginary enables him to map not only the 'internal border and external border of life' but also of the polity. Here, the spectre of Nabruka and Nabruka's death provokes one to seek other ways of living and living together. It is a provocation that resonates with Jacques Derrida's treatment of living and learning in *Spectres of Marx* where he notes that living is something that one learns:

> To live, by definition, is not something one learns. Not from oneself, it is not learned from life, taught by life. Only from the other and by death. In any case from the other at the edge of life. At the internal border or the external border, it is a heterodidactics between life and death.[2]

By apprehending Nabruka's life and the border apparatus complicit in its loss, Rinelli attempts to tell a story that is attentive to migrant lives, faces and stories. A dissensual story that this attentive to the political status of refugees, asylum-seekers and other categories of migrants, as well as the statecraft and the numerous 'states' of being that emerge from the gap between formal declarations of humanity and the empirics of human life that emerges at a border that is not fixed. To live in today's Italy, Rinelli learns, is something one learns from the other.

The death of a Tunisian woman in the Rome that she had called her home for thirty years but never belonged to, raises critical questions about our conception and experience of home, Tunisia and Italy. The story of Nabruka, Rinelli tells us, made him think "that perhaps the externalization of migration control in Africa was just the tip of the iceberg: the most visible feature of a complex European apparatus that is meant to exclude or, better, to differentiate among and to add in, African migrants already in Europe or on their way to it." He then proceeds to ask if we can "define geo-spatially local Roman practices of marginalization as externalization? And to ask where the internal and the external begins and what practices, histories and orientations have created the "geospatial methodologies and conceptions of borders" that make the distinction possible and desirable.

In death, Nabruka, the Tunisian in Rome calls up and calls into question the geopolitical imaginary that marks a sharp distinction between Italy and Tunisia. The imagination that Lampedusa and other CIE sites of migration control try to solidify. Thinking the Tunisia-Italy relation outside of the institutional frame and geopolitical imagination, Rinelli notes that Lampedusa is closer to Tunisia than it is to Sicily. An image that recalls that "an island like Lampedusa is referred to, in contemporary histories, as geologically 'part of Africa' but culturally Italian" and has to be read within the violence underlining the history of Italian nation-state formation where the Italian Northerners made sense of the "South" through colonial metaphors and models that divided "the Italian peninsula and its islands along a North/South, white/black axis."[3] A racial-spatial imaginary that is today used to think and govern migrant presence, Italian ideas of themselves and European conceptions of who belongs and how one belongs to that space.

What, one might ask, is this spirit that the specter of Nabruka reminds us of? What animates the specter embodied by the dead African body on the nude beach in Lampedusa, in the Sahara or the incarcerated migrant body behind bars in Libya? Are these African bodies telling us a story and whose story do they tell? Rinelli offers a clue in his re-reading of externalizations. That is, one cannot read these externalizations as frontal control practices in the Frontex model. While the externalization might seem to begin elsewhere, it also happens at the core of the European metropole. Much like the colonial border/order from which it inherits is force, externalization of migration control is a symptom of something else. The absence of refugee camps, the emergence of city-camps and camp-cities and the bodies in the sand at the bottom of the sea, in the sand on the beach, or in the desert sand all tell us the story of people fleeing the necropolitics in the Horn of Africa, Libya and elsewhere. People who are witnesses and survivors of a post-colonial violence, enclosure and economic problems that Europe is complicit in. In as much as they tell us the story of the postcolony, they also reveal that the West, as Edouard Glissant puts it, " is not in the West. It is a project, not a place."[4]

Nabruka's tragic death reminds us of the violence of the state and unhinges the violent fiction of European space, rights and with it the rights of man and the citizen. The renegotiation of the internal/external borders Europe and Africa and the resultant spatial formations reminds one of the spatial practices that have made Europe, Africa and the modern world possible. It reminds us of the Afro-Asian distinction emerging from the mancraft that cut the isthmus of the Suez creating a canal that at once opens up Africa to European colonization while erasing a geological connection between Africa and Asia. It reminds us that the institution of this violent cartography, its related geopolitical and Hegelian geo-philosophical disunity is constantly being disturbed by migrants who insist on crossing at those points that modern states, modern historiography and FRONTEX say that one must not.

## III

The second person that haunts the text invites us to shift our gaze, to look elsewhere or look otherwise in order to draw other lines and alignments besides those that privilege birth, stasis and limited conceptions of community. Through the story of Dagmawi Yimer, aka Dag and the documentary film, *Like a Man on Earth* (Segre & Yimer 2008), Rinelli enacts an aesthetics that is at once political and ethical. With the moving image, Yimer engages the memories of others who, like him, had journeyed from Ethiopia to Rome via Libya as a means of highlighting the precarious movements and challenges that migrants face as well as the surveillance and carceral practices that keep them outside of the domain of rights, justice and belonging. The documentary film juxtaposes camps, boats, trucks in the desert, containers, technologies and institutions of control and passage in a manner that reveals how transformations in migration control policies in Europe, collaboration and regime change and intervention in Africa are part of a diplomatic formation that brutally keeps migrants from Europe's shores. In addition to presenting migrant memory and stories, the documentary becomes a vehicle for recalling Italian colonialism in Libya, Eritrea and Ethiopia through archival footage that interrupts the presentist representation of Italy-Africa relations that does not acknowledge colonial entanglements characterized by African soldiers fighting along Italian soldiers in Libya and Ethiopia.

The movements in Rinelli's book resonate with the movements in the film and offer a glimpse into the violence and negation surrounding migration control and the negotiations, insistence and resistance characteristic of migration practices. Covering different spaces and the border practices and struggles that characterize them, the book presents a layered critique of the representations and institutions that have come to stand for the experience of migrants in Europe and elsewhere. It also highlights the hopeful forms of activism, solidarity and will to survive that emerge around migrant issues and experiences with attentiveness to the complexity of borders and migrant political subjectivity which is enacted in the very act of moving and transgressing borders.

**IV**

"African migrants wash up on nude beach in southern Spain," these are the opening lines of the Foreword by Nevzat Soguk. "The migrant has no face, status or story", those were the provocative lines through which Kureishi interrogates popular and official discourses on migration in Europe. Doubtless, such stories abound. They take place in Europe and elsewhere. The novelty in Rinelli's work lies in the specific ways in which it highlights the dialectic that underlines the borders and 'grave passages' to and into a fortified Europe that continues to deny refuge, rights and possibilities of cohabitation through practices of externalization not only of migration control, but control in general. Given those it is written in concert with, the book goes beyond mapping and narrating the relationship between externalization of migration control, borders and naked life. It is inspired and haunted by Nabruka and it echoes and shadows Yimer. With attentiveness to migrant lives and the negotiation of migration, Rinelli illustrates the specific ways in which dominant conceptions of borders and naked life cannot account for complexity of migrant lives and the political agency behind them. The migrants name, rather than being a mere exemplar reminds us of a life. A grieveable life. The migrant's status reminds us of the state of the state today — European, African or otherwise. The crisis, if any, is not one of migration but of the way 'we' think and encounter others and familiar reduction of complex encounters to citizenship, security and humanitarian crises that can be managed or migration problems that can be externalized and controlled. The migrant's insistence on the right to move and escape in the closed seas and the adjacent lands serves as a potent venue for reimagining the border and with it the order of modern political life.

**Notes**

1   Kureishi, Hanif. 2014. "The Migrant Has No Face, Status or Story." *The Guardian*, May 30, sec. Immigration and Asylum. Available at: http://www.theguardian.com/books/2014/may/30/hanif-kureishi-migrant-immigration-1. [Accessed May 1st, 2015]
2   Derrida, Jacques. *Specters of Marx: The State of the Debt, the Work of Mourning, and the New International*. New York: Routledge, 1994. p.xvii
3   see Pugliese, Joseph. "Crisis Heterotopias and Border Zones of the Dead." *Continuum*. 23.5 (2009): 663–679. p.655
4   Glissant, Edouard. 1992 [1989] *Caribbean Discourse: Selected Essays*. Edited by A. J. Arnold. Caraf Books. p.2

# Index